CANADIAN BOOKS FOR YOUNG PEOPLE

LIVRES CANADIENS POUR LA JEUNESSE

1980

Canadian Books for Young People

Livres canadiens pour la jeunesse
1980

Edited by
IRMA McDONOUGH

UNIVERSITY OF TORONTO PRESS
Toronto Buffalo London

Toronto Buffalo London
Reprinted 2017
ISBN 978-1-4875-8698-0 (paper)
ISBN 978-0-8020-4594-2 (cloth)

Canadian Cataloguing in Publication Data
Main entry under title:

Canadian books for young people = Livres canadiens pour la jeunesse

"Revision and expansion of Canadian books for children/Livres canadiens pour enfants."
English or French; includes English and French publications.
Includes index.

ISBN 978-1-4875-8698-0 pa.
1. Children's literature, Canadian – Bibliography. I. McDonough, Irma, 1924- II. Title: Livres canadiens pour la jeunesse.

Z1378.C32 1978 028.52 C77-001754-1E

This book has been published with the assistance of the Ontario Arts Council and the Canada Council under their block grant programs.

Contents

Foreword

Children's book production during the last two years has far surpassed its former pace. UNESCO statistics record over 250 new editions published annually in Canada. French language books especially have reached significant numbers - nearly 100 new editions appear each year. Publishers have responded to the expressed needs of the domestic market with titles of significantly higher literary quality, and higher production standards are equally noticeable. This increase in numbers, and improvement in format and content make the need for this new edition of *Canadian Books for Young People/Livres canadiens pour la jeunesse* patently obvious.

The basic criteria still prevail. The selection is inclusive rather than exclusive, and the librarians involved have tried to select the most informative, relevant and excellent books for young people from among titles in print. Books primarily intended for adults have been included if they are relevant and relatively easy to read.

Titles for young people from preschool age to age 14, or of grade nine level, have been included. All of them have been assigned a general age level of reading competence. The English language titles have been marked as suitable for younger, middle, older or mature readers. *Younger* readers are beginners; *middle* readers would include 7- to 10-year-olds; *older* readers are from 10 to 12 years old; *mature* readers read with easy comprehension above the 12 year level. French language titles carry similar age level designations. *Tout-petits* include pre-school children and beginning readers; *débutants* include 7- to 9-year-olds in grades two to three; *moyens* are in grades four to six, probably 9 to 12 years old; *grands* are 12 to 14 years old, likely in grades seven to nine, and *aînés* are mature readers. All of these designations must be construed as flexible. Individual children will find their own levels of reading competence and these will be influenced by the children's interests.

Over 60 English language publishers' series have been listed separately with references from pertinent subject areas. Individual selections from the French language series have been made, however, and included under their subjects.

Only a few Federal and Provincial Government and other institutional publications such as those from the Royal Ontario Museum have been selected. These institutions provide checklists and catalogues free to libraries.

There were five juvenile magazines in the English language listed in the last edition. Although there were two new ones added to the market - *Chickadee* and *Book Times* - two have regrettably disappeared - *Canadian Children's Magazine* and *Jabberwocky*. General interest magazines like *Seasons* and *Tawow*, however, should be available to young people as well. There are seven French language periodicals listed, three of them aimed specifically at a juvenile audience.

Another area of considerable expansion is in professional library tools. These are listed under Professional Media, then under the sub-headings: literary history and criticism, library tools, and periodicals. French language inclusions appear under Outils professionnels and Périodiques. Most of them are useful background reading and professional literature.

Prize-winning authors and their books have all been listed under their appropriate book awards of which we found 17 in the two languages. Five of the awards have been discontinued over the years.

Information regarding omissions and corrections to be incorporated in the next edition is welcome.

The cooperation and enthusiasm of four interested professional librarians reflect their feelings of responsibility and devotion to the national literature. Callie Israel, Windsor Public Library, and Ruth Osler, Toronto Public Library helped to select and annotate the English language titles added to this edition. Micheline Persaud, Eastern Ontario Regional Library System and Danielle Ledoux, Ottawa Public Library selected and annotated the new French inclusions. W.A. Roedde's encouragement, Barbara Smiley's unfailing cooperation and Doris Dowell's assistance reflect the most congenial staff involvement. Thanks are again due to Harald Bohne and other staff of the University of Toronto Press, most notably Kieran Simpson and Diane Egerton, whose expertise has speeded another revision into print.

IRMA McDONOUGH
Co-ordinator, Children's Library Services
Editor, *In Review: Canadian books for young people*
Libraries and Community Information Branch
Ontario Ministry of Culture and Recreation

Avant-propos

Au cours des deux dernières années, la publication de livres pour enfants s'est effectuée à un rythme accéléré. D'après les statistiques de l'UNESCO, plus de 250 nouveaux titres paraissent au Canada tous les ans. Le nombre de parutions en français est particulièrement impressionnant: près de 100 nouveaux titres chaque année. Pour répondre aux besoins souvent exprimés du marché intérieur, les éditeurs ont publié des livres d'une grande valeur littéraire et de présentation soignée. Le nombre de nouvelles publications et les modifications apportées à leur présentation et leur contenu rendaient indispensable la révision du catalogue.

Les critères fondamentaux demeurent les mêmes. La sélection est inclusive plutôt qu'exclusive et les bibliothécaires qui ont participé à la préparation du catalogue ont tenté de choisir, parmi les livres pour la jeunesse encore sur le marché, les meilleurs, les plus instructifs et les mieux adaptés aux besoins des jeunes. Nous avons également inclus des livres pour adultes susceptibles d'intéresser les jeunes mais de lecture relativement facile.

On trouvera des livres s'adressant à des enfants d'âge préscolaire jusqu'aux jeunes de quatorze ans (niveau de la neuvième année). On a précisé la catégorie de lecteurs que vise chaque titre. Les livres anglais portent les indications *younger, middle, older* ou *mature readers. Younger readers* désigne les enfants qui commencent à lire; *middle readers,* les enfants de sept à dix ans; *older readers,* ceux de 10 à 12 ans et *mature readers,* les lecteurs dont la compréhension dépasse le niveau de la 12e année. Des indications semblables accompagnent les titres français. *Tout-petits* désigne les enfants d'âge préscolaire et ceux qui commencent à lire; ***débutants***, les enfants de sept à neuf ans qui sont en deuxième ou troisième année; *moyens,* les élèves de la quatrième à la sixième année, âgés de neuf à douze ans; *grands,* les adolescents de 12 à 14 ans, de la septième à la neuvième année et *aînés*, les lecteurs plus avancés. Est-il besoin d'ajouter que ces désignations ne sont données qu'à titre indicatif. Chaque enfant découvre son propre niveau de compréhension qui dépend d'ailleurs dans une certaine mesure de ses intérêts individuels.

Plus de 60 collections de livres anglais sont cataloguées séparément, avec renvois de domaines pertinents. Pour les livres parus dans des collections françaises, nous avons effectué un choix, et les titres sélectionnés figurent sous la rubrique appropriée.

Nous n'avons retenu que quelques-unes des publications des gouvernements fédéral et provinciaux et d'autres organismes tels que le Musée royal de l'Ontario qui offrent gratuitement aux bibliothèques la liste de leurs publications et leur catalogue.

Dans la précédente édition, nous recensions cinq revues en anglais pour les jeunes. Bien que l'on compte maintenant deux nouvelles publications, *Chickadee* et *Book Times*, deux autres ont malheureusement cessé de paraître: *Canadian Children's Magazine* et *Jabberwocky*. Certaines revues d'intérêt général, comme *Seasons* et *Tawow,* devraient toutefois être mises à la disposition des jeunes. La liste des revues en français comprend sept titres, dont trois s'adressent spécifiquement aux jeunes.

Un autre secteur en pleine expansion est celui des outils professionnels. Les titres anglais pertinents se retrouvent dans la section *Professional Media*, et sous les rubriques *literary history and criticism*, library tools et *periodicals*. En français, ces publications figurent sous les rubriques *outils professionnels* et *périodiques*. La plupart de ces titres sont d'une lecture très instructive et constituent des instruments de travail fort utiles.

Les auteurs ayant gagné des prix sont classés sous la rubrique correspondant à leurs prix respectifs. Il y a en tout, pour les deux langues, 17 de ces prix, dont cinq ne sont plus décernés.

Nous prions instamment nos lecteurs de nous signaler toute erreur ou omission, en vue de la prochaine édition.

La coopération et l'enthousiasme des quatre bibliothécaires professionnelles ayant collaboré au présent catalogue reflètent le profond interêt et le sentiment de responsabilité qui les anime à l'égard de la littérature canadienne. Callie Israel, de la bibliothèque municipale de Windsor et Ruth Osler, de la bibliothèque municipale de Toronto nous ont aidé à choisir et à annoter les titres anglais que nous avons ajoutés à la présente édition. Micheline Persaud, de la Fédération des bibliothèques de l'est de l'Ontario et Danielle Ledoux, de la bibliothèque publique d'Ottawa ont sélectionné et annoté les nouveaux titres français. Nous tenons à remercier les membres du personnel provincial qui ont grandement allégé notre tâche: W.A. Roedde, pour ses encouragements, Barbara Smiley pour son inlassable dévouement et Doris Dowell pour son aide précieuse. Nos remerciements s'adressent également à Harald Bohne ainsi qu'aux autres employés des Presses de l'Université de Toronto, et tout particulièrement à Kieran Simpson et Diane Egerton, dont l'expérience nous a permis d'imprimer aussi rapidement la présente édition.

IRMA McDONOUGH
Coordonnatrice des bibliothèques pour enfants
Rédactrice, *In Review: Canadian Books for young people*
Direction des bibliothèques et des Services d'information communautaires
Ministère des Affaires culturelles et des Loisirs

Canadian Books for Young People

PICTURE BOOKS

PICTURE BOOKS
see also
PUBLISHERS' SERIES
Kids of Canada series
Makwa Books
Mini Books for Mini Hands
Zoo Book Series

Alderson, Sue Ann; Bonnie McSmithers (you're driving me dithers). Garrick, Fiona (illus.); Tree Frog Press, 1975. 53 pages. $2.95 paper [0-88967-008-0]

A lively little girl gets into mischief and her mother goes "blithery blathery out of her mind." *Younger.*

Alderson, Sue Ann; Bonnie McSmithers is at it again! Garrick, Fiona (illus.). Tree Frog, 1979. 41 pages. $5.95 cloth [0-88967-029-3]; $3.95 paper [0-88967-028-5]

This time Bonnie makes pancakes for breakfast with a little Too Much Salt but no help from Mommy. *Younger to middle.*

Alderson, Sue Ann; Hurry up, Bonnie. Garrick, Fiona (illus.). Tree Frog, 1977. 43 pages. $5.95 cloth [0-88967-024-2]; $3.50 paper [0-88967-023-4]

Intrepid, self-directed Bonnie keeps her mother hopping — this time on a trip to get the paper. *Younger to middle.*

Allinson, Beverley, O'Kelly, Barbara and **Lawrence, Judith;** The Dog power tower. Daniel, Alan (illus.). Methuen, 1977. 32 pages. $3.95 paper [0-458-93060-1]

Mr. Dressup's television characters appear in another gentle mystery-adventure for developing sensibilities. *Younger.*

Allinson, Beverley; Mandy and the flying map. Powell, Ann (illus.); Women's Educational Press, 1973. 29 pages. $4.25 cloth; $3.00 paper.

Mandy says "Fly, map" and goes off on a delightful fantasy that proves girls can also do anything. *Younger.*

Allinson, Beverley; Mumbles and Snits. Powell, Ann (illus.); Women's Educational Press, 1975. 29 pages. $7.95 cloth [0-88961-023-1]; $3.00 paper [0-88961-022-3]

Mumbles and Snits roll and tumble, bounce and laugh, spin and twirl - and sing with happiness. *Younger.*

Allison, Rosemary; The Green harpy at the corner store. Garcia, Claire W. (illus.). Kids Can, 1976. 36 pages. $2.95 paper [0-919964-09-5]

A harpy with a damaged wing comes home with Babas and upsets the household. *Younger.*

Allison, Rosemary and **Powell, Ann;** Ms. Beaver travels east. Women's Educational Press, 1978. 27 pages. $7.95 cloth [0-88961-057-6]; $2.95 paper [0-88961-056-8]

Ms. Beaver accompanies the waitress June to Nova Scotia where they help the village people to restore a fish plant destroyed by fire. *Younger.*

Allison, Rosemary and **Powell, Ann;** The Travels of Ms. Beaver. Women's Educational Press, 1973. 31 pages. $2.95 paper [0-88961-056-8]

The story of an enterprising Beaver who dams Toronto's Don River. The new edition has a larger format and printed text. *Younger.*

Anfousse, Ginette; Chicken pox. Romaner, Mayer (tr.); N.C. Press, 1978. 22 pages. $2.95 paper [0-919601-28-6]

The fight. Romaner, Mayer (tr.); NC Press, 1978. 22 pages. $2.95 paper [0-919601-30-8]

Hide and seek. Romaner, Mayer (tr); NC Press, 1978. 22 pages. $2.95 paper [0-919601-10-3]

My friend Pichou. Romaner, Mayer (tr); NC Press, 1978. 22 pages. $2.95 paper [0-919601-08-1]

Jojo and her "honest-to-goodness-baby-aardvark-who-really-eats-ants" visually and verbally involve their reader friends in beguiling childhood antics. *Younger.*

Arnold, Rist; I like birds. Tundra (Collins), 1977. 30 pages. $2.95 [0-912766-76-X]

A cunning counting book in five languages with the months of the year and a simple narrative added. *Younger.*

Atwood, Margaret; Up in a tree. McClelland, 1978. 32 pages. $6.95 [0-7710-0824-4]

The author's illustrations and hand-lettered rhyming text tell a simple story of two children in their treetop retreat. *Younger.*

Barber, James; Once upon Anne Elephant there was a time. Pommier, Claudine (illus.); McClelland, 1974. 32 pages. $4.95 paper [0-7710-1006-0]

Fantastic flights of fancy that banter along at a child's level of hilarious nonsense. Disarmingly fey pictures. *Younger.*

Blades, Ann; The Cottage at Crescent Beach. McClelland, 1977. 32 pages. $4.95 [0-88869-000-2] (A Magook Publication)

Illustrations full of colour and atmosphere reflect the quiet adventures of children on a beach holiday. *Younger to middle.*

Blades, Ann; Mary of mile 18. Tundra (Collins), 1971. 40 pages. $2.95 paper [0-88776-059-7]

The author-artist taught in a backwoods Mennonite community in British Columbia and here shows and tells Mary's story. *Younger.*

Clever, Glenn; Tommy and the ladybug. Yarymowich, Lucy (illus.). Borealis, 1977. 16 pages. $2.95 paper [0-919594-82-4]

A moral tale about a nasty little boy who becomes as small as the insects he torments. *Younger to middle.*

Cook, Lyn; If I were all these . . . Ivens, Peter (illus.); Burns, 1974. 42 pages. $4.95 [0-88768-047-X]

What a little boy would do if he were various animals, told in three-line stanzas, and illustrated with cunning line drawings. *Younger.*

Cook, Lyn; Jolly Jean-Pierre/Voyage extraordinaire de Jean-Pierre. St-Cyr, Micheline (tr.) and Davies, Mary (illus.); Burns, 1973. 35 pages. $6.95 [0-88768-043-7]

Bilingual verses and vivid drawings enhance a tall tale about a bold voyageur. *Younger.*

Côté, Mark; Shakespeare and the flying bed. McClelland, 1979. 32 pages. $6.95 [0-88869-007-X] (A Magook Publication)

A magical bed takes off in amazing flight with the Snozolas and Shakespeare the spider on board. *Younger to middle.*

Csapo, Marg; Charlie Muskox. Coombs, Doris (illus.); Center for Human Development and Research, 1977. 28 pages. $2.25 paper.

The Inuit boy Jeremy meets Charlie on the tundra and shares his dried fish and apples to celebrate Charlie's birthday. *Younger.*

Csapo, Marg; The Christmas Muskox. Coombs, Doris (illus.); Center for Human Development and Research, 1977. 28 pages. $2.25 paper.

This finds Charlie in the unlikely role of a sheep to Jeremy's shepherd at the school Christmas concert. *Younger.*

de Grosbois, Louise and others; Mommy works on dresses. Bayard, Caroline (tr.); Women's Educational Press, 1977. $2.95 paper [0-88961-042-8]

A first book on assembly line work in a dress factory, geared to the sensibilities of very young children. *Younger to middle.*

Donald, David; Hector and the big house. Illustrated. Rhino Books, 1977. 36 pages. $2.95 paper.

Hector wants a little house, but his friends have other ideas - until Hector angrily rejects them, and lives happily ever after in his own little house. *Younger.*

Downie, Mary Alice; Dragon on parade. Baker, Mary Lynn (illus.); PMA, 1974. 44 pages. $3.95 paper [0-88778-176-4]

Lazy summer holidays in Bayfield, Ontario and three sisters who dress up as a dragon in the Lions Club parade. Integral, intimate drawings. *Younger to middle.*

Drawson, Blair; Flying Dimitri. Illustrated. Groundwood, 1978. 32 pages. $7.95 [0-88899-000-6]

Dimitri imagines himself flying in the night sky and lands on Mars where the Queen has been captured by a fierce dragon. A successful fantasy. *Younger.*

Drawson, Blair; I like hats. Illustrated. Scholastic-Tab, 1979. $1.50 paper.

A very small book with a slight story line about a little girl and the different hats she wears. Bright, humorous illustrations. *Younger.*

Elston, Georgia; The Animal's alphabet picnic. Gage, 1977. 31 pages. $3.95 [0-7715-9402-X]

At a picnic the birds, animals and insects choose words whose first letters match their names; for example "the bees and the bears enjoyed the best buns." *Younger.*

Goman, Joan R.; Rebecca's Nancy: a story of a little Mennonite girl. Sand Hills, 1978. 53 pages. $7.95 [0-920446-05-1]

Losing Nancy was a calamity for Rebecca, but finding her favourite doll made life right again. Cunning collages. *Younger.*

Harris, Dorothy Joan; The House mouse. Warne (Saunders of Toronto), 1973. 48 pages. $2.95 [0-7232-6096-6]

Four-year-old Jonathan has secret meetings with a mouse who lives in his doll's house. *Younger to middle.*

Harris, Dorothy Joan; The School mouse. Conover, Chris (illus.); Warne (Saunders of Toronto) 1977. 30 pages. $5.95 [0-7232-6140-7]

Jonathan brings his mouse friend to school and leaves him there when he makes friends with Toby, a boy in his class. *Younger to middle.*

Harris, Dorothy Joan; The School mouse and the hamster. Clifford, Judy (illus.); Warne (Saunders), 1979. 32 pages. $8.95 [0-7232-6172-5]

Toby is home with the mumps so Jonathan cleans the blackboard alone after school and plays the go-between for the class hamster and the school mouse. *Younger to middle.*

Heffernan, Sue; Minoo's family. McGlynn, Frances (illus.); Before We Are Six, (U.T.P.) 1974. 2nd ed. 43 pages. $1.50 paper. 1974, 3rd ed. $2.75 [0-920152-06-6]

Minoo discovers life in a single-parent family after her mother's divorce. *Younger.*

Hopkins, Elizabeth Margaret; The Painted cougar. Talonbooks, 1977. $7.95 [0-88922-125-1]

Enchanting drawings grace this simple fantasy about a cougar in search of his true love. *Younger.*

Howard-Gibbon, Amelia Francis; An Illustrated comic alphabet. Oxford, 1966. 32 pages. $8.75 [0-19-540044-5]

The first Canadian picture book, originally published in 1859. *Younger.*

Itani, Frances; Linger by the sea. Bobak, Molly (illus.); Brunswick, 1979. 32 pages. $4.95 paper [0-88790-108-5]

Molly Bobak's monochromatic blue water colours add a touch of magic to this idyllic interlude by the sea. *Younger to middle.*

Kellerhals-Stewart, Heather; Cricket Christmas. Yaryomich, Lucya (illus.); Borealis, 1978. 26 pages. $3.95 paper [0-919594-70-0]

A graceful, simple story about Stalky the cricket who performed a miracle on Christmas eve. *Younger to middle.*

Kellerhals-Stewart, Heather; Muktu, the backward muskox. Muntean, Karen (illus.); K.E.S., 1975. 31 pages. $1.95 paper.

The antics of a young muskox trying to adapt herself to an adult world are the undoing of an unscrupulous hunter in this appealingly illustrated picture story. *Younger to middle.*

Kilbourne, Frances; Overnight adventure. Powell, Ann (illus.); Women's Educational Press, 1977. 30 pages. $7.95 cloth [0-88961-054-1]; $3.95 paper [0-88961-047-9]

This adventure-without-words involves two self-sufficient youngsters through a night in the backyard tent. *Younger.*

Kilbourne, Frances; The Recyclers. Powell, Ann (illus.); Women's Educational Press, 1979. $9.50 cloth [0-88961-059-2]; $4.95 paper [0-88961-060-6]

This wordless story follows two youngsters who collect neighbourhood cast-offs and recycle them for new uses. *Younger.*

Lasker, David; The Boy who loved music. Lasker, Joe (illus.); Viking (Penguin), 1979. 1st ed. 47 pages. $10.95 [0-670-18385-7]

Karl plays the horn in Joseph Haydn's chamber orchestra whose patron is Prince Nicolaus Esterhazy. Apposite water colours grace this period story. *Younger to middle.*

Layton, Aviva; How the Kookaburra got his laugh. Smith, Robert (illus.); McClelland, 1975. $4.95 paper [0-7710-4868-8]

Another *Just So* kind of story that acquaints children with Australian animals. *Younger to middle.*

Layton, Aviva; The Magic stones. Klunder, Barbara (illus.); McClelland, 1977. 32 pages. $4.95 [0-88869-004-5] (A Magook Publication)

David discovers how to arrange five wailing stones so that they produce sweet songs instead. *Younger to middle.*

Lee, Dennis; The Ordinary bath. McKee, Jon (illus.); McClelland, 1979. 48 pages. $8.95 [0-88869-008-8]

Fantastic creatures pour out of the faucet to overwhelm a youngster in the tub. *Younger to middle.*

Lightfoot, Gordon; The Pony man. Harper's Magazine (Fitzhenry & Whiteside), 1972. 30 pages. $10.20 L.B. [0-06-126325-7]

Surrealistic paintings add new depths to Lightfoot's popular ballad. *Younger to middle.*

McLaughlin, Lorrie; The Furry purry kitten. Gage, 1978. 24 pages. $3.95 [0-7715-9400-3]

A slight story, but the bright illustrations will attract beginning readers. *Younger.*

Mertens, Winnie; My feet roll. Before We Are Six, (UTP) 1977. 32 pages. $2.75 paper [0-920152-16-3]

Realistic drawings reinforce the everyday humanity of a little handicapped girl in this wordless picture book. Excellent concept well realized. *Younger.*

Michailiuk, George; Wayne's wagon. Zenovia, 1971. 33 pages. $6.00 cloth [0-88991-002-2]; $4.50 paper [0-88991-003-0]

Wayne builds a wagon and becomes the envy of his friends. This well-designed picture book was hand set and privately printed. *Younger.*

Michailiuk, Richard; The Wind. Zenovia, 1971. 32 pages. $6.00 cloth [0-88991-000-6]; $4.50 paper [0-88991-001-4]

A simple description of the wind's activities. Colour block prints decorate a private press book. *Younger.*

Millyard, Anne W.; Plato and company. Murata, San (illus.); Annick Press/Books By Kids, 1978. 41 pages. $7.98 [0-920-23608-1]

Well designed, strikingly illustrated, simply told story of how a house cat and some mice become friends. *Younger.*

Moore, Marlene; The Christmas snowmobile. Mycka, John (illus.); Highway Book Shop, 1977. 28 pages. $2.00 paper.

Black and white illustrations and a rhyming text tell how Santa faces a Christmas crisis by using a snowmobile engine on his sled. *Middle.*

Pasternak, Carol and **Sutterfield, Allen;** Stone soup. Campbell, Hedy (illus.); Women's Educational Press, 1975. 32 pages. $7.50 cloth [0-88961-015-0]; $3.00 paper [0-88961-015-0]

An inner city school class makes a stone soup that brings multinational children closer together. Imaginative collages. *Younger to middle.*

Powell, Ann; Strange street. Kids Can, 1975. 28 pages. $2.75 paper [0-919964-01-X].

Sam finds out that his street is not so strange after all. Delightful drawings. *Younger.*

Prather, Ray; The Ostrich girl. Scribner's (Wiley), 1978. 32 pages. $11.50 [0-684-15889-2]

A fantasy based on a Kenyan legend introduces an orphan adopted by a kind family who has to disprove the rumour that she is the child of an ostrich. *Middle.*

Reese, Will; The Money tree. Switzer, Phil (illus.); LeBel, 1977. 32 pages. $5.95 [0-920008-03-8]

Lilting couplets and coloured drawings tell about two brothers' discovery of the Money Tree's riches. *Younger to middle.*

Richards, Jack; Johann's gift to Christmas. Norris, Len (illus).; Douglas & McIntyre, 1972. 32 pages. $5.95 [0-88894-007-6]

About a musical mouse and his involvement in the writing of a Christmas carol, "Silent Night." Also published in French. *Younger to middle.*

Roussan, Jacques de: Au-delà du soleil/Beyond the sun. Tundra (Collins), 1977. 28 pages. $2.95 [0-88776-031-7]

A bilingual picture book about space flight. Eye-catching illustrations allow the imagination to soar. *Younger.*

Roussan, Jacques de; If I came from Mars/Si j'étais Martien. Tundra (Collins), 1977. 28 pages. $2.95 [0-912766-75-1]

Peter takes an imaginary trip from Mars to look at the Earth and decides "how happy the people who live on it must be!" *Younger.*

Shaw, Barbara. Kiki of Kingfisher Cove: a tale of a Nova Scotia cat. Lancelot, 1977. 40 pages. $1.50 paper [0-88999-067-0]

Authentic Nova Scotian fishing village life in words and pictures. *Younger.*

Singer, Yvonne; Little-Miss-Yes-Miss; Wood, Angela (illus.); Kids Can, 1976. 27 pages. $2.95 paper [0-919964-08-7]

Cicely joins her parents in Toronto, but misses Jamaica as she adapts to life in her new home. A sympathetic, intimate portrayal. *Younger.*

Singer, Yvonne; Sara and the apartment building. Powell, Ann (illus.); Kids Can, 1975. 32 pages. $2.75 paper [0-919964-07-9]

Gentle story about the attractions of high rise living through the eyes of two little girls. *Younger.*

Stren, Patti; Bo the constrictor that couldn't. Illustrated. Green Tree, 1978. 32 pages. $6.95 cloth [0-919476-78-3]; $4.95 paper [0-919476-57-0]

Childlike watercolours illustrate this story of a snake who preferred to kiss other animals rather than swallow them. *Younger.*

Stren, Patti; Hug me. Illustrated. Harper (Fitzhenry & Whiteside), 1977. 32 pages. $7.25 [0-06-026080-7]

Line drawings illustrate a small-size book about a porcupine in search of love. *Younger to middle.*

Stren, Patti; Sloan and Philamina; or How to make friends with your lunch. Illustrated. Dutton (Clarke, Irwin), 1979. 40 pages. $8.95 [0-525-39485-0]

Sloan, an anteater and Philamina, an ant live together in peace until Sloan has a birthday party for all their relatives. *Younger to middle.*

Szlavnics, Klara; There were no cats in Goodville. Johnson, Bill (illus.); Black Moss (Firefly), 1979. 24 pages. $4.95 paper [0-88753-060-5]

A droll story demonstrates the gullibility of Goodville's citizens who misinterpret their first cat's feeding instructions. *Younger to middle.*

Taylor, Barbara; I climb mountains. Yacono, Barbara (illus.); Women's Educational Press, 1975. $7.50 cloth [0-88961-021-6]; $3.00 paper [0-88961-020-8]

Annie climbs the mountains of fantasy; Peter scoffs at her, and Lucy is their go-between. *Younger to middle.*

Thurman, Mark; The Elephant's cold. NC Press, 1979. 23 pages. $2.95 paper [0-919601-36-7]

Douglas's friends argue about the best way to cure his cold in this cheerful, colourful and soothing story. *Younger.*

Tolmie, Ken; A Tale of an egg. Oberon, 1975. 54 pages. $6.95 [0-88750-155-9]

About an egg who didn't want to remain an egg, so he ran away. *Younger.*

Vivenza, Francesca; Geranimal, Daddy Lion and other stories. Groundwood, 1978. 33 pages. $6.95 [0-88899-002-2]

Five short involvements in childish pursuits: counting, measuring, inventing, dreaming, playing with words. *Younger.*

Wallace, Ian and **Wood, Angela;** The Sandwich. Kids Can, 1975. 51 pages. $2.95 paper [0-919964-02-8]

Vincenzo's favourite sandwich of provolone and mortadella offends his friends' sense of smell until they taste it and enjoy it too. *Younger.*

Waterton, Betty; A Salmon for Simon. Blades, Ann (illus.); Douglas & McIntyre, 1978. 28 pages. $7.95 [0-88894-168-4]

Simon finally catches a salmon only to free it again. Blades's drawings are award-winning. *Younger to middle.*

Whitaker, Muriel; Pernilla in the perilous forest. Ironside, Jetske (illus.); Oberon, 1979. 24 pages. $9.95 [0-88750-312-8]

Pernilla braves the seven deadly sins to find a horse to eat sugar from her hand and lay its head in her lap. *Middle.*

Wilkins, M.G.; I am a duck. Wakefield, Jeff (illus.); Scholastic-Tab, 1976. $1.05 paper.

In a light-hearted picture story Simon gets his wish and becomes a duck only to discover the life is not what he had supposed. *Younger.*

Wilson, Barbara; ABC & 123. Daigle, Gisèle (illus.); Porcépic, 1980. 38 pages. $4.95 paper [0-88878-165-2]

An ingenious bilingual alphabet and counting book that demonstrates the similarities in our founding languages. *Younger.*

Wood, Angela; Kids can count. Kids Can Press, 1976. 26 pages. $2.95 paper [0-919964-11-7]

A delightful counting book in five languages and arabic numerals which emphasizes Canada's multi-cultural heritage. *Younger.*

Wynne-Jones, Tim; Madeline & Ermadello. Hallam, Lindsey (illus.); Before We Are Six, (U.T.P.), 1977. 30 pages. $2.95 paper [0-920152-14-7]

A delightful but unusual friend called Ermadello enlarges Madeline's gift for fantasy. Just right illustrations in a well designed format. *Younger to middle.*

Wyse, Anne (ed.) and **Wyse, Alex** (ed.); The One to fifty book. U.T.P., 1973. 105 pages. $2.75 paper [0-8020-6222-9]

An imaginative counting book with astonishing illustrations by children. *Younger.*

Young, Chip; Honky the Christmas goose. Clarke, Irwin, 1973. 32 pages. $2.95 [0-7720-0558-3]; 2nd ed. $3.95 [0-7720-1095-1]

Honky eats so much that he can't even honk but manages to diet and become Santa's helper. *Younger.*

FOLKLORE

FOLKLORE
see also
PUBLISHERS' SERIES
Folktale Series

Ahenakew, Beth and **Hardlotte, Sam;** Cree legends, Volumes 1 and 2. Saskatchewan Cultural College, 1973. 55 pages. $1.50 each, paper.

These 12 stories from the oral tradition of the Cree Indians are presented in a rough, authentic translation. A notable addition to the country's folklore. *Middle.*

Anderson, Anne; Legends of Wesakecha. 1976. 44 pages. $4.50 paper.

Cree legends of the great trickster and hero, in authentic tellings. *Older.*

Aubry, Claude; The Magic fiddler and other legends of French Canada. Field, Saul (illus.) and Kane, Alice (tr.); PMA, 1968. 98 pages. $3.95 paper [0-88778-092-X]

Ten French Canadian folktales artfully retold and illustrated; included are *La Corriveau, Le loup-garou* and *La chasse-galerie* among other well known legends. Also published in French. *Older to mature.*

Ayre, Robert; Sketco the raven. Macmillan, 1961. 183 pages. $5.50 [0-7705-0001-3]

Raven's supernatural powers are elaborated in this collection of West Coast Indian legends. *Older to mature.*

B.C. Indian Arts Society; Tales from the longhouse. Gray, 112 pages. $1.95 paper [0-88826-058-X]

Delightful collection of Indian tales from Vancouver Island related by Indian children. *Middle to older.*

Barbeau, Marius; The Golden phoenix, and other fairy tales from Quebec. Oxford, 1980 (c 1958). 144 pages. $4.50 paper [0-19-540345-2]

A reprinting of the 1958 award-winning edition of eight French Canadian folktales retold by Michael Hornyansky, including *The Princess of Tomboso, The Fairy quite contrary*, and *Scurvyhead. Middle to older.*

Bernstein, Margery and **Kobrin, Janet;** How the sun made a promise and kept it; Heffernan, Ed. (illus.); Scribner's (Wiley), 1974. 40 pages. $5.75 [684-13770-4]

Weese-ke-jak captures the sun in a net; Beaver heroically frees him and is left with a hairless tail as a reminder. *Younger to middle.*

Bouchard, Randy and **Kennedy, Dorothy I.D.;** Shuswap stories. CommCept, 1979. 152 pages. $4.35 paper [0-88829-048-9]

Transcribed from taped stories told by elderly story-tellers these 32 tales are typically unvarnished and serious. *Mature.*

Campbell, Maria; Little Badger and the fire spirit. Maclagan, David (illus.); McClelland, 1977. 32 pages. $7.95 [0-7710-1882-7]

Ahsinee visits her grandparents at Lac La Biche and her grandfather tells her the legend about Little Badger, a blind Indian boy, who brought fire home to his people. *Younger to middle.*

Clark, Ella E.; Indian legends of Canada. McClelland, 1960. 177 pages. $7.95 cloth [0-7710-2121-6]; $3.95 paper [0-7710-2122-4]

Brief, simple retellings of Canadian Indian legends, grouped generically. *Older to mature.*

Cleaver, Nancy; How the chipmunk got its stripes. Gal, Laszlo (illus.); Clarke, Irwin, 1973. 28 pages. $4.95 [0-7720-0586-9]

Algonkian How legend simply and wittily told, simply and strikingly illustrated. *Younger.*

Cleaver, Nancy and **Knight, Rosemary;** Snow shoe rabbit and wild rose legends; how the snowshoe rabbit got its white winter coat and how the wild rose got its thorns. Daniel, Alan (illus.); and Smith, Merle (illus.); Highway Book Shop, 1978. 29 pages. $2.00 paper [0-88954-162-0]

Retellings of two legends from the Algonkian Indians. *Middle.*

Clymer, Theodore; The travels of Atunga. Schoenherr, John (illus.); Little, 1973. 31 pages. $6.75 [0-316-14760-5]

Atunga goes on a quest to find food for his people. Stark pictures illustrate this Eskimo legend. *Younger to middle.*

Creighton, Helen; Bluenose ghosts. McGraw, 1957. 280 pages. $7.95 [0-7700-0022-3]; 1976 Rev. ed. $4.95 paper [0-7700-0022-3]

Excellent collection of supernatural tales and folklore from Nova Scotia. *Older to mature.*

Creighton, Helen; Bluenose magic. McGraw, 1968. 297 pages. $8.95 [0-7700-0023-1]

Ghost stories, tales of buried treasure, Indian legends, cures, divinations and fabulous home remedies from Nova Scotia. *Older to mature.*

Csapo, Marg; Nigerian folk tales. Coombs, Doris (illus.); Center for Human Development and Research, 1978. 56 pages. $2.50 paper.

Cunning line drawings illustrate this collection of 23 short tales that illuminate Nigerian folkways. *Middle.*

Csapo, Marg; Ramayana. Coombs, Doris (illus.); Center for Human Development and Research, 1978. 34 pages. $2.50 paper.

A story incorporating a picturesque puppet performance of an Indonesian legend about Ramayana's succession to the throne of Kosala. Line drawings of the puppets. *Middle.*

Cutt, Nancy and **Cutt, W. Towrie;** The Hogboon of hell. Kennedy, Richard (illus.); Deutsch (Collins), 1979. 173 pages. $12.95 [0-233-97020-7]

In a true living tradition Orcadian grandmothers still tell these strange Orkney tales that Towrie Cutt remembers hearing as a child. *Older to mature.*

Fowke, Edith; Folktales of French Canada. NC Press, 1979. 144 pages. $6.95 [0-919601-4]

Jokes, anecdotes, legends, animal tales and folk tales selected from translations that "adhere as closely as possible to the way the original narrators told the stories." *Older to mature.*

Fox, Mary Lou; How the bees got their stingers; an Ojibwe-Odawa legend. Simon, James (illus.); Ojibwe Cultural Foundation, West Bay, Manitoulin Island, 1977. 38 pages. $3.00 paper.

Nannebush gave the bees their stingers to protect their honey from thieves. *Younger.*

Fox, Mary Lou; Ko-Ko-Ko the owl; an Ojibwe-Odawa legend. Panamick, Martin (illus.); Ojibwe Cultural Foundation, West Bay, Manitoulin Island, 1977. 24 pages. $3.00 paper.

A simple legend about how the owl came to be able to "turn his head all the way around." *Younger.*

Fox, Mary Lou; Why the beaver has a broad tail. Highway Book Shop, 1974. 24 pages. $1.50 paper [0-88954-049-7]

An Ojibwe Why legend told in English and Ojibwe by an elder of the Wikwemikong Reserve on Manitoulin Island. *Younger.*

Franko, Ivan; Fox Mykta. Kurelek, William (illus.); Melynk, Bohdan (tr.); Tundra, 1978. 152 pages. $12.95 [0-88776-112-7]

Translation of the 19c Ukrainian poet's version of the mediaeval Reynard the Fox Tales illustrated by a Ukrainian-Canadian artist. *Older to mature.*

Fraser, Frances; The Wind along the river. Parker, Lewis (illus.); Macmillan, 1968. 83 pages. $6.50 [0-7705-0114-1]

Retold with simplicity and dignity these legends of the Blackfoot Indians reflect the harsh realities of their lives. *Older.*

Greene, Alma; Tales of the Mohawks. Miller, R.G. (illus.); Dent, 1975. 186 pages. $7.95 [0-460-95086-X]

Stories told on the Six Nations Reserve near Brantford, Ontario, recalled by a Mohawk clan mother. Beautiful pencil drawings by an artist of Indian heritage. *Older to mature.*

Grisdale, Alex; Wild drums: Indian legends of Manitoba. Shipley, Nan (ed.); Peguis, 1972. 78 pages. $2.50 paper (1974) [0-919566-35-9]

Plains Indian lore collected by an elder as a record of early Indian history. *Older to mature.*

Harris, Christie; Mouse Woman and the mischief-makers. Tait, Douglas (illus.); McClelland, 1977. 115 pages. $7.95 [0-7710-4022-9]

This second volume of North West Indian lore about the Mouse Woman, who was a *narnauk,* a supernatural being, includes seven more stories. *Middle to older.*

Harris, Christie; Mouse Woman and the muddleheads. McClelland, 1979. 131 pages. $10.95 [0-7710-3984-0]

Seven further adventures of the tiny *narnauk* whose special charges are muddleheaded young people whom she helps to choose the proper way to do things. *Middle to older.*

Harris, Christie; Mouse Woman and the vanished princesses. Tait, Douglas (illus.); McClelland, 1976. 155 pages. $7.95 [0-7710-4023-7]

Mouse Woman, that tiny busybody, is the central figure in these six Indian tales. *Middle to older.*

Harris, Christie; Once more upon a totem. Tait, Douglas (illus.); McClelland, 1973. 195 pages. $6.95 [0-7710-3993-X]

Three short traditional tales told by North West Coast Indians, retold and placed in their social context, by a sympathetic white woman. *Middle to older.*

Harris, Christie; Once upon a totem. Reid, Bill (illus.); Atheneum (McClelland), 1963. 148 pages. $6.95 [0-689-20137-0]

Five stories rich in the mythology of the Indians of the North West Coast, illustrated by an Indian artist. *Middle to older.*

Harris, Christie; The Trouble with princesses. Tait, Douglas (illus.); McClelland, 1980. 176 pages. $8.95 [0-7710-3997-2]

Felicitous retellings of the Pacific Northwest Indian tales about princesses that evoke comparisons with Old World princesses. *Older to mature.*

Harris, Kenneth (ed. and tr.)**;** Visitors who never left; the origin of the people of Damelahamid. U.B.C., 1974. 139 pages. $11.95 cloth [0-7748-0033-X]; $5.95 paper [0-7748-0034-8]

Eight readable myths of a Northwest Coast Indian tribe reveal many cultural functions. Retold in English by an Indian for older readers. *Older to mature.*

Hennigar, Ted. R.; Scotian spooks, mystery and violence. Lancelot, 1978. 191 pages. $4.50 [0-88999-079-4]

History and legend are combined in these blood-curdling tales for older readers. *Older.*

Hill, Kay; Glooscap and his magic: legends of the Wabanaki Indians. McClelland, 1963. $5.50 cloth; $2.79 paper [0-7710-4117-9]

Hill, Kay; More Glooscap stories. McClelland, 1970. 178 pages. $5.95 [0-7710-4090-3]

Two volumes of Micmac legends about the great chief Glooscap who guided his people in living wisely and well. *Older.*

Hooke, Hilda Mary; Thunder in the mountains. Oxford, 1947. 217 pages. $8.75 [0-19-540043-7]

Seventeen Canadian folktales include white men's lore and Indian legends. *Older to mature.*

Houston, James; Ghost paddle. Academic, 1972. 64 pages. $4.95 [0-15-230760-5]

With a magic paddle Hooits of the Raven people fights a great duel and wins peace for his tribe. *Middle to older.*

Houston, James; Kiviok's magic journey: an Eskimo legend. Academic, 1973. 40 pages. $5.95 [0-7747-0130-7]

Because Raven took her white feather coat, Kungo, the beautiful goose girl, retained her human form and married Kiviok. *Middle to older.*

Houston, James; Tikta'liktak: an Eskimo legend. Academic, 1965. 63 pages. $7.25.

A young Eskimo hunter adrift on an ice pan survives and returns to his people. *Middle to older.*

Johnston, Patronella; Tales of Nokomis. Kagige, Francis (illus.); Musson, 1970. 64 pages. $4.95 [0-7737-0016-1]

Sixteen simply told Ojibway legends stunningly illustrated in colour. *Middle to older.*

Keller, Betty (ed); Legends of the River People. November House, 1976. 127 pages. $6.95 paper [0-88894-115-3]

Culture and traditions of the Chilliwack Indians are revealed in this collection of their myths, folk tales and legends, originally recorded by anthropologist Norman Lerman. *Older to mature.*

Leach, Maria; The Lion sneezed. Siegl, Helen (illus.); Crowell (Fitzhenry), 1977. 102 pages. $10.50 [0-690-01364-7]

Anecdotes, proverbs, riddles and folklore about the domestic cat, collected by a noted folklorist, will please cat lovers. *Older.*

Lunn, Janet; The Twelve dancing princesses. Gal, Laszlo (illus.); Methuen, 1979. 32 pages. $10.95 [0-458-93890-4]

A graceful retelling of an old French tale also retold by the Grimm Brothers, with illustrations enchanting and romantic. *Middle.*

MacDonald, Margaret (ed.); The Magic fife. McGraw, 1968. $6.30 [0-7700-3078-5]

These are folk tales that settlers from 18 nations brought to Canada. *Older.*

Macklem, Michael; Jacques the woodcutter. Blades, Ann (illus.); Oberon, 1977. 36 pages. $9.95 [0-88750-239-3]

The ribald tale of the woodcutter's unfaithful wife appropriately illustrated. *Middle.*

McLaughlin, Lorrie; Shogomoc Sam. Macmillan, 1970. 61 pages. $2.95 paper [0-7705-1014-0]

Hilarious tall tale about the sidekick of New Brunswick's version of Paul Bunyan. *Middle to older.*

MacMillan, Cyrus; Canadian wonder tales. Cleaver, Elizabeth (illus.); Clarke, Irwin, 1974. 276 pages. $14.75 [0-7720-0739-X]

Retellings in the European folk tradition of Indian legends and French Canadian stories made by the author in 1918 and 1922. Distinguished chapter heads. *Older to mature.*

Macpherson, Jay; Four ages of man. Macmillan, 1971. 205 pages. $2.25 paper [0-7705-0669-0] (St. Martin's Classic Series)

Classical myths fittingly retold. *Older.*

Martin, Fran; Raven-who-sets-things-right. McEntee, Dorothy (illus.); Harper (Fitzhenry & Whiteside), 1975 (c1951). Rev. ed. 96 pages. $8.65 L.B. [0-06-024071-7]

Revision of *Nine tales of raven* with an informative introduction and new drawings. *Middle to older.*

Mason, Patricia F.; Indian tales of the Northwest. Morgan, Joey (illus.); CommCept, 1976. 102 pages. $6.45 paper.

The origin of each of these simply told stories is clearly indicated. Linguistic area map and bibliography included. *Middle to older.*

An excellent teachers' guide is also available. ($4.00)

Melzack, Ronald; The Day Tuk became a hunter and other Eskimo stories. McClelland, 1967. 92 pages. $5.95 [0-7710-5842-X]

Ten Eskimo legends of witches, wild beasts and courageous deeds, simply told, imaginatively illustrated. *Middle to older.*

Melzack, Ronald; Raven, creator of the world. McClelland, 1970. 91 pages. $4.95 [0-7710-5833-0]

A further collection of simple Eskimo legends, dramatically illustrated. *Middle to older.*

Melzack, Ronald; Why the man in the moon is happy: and other Eskimo creation stories. Gal, Laszlo (illus.). McClelland, 1977. 64 pages. $6.95 [0-7710-5832-2]

Effective colour illustrations enhance eight Inuit creation stories that evoke other primitive explanations of human origins. *Older.*

Metayer, Maurice; Tales from the igloo. Nanogak, A. (illus.); Hurtig, 1972. 127 pages. $4.95 cloth [0-88830-062-X]; $3.95 paper [0-88830-088-3]

Twenty-two stories from the Copper Eskimo, illustrated in rich colours by an Eskimo artist. *Older.*

Morgan, John S.; When the morning stars sang together. Beardy, Jackson (illus.) and Hamilton, Ron (illus.); Book Society, 1974. 201 pages. $8.95 cloth [0-7725-5080-8]; $4.50 paper [0-7725-5079-4]

Comparative study of Greek and Indian legends which effectively presents the culture and heritage of North American Indians. *Older to mature.*

Morriseau, Norval; Legends of my people, the great Ojibway. Dewdney, Selwyn (ed.); McGraw, 1965. 130 pages. $7.95 [0-7700-0110-6]; 1977, $4.95 paper [0-07-077714-4]

Beliefs, tales and lore of the Ojibway nation of Lake Nipigon and Thunder Bay District. *Older to mature.*

National Museum of Canada and **Jenness, Diamond;** The Corn goddess and other tales from Indian Canada. Canadian Government, 1966, 111 pages. $3.25 paper (Anthropological Series)

Twenty-five Indian legends give an insight into Native social customs. *Older to mature.*

Newfeld, Frank; The Princess of Tomboso. Oxford, 1960. 24 pages. $5.95 [0-19-540066-6]

Based on the French-Canadian tale of the king's son who loses his inheritance to a wily princess. Vigorous drawings. *Younger.*

Newfeld, Frank; Simon and the golden sword. Oxford, 1976. 24 pages. $4.95 [19-540270-7]

A traditional wonder tale beautifully illustrated and retold, adapted from a New Brunswick source recorded by Helen Creighton. *Middle.*

O'Neill, Paul; Legends of a lost tribe. McClelland, 1976. 95 pages. $3.95 paper [0-7710-6878-6]

Folk tales of the Beothuck Indians of Newfoundland reconstructed from what is known of their life and beliefs and told through the author's imagination. *Older to mature.*

Perrault, Charles and **Macklem, Michael** (adapter); The Sleeping beauty. Moiseiwitsch, Carel (illus.); Oberon, 1974. 48 pages. $9.95 [0-88750-097-8]

A mediaeval mood permeates the pictures of this familiar tale first set down by Perrault. *Younger to middle.*

Perrault, Charles and **Suddon, Alan** (adapter)**;** Cinderella. Aubry, Claude (tr.); Oberon, 1969. Bilingual ed. 57 pages. $9.95 [0-88750-013-7]

Exciting contemporary collages illustrate the old story which is engagingly retold in bilingual versions. *Younger to middle.*

Reid, Dorothy M.; Tales of Nanabozho. Oxford, 1979. (c1965) 128 pages. $3.95 paper [0-19-540322-3]

A felicitous retelling of 21 Ojibway trickster hero legends, ideal for storytelling sessions and private enjoyment. *Middle to older.*

Robertson, Marion; Red earth. Scott, Fred (illus.); Nova Scotia Museum, 1969. 98 pages. $2.50 paper.

Stories from the oral tradition of the Micmac Indians are prefaced by a description of the way of life which they portray. *Middle.*

Robins, Patricia; Star maiden: an Ojibwa legend of the first water lily. Day, Shirley (illus.); Collier-Macmillan, 1975. 32 pages. $5.95 [0-02-976690-7]

Why a star becomes a water lily. Effectively illustrated in earth colours. *Younger.*

Robinson, Gail and **Hill, Douglas;** Coyote the trickster. Chatto and Windus (Clarke, Irwin), 1975. 124 pages. $8.95 [0-7011-5023-8]

A readable rendition of 12 legends from Eskimo and Indian peoples whose trickster hero has all-too-human attributes. *Older.*

San Souci, Robert; The Legend of Scarface: a Blackfeet Indian tale. San Souci, Daniel (illus.). Doubleday, 1978. 40 pages. $9.95 [0-385-13247-6]

In this Blackfoot tale Scarface's love for the chief's daughter, Singing Rain, takes him to the sun's lodge to seek a release from her promise never to wed. Beautifully illustrated. *Younger to middle.*

Schwarz, Herbert T.; Elik and other stories. McClelland, 1970. 79 pages. $6.95 [0-7710-7976-1]

Legends retold by living Eskimos and rendered into English by a white man who includes biographies of the story tellers. *Mature.*

Schwarz, Herbert T.; Windigo and other tales of the Ojibway. McClelland, 1969. 40 pages. $5.95 [0-7710-7975-2]

Eight short Ojibway tales retold from Norval Morriseau's written tales and pictures. Stark compelling paintings accompany the text. *Older to mature.*

Simeon, Anne; The She-wolf of Tsla-a-wat: Indian stories from British Columbia. Tait, Douglas (illus). Douglas & McIntyre, 1977. 80 pages. $7.95 [0-88894-145-5]

Six transformation tales told to young Coast Salish children, prefaced by an introductory chapter on life centred in the *thee laylum* or Big House, their tribal home. *Middle to older.*

Snake, Sam and others; The Adventures of Nanabush: Ojibway Indian stories. Kagige, Francis (illus.). Doubleday, 1979. 84 pages. $12.95 cloth [0-385-14248-X]; $7.95 paper [0-385-14249-8]

Elders of the Rama Ojibway Band dip into the treasury of legends about their mighty trickster-hero and retell 16 stories that recall Nana's supernatural abilities and human frailties. Appropriate full-colour paintings enhance the traditional tales. *Older to mature.*

Spray, Carole; Will O' the wisp: folk tales and legends from New Brunswick. Brunswick, 1979. 132 pages. $4.95 paper [0-88790-106-9]

Folk tales and legends, yarns and tall tales about devilish bears and red-haired ghosts, buried treasure and legendary cures, collected in New Brunswick from English language sources. *Older to mature.*

Symchych, Victoria and **Vesey, Olga;** The Flying ship . . . and other Ukrainian folk tales. Kuch, Peter (illus.); Holt, 1975. 93 pages. $8.95 [0-03-929950-3]

Both the colourful drawings and the simple translations impart an authentic flavour to these Ukrainian folk tales retold for Canadian children. *Middle.*

Toye, William; The Fire stealer. Cleaver, Elizabeth (illus.); Oxford, 1979. 24 pages. $6.95 [0-19-540321-5]

Scintillating collage pictures interpret this Ojibway legend of how humans received the gift of fire. *Younger to middle.*

Toye, William; How summer came to Canada. Cleaver, Elizabeth (illus.); Oxford, 1969. 32 pages. $7.95 [0-19-540158-1]

Micmac legend explains the occurrence of the seasons in simple words and dramatic collages. *Younger.*

Toye, William; The Loon's necklace. Cleaver, Elizabeth (illus); Oxford, 1977. 24 pages. $5.95 [0-19-5402782]

A simple retelling of a Tsimshian legend beautifully illustrated by a prize winning artist. *Younger.*

Toye, William; The Mountain goats of Temlaham. Cleaver, Elizabeth (illus.); Oxford, 1969. 32 pages. $7.95 [0-19-540159-X]

Tsimshian Indian legend recreated simply and dramatically. *Younger.*

Trueman, Stuart; Tall tales and true tales from down east. McClelland, 1979. 171 pages. $12.95 [0-7710-8598-2]

Readable and amusing retellings of New Brunswick tall tales and historical events that will have a popular following. *Older to mature.*

Weatherby, Hugh; Tales the totems tell. Macmillan, 1976 (c1944). 97 pages. $4.95 paper [0-7705-1449-9]

Ten West Coast Indian legends retold in a simple narrative style by a white admirer. *Middle.*

Wilson, Marie (ed.); We-gyet wanders on: fables of the Northwest. Mowat, Ken (illus.) and Stephens, Vernon (illus.). Hancock House, 1977. $9.95 [0-919654-99-1]

A Tsimshian people, the Gitksan, live on the Skeena River and once hunted mountain goats and bears, fished for salmon and held potlatches, which all figure in their mythology. *Mature.*

MONSTERS

Garner, Betty Sanders; Canada's monsters. Potlatch, 1976. 95 pages. $4.95 paper [0-919676-06-5]

Imaginative illustrations and dramatic descriptions make this an exciting compendium of Canadian monsters. There is even a page for "My personal sighting record," and a comprehensive bibliography. *Middle.*

Green, John: Sasquatch: the apes among us. Cheam (Hancock House), 1978. 492 pages. $14.95 [0-920044-03-4]

Legends, newspaper accounts, and other sources compiled to bring together all that is known about the sasquatch. *Mature.*

Hunter, Don and **Dahinden, Rene;** Sasquatch. McClelland, 1973. 192 pages. $7.95 [0-7710-4297-3]

The fascination of Canada's Abominable Snowman has attracted many hunters; their findings are gathered together here. *Mature.*

Moon, Mary; Ogopogo, the Okanagan mystery. (illus.); Douglas & McIntyre, 1977. 195 pages $5.95 paper [0-88894-108-0]

From Indian lore to contemporary evidence Moon traces the facts about the legendary monster of Lake Okanagan in British Columbia. *Mature.*

SOCIAL SCIENCES

TRANSPORTATION AND COMMUNICATIONS

Berton, Pierre; The Great railway, McClelland, 1971. 2 vols. (boxed) 336 pages. $28.50 [0-7710-1328-0]

Pictorial history of the CPR is a condensation of the author's *The National Dream* and *The Last Spike*. *Older to mature.*

CN Tower; the world's tallest book about the world's tallest freestanding structure; Sevier, Gerry (illus.); Greey de Pencier, 1975. 15 pages. $2.95 paper [0-919872-19-0]. *All ages.*

Collins, David H.; Wings across time: the story of Air Canada, illustrated. Griffin, 1978. 94 pages. $8.95 [0-88760-090-5]

Uncritical history of Air Canada from its beginnings in 1937 to 1977 describes the progress made by the company to serve Canadians in peace and war. *Mature.*

Collins, Robert; A Great way to go. McGraw, 1973. 152 pages. $5.95 paper [0-07-092977-7]

Illustrated history of the motor car in Canada. *Older to mature.*

Collins, Robert; A Voice from afar; the history of telecommunications in Canada. McGraw, 1977. 304 pages. $14.95 [0-07-082536-X]

An illustrated history of telephones, cables, microwave, high-frequency radio and Anik satellites. Chronology, extensive bibliography and index. *Older to mature.*

Grayson, Linda and **Grayson J. Paul;** Paddles and wheels: everyday life and travel in Canada. Oxford, 1974. 192 pages. $4.75 paper [0-19-540216-2]

A useful survey from Indian canoes to modern transport. *Older.*

Guillet, Edwin C.; Pioneer travel. U.T.P., 1966. 241 pages. $3.95 paper [0-8020-6052-8]

Various modes of travel and how they affected the development of Upper Canada. *Middle to older.*

Italiano, Carlo; The Sleighs of my childhood/Les traîneaux de mon enfance (bilingual text). Chicoine, René (tr.); Tundra (Collins), 1974. 48 pages. $9.95 [0-88776-050-3]

Bilingual text, superb design and vital illustrations celebrate the variety and charm of Montreal's horse-drawn sleighs. *Younger to middle.*

MacEwan, J.W. Grant; Power for prairie plows. Prairie Books, 1971. 115 pages. $9.95 [0-919306-32-2]

Photographs enhance the story of mechanization in Western Canada and its effect on transportation and agriculture. *Older to mature.*

Mika, Nick and **Mika, Helma;** Railways of Canada: a pictorial history. McGraw, 1972, 1978. 176 pages. $12.50 cloth [0-07-092776-6]; $6.95 (1978) paper [0-07-082815-6]

A pictorial and chronological survey of the development of railways from the Champlain and St. Lawrence Railroad to the Canadian National Railways. *Older to mature.*

Stewart, Sandy; A Pictorial history of radio. Gage, 1975. 154 pages. $12.95 cloth [0-7715-9948-X]

Nostalgic recreation of Canada's enviable radio network history. Well illustrated. *Mature.*

Tucker, Albert; Steam into wilderness; Ontario Northland Railway, 1902-1962, illustrated. Fitzhenry, 1978. 216 pages. $19.95 cloth [0-88902-444-8]; $9.95 paper [0-88902-558-4]

An illustrated history of the development of the Ontario Northland Railway from its beginnings in 1902 to 1962 when it joined the cities of the south with Moosonee, Haileybury, North Bay and the Northern hinterland. *Older to mature.*

Vachon, Georgette; Goggles, helmets and airmail stamps. Clarke, Irwin, 1974. 150 pages. $8.95 [0-7720-0619-9]

Canada's aviation history includes the exploits of daredevil war flyers, bush pilots, and commercial aviators. *Mature.*

POLITICS AND GOVERNMENT

see also
PUBLISHERS' SERIES
Canadian Critical Issues

The Arms, flags and emblems of Canada. Canada. Secretary of State; Deneau, 1978. 65 pages. $3.50 paper [0-88879-006-6]

Comprehensive, informative guide to the significance and uses of Canadian arms, flags and emblems. *Older to mature.*

Borovoy, A.A.; The Fundamentals of our fundamental freedoms: a primer on civil liberties and democracy. Canadian Civil Liberties, 1979. 31 pages. $1.50 paper.

Also available in French as *Principes de nos libertés fondamentales. Older.*

Carlton, Alex; Here's how it happens. Gage, 1978. 86 pages. $5.50, paper [0-7715-8507-1]

How municipal, provincial and federal governments work in Canada. *Middle.*

Greason, George K. and **King, Roy C.;** Canadian democracy at work. 3rd ed. Macmillan, 1977 (c1962). 119 pages. $2.75 paper [0-7705-0514-4]

Written to provide a working knowledge of Canadian federal, provincial and municipal systems of government with an outline of comparisons with those of Great Britain and the U.S.A. *Older to mature.*

Hill, Daniel G.; Human rights in Canada: a focus on racism. Canadian Labour Congress, 2841 Riverside Dr., Ottawa, 1977. 44 pages. $1.00 paper.

Explains how Canadians allow racism to prevail, giving positive ways to stem the growth of this inhuman practice.

Available in French as *Les droits de la personne au Canada: regard sur le racisme. Older.*

Monet, Jacques; The Canadian crown. Clarke, Irwin, 1979. 95 pages. $9.95 [0-7720-1252-0]

This profusely illustrated popular history shows the relationship of Canada's form of government to its continuing British connection. *Mature.*

Stanley, George F.G.; The Story of Canada's flag. McGraw, 1965. 96 pages. $6.95 [0-7700-0197-1]

How it was designed, how it was chosen, how it is to be used. *Older.*

Tooke, Moyra (ed.); Politics are people: an illustrated guide to Canadian elections. Griffin, 1974. 73 pages. $5.95 paper [0-88760-050-6]

Lively, informative guide to Canadian politics. *Older.*

LAW

see also
PUBLISHERS' SERIES
In the Public Interest Law Series

Copeland, Paul; Ruby, Clayton; King, Greg; King, Lynn; Law law law. Anansi, 1976. 4th ed. $2.95 paper [0-88784-611-4]

This up-to-date citizen's pocket manual makes Canadian law easily accessible through its plain, straightforward style. Use the newest edition only. *Older to mature.*

Jarman, Fred; In pursuit of justice. Wiley, 1976. 287 pages. $9.25 [0-471-02384-1]

Arguments for both sides show the complexities involved in capital punishment, women's rights, abortion, euthanasia and other controversial issues. *Mature.*

Ontario. Provincial Secretariat for Justice; The Growth of the laws we live by. Ontario. Publications Centre. [n.d.] 15 pages. $0.15 paper.

A simple introduction to Canadian law, illustrated with colour drawings. *Middle.*

Rivard, Glenn; Youth and the law. Community Legal Education Ontario, 2nd rev. ed. 43 pages. $2.00 paper [0-88903-022-7]

A well written booklet aimed at teenagers supplies information on how the law can and does affect them while encouraging young people to examine the reasons laws are necessary. *Mature.*

Wilson, Jeffery; Children and the law. Butterworth, 1978. 367 pages. $30.00 [0-409-87760-3]

Lacking a set of legal rules for children or a children's legal code in Canada the author presents "a collection of our existing laws affecting, in various degrees, the interest of the child." *Mature.*

Wilson, Jeffery; Up against it: children and the law in Canada. Anansi, 1980. 166 pages. $6.95 paper [0-88784-076-0]

A founding member of Justice for Children writes an informal, practical guide to the legal rights of Canadian children. *Mature.*

ECONOMICS

Mitchell, Alison Kemp and **Millard, Mary Austin;** Economics: a search for patterns. Gage, 1971. 311 pages. $7.75 [0-7715-8763-5]; Bibliography (1972) $1.60 [0-7715-8764-3]

Taxation, banking, trade, welfare and employment based on Canadian examples. *Older to mature.*

OCCUPATIONS

see also
PUBLISHERS' SERIES
Canada at Work
Careers Canada
Women at Work

Davison, Catherine V. and **Tippett, L. Glen;** A Career planning guide/a job search guide. Printing and Publishing Supply and Services Canada, Ottawa, K1A 0S9, 1977, 1978. 123 pages/130 pages. $2.95 paper each; $3.95 outside Canada. [0-660-00766-5]; [0-660-00765-7]

Two booklets to aid the junior high reader - choosing a career, taking the appropriate courses, and some strategies for finding work. *Older.*

SOCIAL SERVICES

see also
PUBLISHERS' SERIES
In Your Community

Barnes, Michael; In the public service; the Ontario Provincial Police. Highway Book Shop, 1974. 82 pages. $2.00 paper [0-88954-046-2]

Photos illustrate this comprehensive yet concise guide which focuses on aspects of prime interest to children. *Middle to older.*

Charters, Dean; Mountie: a golden treasury of those early years. Collier-Macmillan, 1973. 253 pages. $7.95 cloth [0-02-973420-7]; $3.95 paper [0-02-973400-2]

Photographic essay on the North West Mounted Police from its formation in 1870 until it became the Royal Canadian Mounted Police in 1920. *Older to mature.*

Coughlin, T.G.; The Dangerous sky. McGraw, 1968. 214 pages. $9.95 [0-7700-0241-2]

Highly entertaining book of tales about the Canadian flyers of the second World War. *Mature.*

Darrach, Jim; Fingerprinting: a science at your fingertips. Book Society, 1977. 30 pages. $2.25 net. [0-7725-5117-0]

Attractive, succinct yet comprehensive study of fingerprinting. *Middle.*

Horrall, Stanley; The Pictorial history of the R.C.M.P. McGraw, 1973. 256 pages. $14.95 [0-07-077366-1]

Factual history of the Royal Canadian Mounted Police from 1873-1973, liberally illustrated. *Older.*

DISCRIMINATORY PRACTICES

Morton, Tom and **McBride, John;** Look again: the process of prejudice and discrimination. CommCept, 1977. 90 pages. $6.75 paper [0-88829-020-9]

Readings in the causes and effects of prejudice that will make children more aware of their own perceptions. *Older to mature.*

An excellent teachers' guide is also available. ($4.00).

Populot Educational Resources. Detecting prejudice. Williams-Wallace, 1979. 52 pages. $2.95 paper [0-88795-004-3]

This handbook on discrimination in visual materials aims to teach young people how to become more aware of prejudice in their daily lives and how to fight it. *Older to mature.*

MULTICULTURALISM

see also
PUBLISHERS' SERIES
Kids Like Us
Multiculturalism Canada Series

Andrew, Robert and **Mason, Trishia;** We are their children: ethnic portraits of British Columbia. Branch, Doug. (illus.). Commcept, 1977. 162 pages. $6.75 [0-88829-003-9]

An introduction to the B.C. ethnic communities that figure in the history of the province. *Older.*

Canada. Multiculturalism Directorate; The Canadian family tree: Canada's peoples. Corpus, 1979. Rev. ed. 250 pages. $19.95 cloth [0-919217-13-3]; $12.95 paper [0-919217-14-1]

Short, well written and pertinent articles on about 80 national groups of immigrants to Canada. *Older to mature.*

Findley, Timothy and **others;** The Newcomers: inhabiting a new land. McClelland, 1979. 228 pages. $24.95 [0-7710-0158-4]

Photographs from the videotape illuminate this book that complements the television series. *Mature.*

Identity; the black experience in Canada. O.E.C.A. (Gage), 1979. 163 pages. $4.95 paper [0-7715-8328-1]

This excellent resource deals with Canadian Black history and contemporary Black Canada. Bibliography, filmography and other lists of Black cultural endeavours. *Mature.*

Ontario ethnocultural profiles. Ministry of Culture and Recreation, Multicultural Development Branch, 5th Floor, 77 Bloor St. West, Toronto M7A 2R9, 1979. 38 sheets. Free from the above address.

Fact sheets on Austrians, Finns, Japanese and 35 other ethnic groups who have made Canada their home. *Middle to older.*

Wood, Dean D.; Multicultural Canada; a teacher's guide to ethnic studies. OISE, 1978. 136 pages. $10.50 paper [0-7744-0175-2]

For help in developing and implementing special programs to promote intercultural understanding, multiculturalism and positive race relations. *Older to mature.*

HOLIDAYS

Allen, G.P.; Days to remember, illustrated. Ontario Ministry of Culture and Recreation Multicultural Development Branch, 1977. 78 pages. $1.50 paper.

Holidays observed by over 70 ethnic cultures represented in Ontario celebrate events significant to them and their history. *Middle to mature.*

Barber, Mary; Christmas in Canada. Dent, 1972. 134 pages. $2.50 list paper [0-460-90553-8]

Stories, poems, articles of Christmas past and present from sea to sea. *Older to mature.*

Carver, Caroline; Caroline Carver's merry Christmas book: a gift from Canada's past. Tundra, 1975. 96 pages. $4.95 paper [0-88776-066-X]

A handsel from Canada's Victorian past - a collection of pictures and stories from Canadian newspapers and magazines, 1837-1901. *All ages.*

Newman, Fran and **Boulanger, Claudette;** Hooray for today. Scholastic-Tab, 1979. 52 pages. $7.95 [0-590-07623-X]

A short note, an appropriate quote and a full-page colour painting on 24 days special to Canadians, starting with Canada Day and including Octoberfest and Chinese New Year. *Older.*

Nickerson, Betty; Celebrate the sun: a heritage of festivals interpreted through the art of children from many lands. McClelland, 1969. 128 pages. $8.95 [0-7710-6803-4]

Children paint their festival impressions and Nickerson explains the import of the holidays. *Older.*

SCIENCE

PHYSICAL SCIENCES
see also
PUBLISHERS' SERIES
Geological Guide Books

Baird, D.M.; A Guide to geology: for visitors in Canada's national parks. Macmillan, 1974. Rev. ed. 160 pages. $2.95 paper [0-7705-1010-8]

Pocket-sized, well-illustrated guide to rocks and other geologic phenomena. *Older to mature.*

Baird, D.M.: Our earth in continuous change. McGraw, 1971. 128 pages. $12.95 [0-7700-0316-8]

Excellent introduction to the earth sciences. *Mature.*

Gait, Robert I.; Exploring minerals & crystals. McGraw, 1974. 119 pages. $7.95 [0-07-077395-5]

Mineralogy for middle and older readers. *Middle to mature.*

Gait, Robert I. and **Meen, V.B.;** The Gallery of mineralogy. Royal Ontario Museum, 1968. 2 vols. 33 pages. $1.00 paper [0-88854-070-1] [0-88854-071-X]

Of most use to people having access to the Museum's facilities. *Middle to older.*

Hornstein, R.A.; Weather and why. Steinhaur, Norm (illus.). Environment Canada, 1978. 61 pages. $1.75 paper.

A compilation of frequently-noted questions and answers about weather phenomena under alphabetically arranged topics for quick reference. *Older.*

Hornstein, Reuben A.; The Weather book. McClelland, 1980. 95 pages. $7.95 paper [0-7710-4216-7]

Lore, legend and scientific facts about weather help the layman to forecast his own weather. *Mature.*

Ontario Department of Mines and **Hewitt, D.F.;** Rocks and minerals of Ontario. Queen's Printer, Ont., 1972. Rev. ed. 108 pages. $1.00 paper.

Comprehensive list of rocks and mineral deposits in Ontario, their physical properties, occurrence, location, with descriptions of the province's geological regions. *Older to mature.*

Penrose, Gordon; Dr. Zed's brilliant book of science experiments. Bucholtz-Ross, Linda (illus.). Greey de Pencier. 64 pages. $3.95 paper [0-919872-34-4]

Tested, illustrated, entertaining experiments that make learning scientific facts enjoyable. *Middle to older.*

Sabina, Ann P.; Rock and mineral collecting in Canada. Vol. 3. New Brunswick, Prince Edward Island and Newfoundland. Supply and Services Canada, 1973. $2.75 paper. *Mature.*

Spivak, Michael (ed.); What will they think of next? Condy, Roy C. (illus.). McClelland, 1979. 124 pages. $7.95 paper [0-7710-8221-5]

Based on the popular television series these "wacky inventions, startling discoveries, surprising medical developments and ingenious solutions to old problems" will delight young readers. *Middle to older.*

Swinton, William; The Earth tells its story. Hardy, David A. (illus.); Bodley Head (Clarke, Irwin), 1966. 32 pages. $6.25.

A Canadian scientist explains the dynamics of geology in a picture story. *Middle.*

Watts, Alan; Instant weather forecasting in Canada. General, 1968. 62 pages. $4.95 [0-7736-0010-8]

Twenty-four coloured photographs of clouds and sky interpreted for the layman who wants to know how to forecast the weather. *Older.*

THE ENVIRONMENT

see also
PUBLISHERS' SERIES
Elements Series

Chant, Donald A. (ed.); Pollution probe. New Press, 1970. 209 pages. $8.50 cloth [0-88770-054-3]; $2.50 paper [0-88770-055-1]; $1.75 paper [0-88770-167-1]

A handbook on pollutants and means of controlling them. *Mature.*

Holloway, Paul D. and **Tiesma, Peter P.;** One small step . . . an introduction to environmental studies. NC Press, 1977. 104 pages. $2.95 paper [0-919600-60-3]

Produced by the Laurentian Project of the Canada Studies Foundation, this book explores the impact of technology on the quality of life in Canada. *Mature.*

Morgan, Frank and **Forrester, James;** Pollution. McGraw, 1970. 137 pages. $5.85 paper [0-7700-3217-6] (Shaping Canada's Environment Series)

Well-written survey of Canada's pollution problems and the steps to be taken to solve them. *Mature.*

Sturmanis, Karl and **Sturmanis, Dona;** The Greenpeace book. Intermedia, 1978. 71 pages. $6.95 paper [0-920616-00-3]

Statement of the origins, purpose and history of the Greenpeace movement interspersed with photographs, poetry, maps and drawings. *Mature.*

NATURAL HISTORY

see also
PUBLISHERS' SERIES
Edible Wild Plants of Canada Series
The Illustrated Natural History of Canada Series
Natural History Notebook Series

Blood, Don and **Hall, Tom W.;** Rocky Mountain wildlife, illustrated. Hancock, 1976. 130 pages. $24.95 [0-919654-37-1]

Describes climate, vegetation and fauna of the Rocky Mountains and contains full descriptions of animals found there. Lavishly illustrated. *Older.*

Brooks, Bill; Wildlife of Canada in colour. Hounslow, 1976. 93 pages. $9.95 [0-88882-010-0]

Striking full-colour pictures of Canadian birds and animals that will encourage their conservation. *All ages.*

Gilroy, Doug; Parkland portraits: some natural history of the prairie parklands. Western Producer Prairie, 1979. 127 pages. $24.95 cloth [088833-019-7]; $14.95 paper [0-88833-031-6]
Flora and fauna beautifully photographed in colour and carefully captioned. *Older to mature.*

Groves, J. Walton; Edible and poisonous mushrooms of Canada. Canadian Government, 1972. 316 pages. $9.95.
Detailed reference guide for those who wish to make use of the edible wild. *Older to mature.*

Hosie, R.; Native trees of Canada. Fitzhenry and Whiteside, 1979. 383 pages. $16.95 cloth [0-88902-572-X] $9.95 paper [0-88902-550-9]
The definitive work on indigenous trees, not ones introduced to our country, well illustrated. *Mature.*

Karstad, Aleta; Canadian nature notebook. McGraw, 1979. 144 pages. $12.95 [0-07-082782-6]
A field naturalist-artist collects material from 25 communities of animals and plants and records their relationships in an easily understood text and meticulously detailed drawings. *Older to mature.*

Keenan, Noel and **Clery, Val;** A Day in the woods, illustrated. Greey de Pencier, 1978. 32 pages. $6.95 [0-919872-41-7] (An Owl Book)
Stunning colour photos provide felicitous encounters with dragonflies, turtles, snakes and other wildwood denizens. *Younger to middle.*

Lawrence, Louise de K.; The Lovely and the wild. McGraw, 1973. 2nd ed. 228 pages. $5.95 paper [0-07-077445-5]
Reflects an infinite understanding of the bird and animal world of Northern Ontario. *Older to mature.*

Livingston, John and **Sinclair, Lister;** Darwin and the Galapagos. C.B.C., 1966. 64 pages. $4.20 [0-88794-021-8]
Succinct statement on Darwin's Galapagos studies which led to the formulation of his theory. *Older to mature.*

MacKay, H.H.; Fishes of Ontario. Ontario Department of Wildlife, Fish and Wildlife Branch, 1963, 1969. 292 pages. $2.50.
"Thousands of miles of our fishing waters contain some of the best species of fish known to man." Colour plates. *Mature.*

McKay, Sheila and **Catling, Paul;** Trees, shrubs and flowers to know in Ontario. Gordon, Betsy (illus.). Dent, 1979. 208 pages. $6.95 [0-460-95304-4]
Black-and-white line drawings and short notes cover Ontario's flora. *Older to mature.*

Montgomery, F.H.; Weeds of Canada and the northern United States. McGraw, 1973. 226 pages. $4.95 paper [0-07-092970-X]
All you want to know about weeds; only colour illustrations are missing. *Middle to mature.*

Mulligan, Gerald A.; Common weeds of Canada/Les mauvaises herbes communes du Canada. Illustrated with colour photographs. McClelland in association with Information Canada, 1976. 140 pages. $7.95 paper [0-7710-6653-8]
Bilingual information describing each plant is short, to the point and uncomplicated. Colour illustrations for easy identification. *Older.*

Prescott, Christine and **Cavin, Betty;** A Nature walk in Stanley Park. Mitchell, 1977. 114 pages. $6.50 paper [0-88836-016-9]
A guide to plants, birds and small animals including glossary, scientific names, and bibliography. *Mature.*

Rising, Trudy L.; Snails, slugs, spiders and bugs. Miller, Kathryn De Vos (illus.). McClelland, 1977. 32 pages. $4.95 [0-88869-002-9] (A Magook Publication)
A child's guide to Canadian animals, birds, insects, fish, trees, bushes, flowers and ponds, beautifully illustrated. *Younger to middle.*

Stewart, Darryl; Canadian endangered species. Gage, 1974. 172 pages. $12.95 [0-7715-9313-9]; $7.95 paper [0-7715-9309-0]

An impassioned appeal to conserve Canadian wildlife - mammals, birds, reptiles and amphibians. Descriptions of extinct species become cautionary tales for the aware reader. *Older.*

Van Camp, J.L.; Fifty trees of Canada east of the Rockies. Book Society, 1952. 64 pages. $1.25 [0-7725-1099-7]

Brief, illustrated notes. *Middle to older.*

FLOWERS

Courtenay, Booth; A Guide in full colour: wild flowers and weeds. Van Nostrand, 1976. 144 pages. $9.95 paper [0-442-21704-8]

Includes family-group charts and geographical range map. *Middle to older.*

Ferguson, Mary and **Richard Saunders;** Canadian wildflowers. Van Nostrand, 1976. $19.95 [0-442-29859-5]

A treasury of native flowers beautifully illustrated and clearly described. *All ages.*

Ferguson, Mary; Canadian wildflowers 1976. Fleming, Allan (design); Van Nostrand, 1975. 86 pages. $19.95 [0-442-29851]

A historical commentary on the flora of Canada as it was over one hundred years ago. Beautiful full-page illustrations. *Older to mature.*

Gillet, John M; Spring flowers of the national capital region, illustrated. National Capital Commission, 1973. 116 pages. $1.50.

Arranged by their scientific names, 50 flowers found in the Ottawa-Hull and Gatineau areas. An illustrated guide. *Mature.*

Mackenzie, Katherine; Wild flowers of eastern Canada. Tundra (Collins), 1973. 96 pages. $2.95 paper.

Short notes of little known facts about 90 wild flowers, grouped by flowering season and accompanied by beautiful watercolours. *All ages.*

Neufeld, J.B.; Wild flowers of the prairies. Prairie Books, 1968. 33 pages. $3.95 [0-919306-17-9]

Close-up colour photos and brief descriptions of prairie flowers, more suited for identification than scientific study. *All ages.*

Porsild, A.E.; Rocky Mountain wild flowers. Lid, Dagny Tande (illus.). Published jointly by the National Museum of Natural Sciences, National Museums of Canada and Parks Canada, Department of Indian and Northern Affairs, 1976. 454 pages. Available by mail from the National Museums of Canada, Marketing Services Division, Ottawa, Ontario, K1A 0M8. $5.00

Well arranged and illustrated with minutely detailed water-colours. This will introduce lowland children to a wide variety of mountain flora. *Older to mature.*

Sherk, Lawrence C.; Growing Canada's floral emblems. Canadian Government, 1971. 28 pages. $0.75 paper.

Transplanting and care of Canadian wildflowers, the emblems of the provinces. *Middle.*

Vance, F.R.; Jowsey, J.R. and **McLean, J.S.;** Wildflowers across the prairies. Western Producer, 1977. 214 pages. $14.95 cloth [0-919306-74-8] $8.95 paper [0-919306-73-X]

This useful guide to 270 species of Western wildflowers includes a glossary and coloured photos. *Older to mature.*

White, Helen A. and **Maxcine Williams.** The Alaska-Yukon wild flowers guide. Howie, Virginia (illus.). Alaska Northwest Publishing, Anchorage, Alaska, 1974. 218 pages. $8.95 paper [0-88240-032-0]

An excellent introduction to the flora of the Far North includes a chapter on wild flowers in your garden which gives instruction on collecting flowers, how to transport them, etc. *Older to mature.*

ANIMALS

see also
PUBLISHERS' SERIES
Paper sculptures
Zoo Book Series

Berrill, Jacquelyn; Wonders of animal nurseries. Dodd, 1968. 66 pages. $5.25 [0-396-05766-7] (Wonders Series)

Berrill, Jacquelyn; Wonders of the monkey world. Dodd, 1967. 88 pages. $5.25 [0-396-06394-2] (Wonders Series)

Berrill, Jacquelyn; Wonders of the woods and desert at night. Dodd, 1963. 96 pages. $5.25 [0-396-06395-0] (Wonders Series)

Berrill, Jacquelyn; Wonders of the world of wolves. Dodd, 1970. $5.25 [0-0-396-07155-4] (Wonders Series)

Excellent titles in a series on different aspects of wildlife. *Middle to older.*

Braithwaite, Max; Voices of the wild. McClelland, 1962. $5.95 [0-7710-1638-7]

Betty and Bob learn about bears and skunks, herons and sparrows, frogs and moose from Uncle Jack. *Middle to older.*

Burns, Florence McLaughlin; Jumbo: the biggest elephant in all the world, illustrated. Scholastic, 1978. 64 pages. $1.50 paper.

A short readable life story of the "biggest elephant in all the world." His great size and his playfulness and love for children endeared him to all Regent's Park Zoo visitors. *Middle.*

Campbell, Craig A. and **Dagg, Anne Innis;** Mammals of Waterloo and South Wellington counties. Gartshore, Mary (illus.) and Dyer, Michaël (maps); Otter, 1972. $3.50 paper. *Older to mature.*

Dagg, Anne Innis; Mammals of Ontario. Alexander, Roslyn A. (illus.); Otter, 1974. 159 pages. $10.00 cloth; $3.50 paper.

Scientific data, short items of research and excellent drawings familiarize readers with all common animals from the vole to the ringed seal. *Older to mature.*

Froom, Barbara; The Snakes of Canada. McClelland, 1977. 128 pages. $5.95 paper [0-7710-3186-6]

Illustrations, description, folklore, and geographic habitat. *Older to mature.*

Froom, Barbara; The Turtles of Canada. McClelland, 1976. 120 pages. $8.95 [0-7710-3183-1]

This companion to *The Snakes of Canada* is another excellent, readable guide, well illustrated. *Older to mature.*

Grainger, David; Animals in peril: a guide to the endangered species of North America. Pagurian, 1978. 192 pages. $14.95 [0-88932-082-9]

Clear and straight forward information on 20 mammals indigenous to Canada and the USA in danger of extinction. Distinctive illustrations, some in colour. *Older to mature.*

Hampson, Cy; Into the woods beyond. Macmillan, 1971. 117 pages. $7.95 [0-7705-0163-X]

Informative study of Canadian mammals. Excellent photographs. *Older.*

Horwood, Harold; The Foxes of Beachy Cove. PaperJacks, 1975. 190 pages. $1.75 paper [0-7737-7082-8]

The natural beauties of Newfoundland unfold in these wild life observations by a partisan writer. *Older to mature.*

Lawrence, R.D.; Paddy: a naturalist's story of an orphan beaver. Elliot, Bill (illus.). Knopf (Avon), 1977. $11.75 cloth [0-394-40403-3]; $1.95 paper [0-380-42580-7]

Lawrence adopted an orphan beaver, raised it to full independence in four months, then returned it to its natural environment. His observations make an interesting record of *Castor Canadensis. Older to mature.*

Logier, E.B.S.; The Snakes of Ontario. U.T.P., 1958. 94 pages. $4.75 paper [0-8020-6069-2]

A general account of snakes followed by a section dealing with various species. *Older to mature.*

McAllister, D.E. and **Crossman, E.J.;** A Guide to the freshwater sport fishes of Canada. National Museums, 1973. 89 pages. $3.75 paper. (Natural History Series, No. 1)

Succinct, practical coverage with clear illustrations of one of Canada's bountiful natural resources. *Older to mature.*

May, Charles Paul; A Second book of Canadian animals. Macmillan, 1964. 115 pages. 1977. $4.95 [0-7705-1521-5]

Informal descriptions of 26 Canadian mammals. *Middle to older.*

Mowat, Farley; Never cry wolf. McClelland, 1973. Rev. ed. 247 pages. $8.95 [0-7710-6584-1]; Text ed. $2.75 paper [0-7710-6582-5]

Fascinating account of a man's attempt to study the wolf through a summer of daily observation. *Older to mature.*

Mowat, Farley; A Whale for the killing. McClelland, 1972. 239 pages. $6.95 [0-7710-6570-1]

An attempt to save a trapped whale on the Newfoundland coast results in a crusade to save this endangered species. *Older to mature.*

Peterson, Randolph L.; Mammals in profile. Loates, Martin Glen (illus.); cartography by G.J. Mathews, 2 volumes, Cerebrus (Prentice-Hall), 1975. 36 pages each. $2.95 each paper [0-920016-00-6]

Beautiful illustrations illumine detailed descriptions of habitat, diet, habits and reproduction of each species. Fine coated paper and small format make these titles ideal for children. *Middle to older.*

Russell, Andy; Adventures with wild animals. Savage, Harry (illus.); Hurtig, 1977. 183 pages. $9.95 [0-88830-143-X]

Elks, otters and friendly owls are among the wild animals that live through the author's pen. *Mature.*

Scott, W.B.; Freshwater fishes of eastern Canada. U.T.P., 1967. 2nd ed. 137 pages. $4.50 paper [0-8020-6074-9]

Detailed reference work with complete descriptions. *Older to mature.*

Seton, Ernest T.; Animal tracks and hunter signs. Doubleday, 1958. 160 pages. $7.95 [0-385-06862-X]

Habits and behaviour of animals as revealed by their trails. *Middle to mature.*

Shuh, John Hennigar; Crabs wear their skeletons on the outside. Stobie, Nancy (illus.). Nova Scotia Museum, 1979. 40 pages. $3.00 paper [0-919680-17-8]

A simple explanation of this crustacean's life cycle carefully illustrated with line drawings. *Younger.*

Smith, David Allenby; Sharptooth: a year of the beaver. Kebic, Robert (illus.); 1974. 54 pages. $6.95 [0-88778-107-1]

Two beavers follow the natural round as integral components of the Canadian ecology. *Middle to older.*

Solandt, Barbara M. and **Hatton, Norman;** Children of the ark. U.T.P., 1973. 95 pages. $7.95 [0-8020-2101-8]

A review of the educational role which zoos fulfil and their potential. *Mature.*

Stewart, Miller and **Stewart, Margaret;** Bright world around us. Simon & Schuster (PaperJacks) 1971. 183 pages. $1.25 paper [0-671-78091-3]

Personal observations of animals and birds that delighted the authors. *Older to mature.*

Terhune, David; The Harp seal. Burns, 1973, 48 pages. $7.95 [0-88768-042-9]

An illustrated study. *Older.*

Theberge, John B.; Wolves and wilderness. Theberge, Mary (illus.). Dent, 1975. 159 pages. $4.95 paper [0-460-95829-1]

First-hand experiences with wolves in different parts of Canada. *Older to mature.*

Trueman, Stuart; The Wild life I've led, illustrated. McClelland, 1976. 160 pages. $8.95 [0-7710-8600-8]

Encounters with a bull moose in mating season, a bat in a bedroom and other animals, told with a chuckle by a winner of the Stephen Leacock Memorial Medal for Humour. *Older to mature.*

Vevers, Gwynne; Animals of the Arctic. Wilson, Maurice (illus.); Bodley Head (Clarke, Irwin), 1964. 32 pages. $2.25 [0-370-00858-8]

Short text and clear attractive drawings present northern wildlife. *Middle.*

Wooding, Frederick; The Book of Canadian fishes. McGraw, 1973. 2nd ed. 303 pages. $5.95 paper [0-07-077635-0]

A comprehensive illustrated catalogue. *Older to mature.*

BIRDS

Angell, Tony; Owls. Hancock House, 1975. 80 pages. $12.95 [0-919654-25-8]

Sixty beautiful drawings and short informative descriptions of the 18 North American species, by an owl lover. *Middle to older.*

Bodsworth, Fred; Last of the curlews. McClelland, 1963. 126 pages. $1.95 paper (New Canadian Library)

Realistic portrayal of the migrating Arctic curlews, beautifully written. *Mature.*

Gilroy, Doug; Prairie birds in colour. Western Producer, 1976. 113 pages. $14.95 cloth [0-919306-48-9]; $9.95 paper [0-919306-59-4]

Over 90 captioned pictures of western birds heighten the viewer's appreciation of our wild fowl. *Middle to older.*

Godfrey, W. Earl; The Birds of Canada. Crosby, John (illus.); and MacDonald, S.D. (illus.). National Museums, 1966. 428 pages. $22.50 [0-660-00126-8]

The definitive work on the birds of Canada including over 400 species, beautifully illustrated in colour. *Older to mature.*

Godfrey, W. Earl; Some Canadian birds. Crosby, John (illus.). National Museums, 1966. 44 pages. Rev. ed. 1975. $1.95 paper [0-660-02426-8]

An inexpensive illustrated account of common Canadian birds. *Middle to older.*

Hancock, David A.; Adventure with eagles. Wildlife Conservation, 1970. 40 pages. $4.95 cloth [0-919654-22-3]; $2.50 paper [0-919654-23-1].

Biological survey of the bald eagle indigenous to the British Columbia coast. *Older.*

Hancock, David A.; and **Hancock, Susan;** Guide to western wildlife. Hancock House, 1977. 33 pages. $2.50 paper [0-919654-81-9]

A brief text and attractive illustrations serve as an introduction to animals and birds. *Middle to older.*

Lawrence, Louise de Kiriline; Mar. Clarke Irwin, 1976. 103 pages, $8.50 [0-7720-1034-0]

Two years in the life of a yellow-bellied sapsucker, sensitively and knowledgeably observed. *Older.*

Loates, Glen and **James, Ross;** Glen Loates birds of North America. Prentice, 1979. $24.95 [0-13-357103-3]

Sketches and coloured plates of 24 North American birds in folio format show off Glen Loates's precision and artistry. *Older to mature.*

MacKay, Barry; Eighty more land birds to know. Book Society, 1968. 83 pages. $4.95 [0-7725-1093-8]

Land birds of the Great Lakes area. Data for identification with illustrations and profiles. *Older.*

Mackenzie, John P.S.; Birds in peril: a guide to the endangered species in Canada and North America. Shortt, Terence (illus.). McGraw, 1976. 191 pages. $9.95 [0-07-082375-8]

The history and habitat of 20 of the 32 North American bird species whose future is predictably limited. Superb illustrations. *Older to mature.*

Rising, Trudy L.; Songbirds of eastern Canada; Manitoba, Ontario, Quebec, Atlantic provinces. DeVos-Miller, Kathryn (illus.). Tundra, (Collins) 1977. 96 pages. $3.95 paper [0-8876-037-6]

Descriptive texts with facing paintings identify 44 songbirds. *All ages.*

Salt, W. Ray and **Jim R. Salt;** The Birds of Alberta with their ranges in Saskatchewan and Manitoba. Hurtig, 1976. 498 pages. $10.00 [0-88830-108-1]

Beautiful colour photographs, clear and well-detailed, enhance an accurate and informative text. "The birds give the impression that they have flown onto the pages and are merely resting before flying off again." *All ages.*

Scott, Jack D.; Canada geese. Sweet, Ozzie (illus.) Putnam's (Academic), 1976. 64 pages $8.95 [0-339-20492-X]

Black and white photos and an up-to-date commentary explore the life cycle of the Canada goose. *Middle.*

Tufts, Robie W.; Nova Scotia birds of prey. Lancelot, 1978. 88 pages. $2.95 paper [0-88999-085-9]

Small black and white drawings accompany concise descriptions of birds of prey - eagles, hawks, owls and vultures. *Middle to mature.*

Tufts, Robie W. 20 favourite birds of Nova Scotia, illustrated. Lancelot, 1975 47 pages. $2.00 paper. [0-88999-036-0]

Brief but well written guide contains descriptions which "reveal a professional knowledge of birds, an appreciation of their differing qualities and an enthusiasm for their existence in nature." *All ages.*

HEALTH

see also
PUBLISHERS' SERIES
Charlie Choppers Series

Can you babysit tonight? Ontario Government Publications, Ont., 1970. $0.25 paper.

This small pamphlet has safety hints and child care instructions for the beginning sitter. *Older.*

Clarkson, Margaret; Susie's babies. Eerdmans (Canterbury House), 1960. $2.25 paper [0-8028-4005-1]

A first book of sex instruction for the very young. *Younger to middle.*

Cotter, Graham; Powell, Marion and **Vichert, Bruce;** Youth hotline: letters to the Toronto Star Hotline. Musson, 1979. 192 pages. $4.95 paper [0-7737-1032-9]

A social worker, a medical doctor and an Anglican priest answered young people's questions in a Toronto Star column. They are collected here to help a new audience of troubled teenagers. *Older to mature.*

Gendron, Lionel; Birth: the story of how you came to be. Cowan, Alice (trans.); Harvest, 1970. 93 pages. $3.50 paper [0-88772-112-5]

Large print, simple explanations and clear diagrams. *Middle.*

Keyl, Anne; VD: the people to people diseases. Anansi, 1971. 113 pages. $1.95 paper [0-88784-610-6]

Detailed, accurate and straight-forward account of a prevalent problem. *Older.*

Leibel, B.S. and **Wrenshall, G.A.;** Insulin. Canadian Diabetic Association, 1971. 45 pages. $3.00.

History of diabetes, and the discovery of insulin - a Canadian accomplishment. *Middle.*

Robson, Bonnie Edna; My parents are divorced, too: what teenagers experience and how they cope. Dorset, 1979. 211 pages. $7.95 paper [0-88893-010-0]

A group of young people (ages 11-19) who have all experienced the traumas of divorce discuss them openly with a child psychologist. The result is a sympathetic approach to a prevalent social problem. *Older to mature.*

Vandermaas, A.; Sex education in home and school. Norris Place, 1973. 140 pages. $3.95 paper.

Factual, common-sense guide for parents and teachers. *Mature.*

THE METRIC SYSTEM

Bates, W.W. and **Fullerton, O.;** How to think metric. Copp, 1974. 73 pages. $1.25 paper [0-7730-4023-4]

Amusing illustrations help readers to convert their way of thinking about measurement. *All ages.*

Black, Gerald J.; Thinking metric for Canadians. Brown, Robert (illus.); Doubleday, 1975. 93 pages. $1.95 paper.

Advanced guide to the history of the metric system, its various components and their uses. *All ages.*

The Canadian metric conversion handbook. Hurtig, 1977. $1.95 paper [0-88830-149-9]

A useful quick reference tool on the basic terms and conversion tables. *Older to mature.*

Council of Ministers of Education, Canada. The Metric guide. Council of Ministers of Education, 1976. 2nd ed. 31 pages. $3.00 paper [0-7744-0127-3]

A comprehensive guide to metric measurement based on Canada's official Metric Practice Guide. *Mature.*

DelGrande, J.J.; The Great Canadian how to go metric . . . and like it book. Gage, 1975. 64 pages. $3.95 [0-7715-9933-1]

Comparative photographs of familiar products particularize their metric measurements in many everyday situations - shopping, driving, cooking. An excellent introduction to the metric system. *All ages.*

Hallamore, E. and **Bucholtz, Ross L.;** The Metric book of amusing things to do. Greey de Pencier, 1974. 96 pages. $2.95 paper. [0-919872-06-9]

Metric mice introduce 46 ways to use the metric system without converting to imperial measurement. *Middle.*

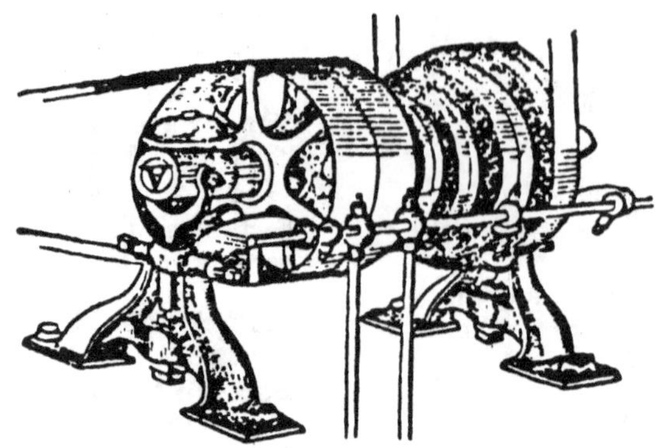

APPLIED SCIENCES

INVENTIONS

Nostbakken, Janis and **Humphrey, Jack;** The Canadian inventions book; innovations, discoveries and firsts. Greey de Pencier, 1976. 159 pages. $6.95 paper. [0-919872-24-7]

With over one million patents to their credit since 1824, Canadians have a right to be proud of their collective creativity which is well documented in this valuable account. *Middle to older.*

INDUSTRIES

see also
PUBLISHERS' SERIES
Canada at Work

Forester, Joseph E. and **Forester, Anne D.;** Fishing, British Columbia's commercial fishing history. Hancock, 1975. 224 pages. $14.95. [0-919654-43-6]

A well-researched account comprehensive of Indian and early settlers' fishing methods, sealing, whaling, canning and modern techniques. *Older to mature.*

Gould, Ed. Logging; British Columbia's logging history. Hancock, 1975. 224 pages. $14.95 [0-919654-44-4] (Resource Series)

A large, profusely illustrated history of the B.C. lumbering industry. *Mature.*

Le Messurier, Sally Lori; The Fishery of Newfoundland and Labrador. Memorial University, St. John's, A1C 5S7, 1980. 151 pages. $6.25 paper [0-88901-041-2]

Vital to the economy of Canada, the fishing industry sustains about 15% of the people in Newfoundland and Labrador. *Mature.*

Lind, Carol J.; Big timber! Big men!: a history of loggers in a new land. Hancock House, 1978. 153 pages. $14.95 [0-88839-020-3]

The colourful history of the lumbering industry (1800-1930) as it progressed across Canada emphasizes the lumberjack, not the technology. *Mature.*

Stanton, Charles R.; Canadian forestry: the view beyond the trees. Macmillan, 1976. 70 pages. $5.95 paper [0-7705-1417-0]

Forest management for the benefit of all Canadians is the imperative message of this informative book. *Older to mature.*

THE ARTS

Fulford, Robert; Arts Canada today. Copp, 1977. 135 pages. $9.95 cloth [0-7730-4029-3]; $5.95 paper [0-7730-4028-5]

Brief survey of music, theatre, painting and sculpture, dance, film, architecture, broadcasting, native art and literature in Canada. *Older and mature.*

ART

see also
PUBLISHERS' SERIES
Canadian Artists' Series (Gage)
Canadian Artists' Series (The National Gallery)

Arts of the raven; masterworks by the Northwest Coast Indians. Vancouver Art Gallery, 1974 (c1967). 109 pages. $7.50. *Older to mature.*

Comins, Jeremy; Eskimo crafts and their cultural backgrounds. Lothrop, (Gage), 1975. 125 pages. $8.55 L.B. [0-688-41705-1]

Gives simple directions for many Eskimo crafts which will encourage young people to copy them and spark their interest in the Inuit. *Older to mature.*

Duval, Paul; The Art of Glen Loates. Cerebrus/Prentice, 1977. 189 pages. $35.00 [0-920016-05-7]

Colour reproductions of Loates's nature paintings and an inspiring biography by Duval will delight young readers. *Mature.*

Fleming, Marie; 100 years: evolution of the Ontario College of Art. AGO, 1976. $4.95 paper [0-919876-21-8]

A representative selection of works by faculty and students through the first century. *Older to mature.*

Folk art of Nova Scotia. Art Gallery of Nova Scotia, 1976. 59 pages. $3.00 paper.

"A travelling exhibition of 20th century folk art of Nova Scotia" which displays the spontaneity, simplicity and humour inherent in native art. Includes profiles of 18 artists and illustrations of their work. *Older to mature.*

Gidmark, David; The Indian crafts of William and Mary Commanda. McGraw, 1980. 144 pages. $12.95 cloth [0-07-092359-0]; $7.95 paper [0-07-092360-4]

These well known Algonkian craftsmen excel in beadwork, quill work, snowshoe making, and hide tanning as well as in constructing birchbark canoes. *Mature.*

Glubok, Shirley; The Art of the Woodland Indians. Collier-Macmillan, 1976. 48 pages. $9.95 [0-02-736440-2]

Describes the art, architecture, traditions and customs of these inhabitants of the Northeastern forests of Canada and the United States. Beautiful handiwork is shown in the photographs. *Middle.*

Guillet, Edwin C.; Pioneer arts and crafts. U.T.P., 1968. 2nd ed. 97 pages. $2.50 paper [0-8020-6081-1]

How the early settlers made soap, candles, quilts and other necessities of domestic life. *Older to mature.*

Houston, James; Eskimo prints. Academic, 1971. 112 pages. $14.95 cloth; $7.50 paper.

Stone cut and stencil prints by Eskimos reflect their simple life. *Older to mature.*

Hunkin, Harry. A Story of the Group of Seven. McGraw, 1976. 160 pages. $10.95 [0-07-082418-5]

A reissue of *There is no finality,* published in 1971 by Burns, a fine visual introduction to an important segment of Canadian art. *Older.*

'KSAN breath of our grandfathers; an exhibition of 'KSAN art. National Museum, 1972. 108 pages. $2.50 paper.

A catalogue of captioned photographs of feast houses, regalia and masks of Skeena River people. *Older to mature.*

The Laurentians: painters in a landscape. Gage, 1977. 88 pages. $8.95 [0-7715-93953]

An illustrated catalogue of a special exhibition of the works of 15 artists working north of Montreal during the past 50 years. *Older to mature.*

MacDonald, Thoreau; The Group of Seven. McGraw, 1944. 34 pages. $2.95 paper [0-7700-0007-X]

The son of one of the Group produces a brief illustrated account of its members. *Middle to older.*

Patterson, Nancy-Lou; Canadian native art. Collier-Macmillan, 1973. 180 pages. $12.50 [0-02-975610-3]

Concise, comprehensive and analytical history of Native arts from coast to coast, profusely illustrated. *Older to mature.*

Sculpture of the Inuit: masterworks of the Canadian Arctic/La sculpture chez les Inuit: chefs-d'oeuvre de l'Arctique canadien. U.T.P.; 1971. 493 pages. $20.00 cloth [0-8020-1845-9]

An impressive tribute to an artistically talented people. *Mature.*

Spencer, Audrey; Spinning and weaving at Upper Canada Village. McGraw, 1964. 40 pages. $2.95 (text) [0-7700-0024-X]

Raising flax and sheep is only part of the skill involved in this ancient craft. *Middle to older.*

Steltzer, Ulli; Indian artists at work. Douglas & McIntyre 1976. 163 pages. $13.95. [0-88894-116-1]

Dedicated West Coast Native artists pictured at work on the knitting, weaving, carving that distinguish their creative bent. *Older to mature.*

Stewart, Hilary; Looking at Indian art of the Northwest Coast. Douglas & McIntyre, 1979. 111 pages. $6.95 paper [0-88894-229-X]

Excellent photographs and drawings illustrate the basic line forms preferred by the six West Coast Indian groups to elaborate their distinctive art work. *Older to mature.*

Wallace, George; The Artists' zoo. Holt, 1970. 92 pages. $1.95 [0-03-926555-2] (Themes in Art)

The plastic arts from prehistoric cave paintings to the caustic drawings of George Grosz. *Older.*

Wallace, George; Sailing ships: themes in art. Holt, 1972. 92 pages. $2.50 cloth [0-03-926558-7]; $1.95 paper [0-03-928277-5] (Themes in Art)

Traces design in the development of ships. *Mature.*

MUSIC

Barbeau, Marius; Lismer, Arthur and **Bourinot, Arthur;** Come a singing: Canadian folksongs. Canadian Government. 1974 (c1963). $1.25 paper.

Thirty Canadian folksongs adapted from original English and French sources, including The Gay Raftsmen, Mary Anne and Alouette, illustrated with line drawings by one of The Group of Seven. *All ages.*

Barber, Lois; Twelve days of Christmas north. Chaplin, Carl (illus.). Northern Times Press, 1978. 28 pages. $3.75 paper.

In this Northern version of a favourite Christmas song "three bull moose, six beavers swimming and a blue grouse in a spruce tree" among other forest denizens capture an authentic Canadian feeling. Green monochromes and clever design add to this ingenious rendition. *Younger to middle.*

Byrne, Pat (ed.); The Ryan's fancy. Breakwater, 1977. 122 pages. $5.95 paper [0-919948-26-X]

Songbook–photo-album–biography of this popular folk singing group. *Mature.*

Canadian vibrations canadiennes. Macmillan, 1972. 154 pages. Educ. ed. $2.80 paper [0-7705-0975-4]

Seventy popular and singable Canadian songs with words, chords and historical notes. *Older to mature.*

Cass-Beggs, Barbara; Canadian folk songs for the young. Douglas & McIntyre 1975. 48 pages. $6.95 [0-88894-065-3] $5.95 paper. [0-88894-266-4]

Humorous drawings, simple musical notation and pertinent comments embellish 32 Canadian folk songs. *Younger to middle.*

Cass-Beggs, Barbara; Your baby needs music. Douglas & McIntyre Ltd., 1978. 144 pages. $9.95 [0-88894-213-3]

Using music with children from birth to two years; why, how, and a selection of songs, finger plays and singing games to choose from. *Younger to middle.*

Creighton, Helen; Songs and ballads from Nova Scotia. General, 1966. 333 pages. $4.95 paper [0-7736-1001-4]

150 folk songs from Down East. *All ages.*

Davis, Bob; Singin' about us. Lorimer, 1976. 144 pages. $11.95 Spiral-bound [0-88862-109-4]; $5.95 paper [0-88862-108-6]

"Fine contemporary songs being sung across Canada today." *Older to mature.*

Fowke, Edith; The Penguin book of Canadian folk songs. Penguin, 1973. $2.95 paper.

Songs that evoke the history, the land and the people of Canada. Guitar chords. *All ages.*

Fowke, Edith; Ring around the moon. Brown, Judith Gwyn (illus.); McClelland, 1977. 160 pages $6.95 [0-7710-3200-5]

A continuation of *Sally go round the sun* for older children. The section, Dopey Ditties, ought to be vetted before the book is given to children. *Older.*

Fowke, Edith; Sally go round the sun. Marchiori, Carlos (illus.); McClelland, 1969. 160 pages. $9.95 book [0-7710-3165-3]; $4.95 record; $11.95 book & record.

Sandlot, street-corner, and playroom poetry that Canadian children chant as they play. *Middle to older.*

Fowke, Edith (literary ed.) and **Hoey, Elizabeth Wilkes** (illus.); More folk songs of Canada. Johnston, Richard (music ed.); Waterloo Music, 1967. 207 pages. Library edition $7.50.

Easy musical arrangements of Canadian folk songs. This publisher's catalogue lists many other Canadian music books suitable for children. *All ages.*

Fowke, Edith (literary ed.), **Johnston, Richard** (music ed.) and **Hoey, Elizabeth Wilkes** (illus.); Folk songs of Canada. Waterloo Music, 1954. 4th ed. 198 pages. Library edition $7.50; Choral ed. $2.50.

Songs of French and English Canada: variants of traditional folksongs and popular songs mating familiar tunes and topical lyrics. *All ages.*

Fowke, Edith (trans.), **Johnston, Richard** (arr.) and **Hoey, Elizabeth Wilkes** (illus.); Folk Songs of Quebec (Chansons de Québec). Waterloo Music, 1957. Library edition $4.95.

Familiar French-Canadian folk songs, in French and English, collected by Canada's foremost authority in the field. *All ages.*

Fowke, Edith and **Mills, Alan;** Canada's story in song. Gage, 1965. Rev. ed. 230 pages. $8.00 [0-7715-4540-1]

A collector and a singer combine their talents to give children an historical survey of folk songs from Eskimo chants to French *chansons.* A recording by Alan Mills is available: Folkways, FW 3000. *All ages.*

Garshowitz, S.G.; Play to music. Ministry of Culture and Recreation, Sports and Fitness Division, 1978. 102 pages. $2.00.

Songs (with scores), games and dances (with instructions) suitable for children from age five to teenage make this a valuable guide. *All ages.*

Glatt, Louise; What to do until the music teacher comes. Cockburn, Kitty (illus.). Berandol Music, 1978. 94 pages. $7.95 paper.

A sensitive introduction to using music as an integral part of a young child's life. There are chapters on listening, games, instruments, songs and recommended books and records. *Middle to mature.*

Houston, James; Songs of the Dream People: chants and images from the Indians and Eskimos of North America. Academic, 1972. 83 pages. $6.95.

These songs enlarge the reader's appreciation of our Native singers. *Older.*

MacNeil, Rita; Born a woman: songs. Bourque, Pat (design); Women's Educational Press, 1975. 41 pages. $4.00 paper. [0-88961-019-3]

Songs composed to celebrate woman's fight for freedom and recognition. A recording is also available on the Boot label and distributed by the London Record Company at $7.29. *Mature.*

Manny, Louise (ed.)**;** Songs of Miramichi, Brunswick, 1968. 330 pages. $7.50 [0-88790-022-4]

Over 100 songs handed down by the early European settlers in the "land of the Micmacs," New Brunswick's Miramichi river country. *Older to mature.*

Offenheim, Sandy Tobias; Honey on toast. Berandol, 1977. 108 pages. $5.95 paper.

This song book illustrated by the author's daughter includes 15 songs with piano and autoharp, guitar or banjo arrangements. A recording of the songs is available on Berandol (BER 9021) at $7.98. *Younger to middle.*

Panabaker, Lucile; Lucile Panabaker's second song book. Dacey, Pat (illus.); PMA, 1975. 65 pages. $6.50 [0-88778-123-3]

Panabaker, Lucile; Lucile Panabaker's song book. PMA, 1968. 68 pages. $6.50 saddle-stitched [0-88778-020-2]

Delightful songs and rhyming games for pre-schoolers. *Younger.*

Usher, Bill and **Page-Harpa, Linda** (eds.)**;** For what time I am in this world. PMA, 1977. 240 pages. $15.00 cloth [0-88778-166-7]; $8.95 paper [0-88778-167-5]

The personal responses of dozens of contributors as they talk of their own lives, folk music and cultures in relation to the Mariposa Folk Festival which started in 1961 in Orillia, now grown to a major North American folk music event. *Mature.*

Waring, Dennis; Folk instruments; make them and play them. Hyperion, 1979. 168 pages. $14.00 paper [0-920534-06-6]

Complete guide to making musical instruments -pan pipes, glockenspiel, dulcimer and more. Detailed simple instructions and clear photographs and diagrams. *Older to mature.*

BALLET

Darling, Christopher; Kain and Augustyn. Macmillan, 1977. 160 pages. $10.00 paper [0-7705-1612-2]

Stunning photographs capture the star quality of these world-renowned National Ballet dancers. *Middle to mature.*

Mason, David; Karen Kain; lady of dance. Street, David (illus.). McGraw, 1978. 127 pages. $14.95 [0-07-082705-2]

Kain's career from its earliest beginnings to her world-wide acclaim seen through the masterly photographs taken while she performed and rehearsed. *Middle to mature.*

SPORTS AND RECREATION

GAMES

Bereiter, Carl and **Anderson, Valerie;** Thinking games. Della-Vedova, Rod (illus.). O.I.S.E., 1975. vol. 1. $3.50 paper [0-7744-0118-4]; vol. 2 $3.50 paper [0-7744-0119-2] (Curriculum Series)

Children are involved in thinking, problem solving and group participation while they enjoy playing games of varying difficulty. Vol. 1 is for ages 5-9; vol. 2 for ages 9–older. *Middle to mature.*

Estrada, Billie; How to play hopscotch: a game created by children. Estrada, 1974. $3.95 paper [0-9690490-0-5]

Photographs and drawings illustrate players and diagrams for 20 variants of the game. *Younger.*

Orlick, Terry; The Cooperative sports and games book. Pantheon (General), 1978. 129 pages. $11.95 [0-394-42215-5]

A professor of sports psychology introduces the concept of cooperation as opposed to competition in children's games. For parents and teachers. *Mature.*

Owens, Judy; Hallowe'en fun. Cole, Kathryn (illus.) and Brooks, Terry (illus.); Scholastic-Tab, 1972, 2nd ed. 32 pages. $1.35 paper.

Gaily illustrated paperback offers games, decorations and costumes for celebrating Hallowe'en. *Younger to middle.*

Robson, Ann and **Robson, J.M.;** Word games for families who are still speaking to each other. PaperJacks, 1974. 140 pages. $1.95 paper [0-7737-7057-7]

Fun for crossing generational boundaries. *Middle to mature.*

Scargall, Jeanne; 1001 ways to have fun with children. Pagurian, 1973. 159 pages. $7.95 cloth [0-919364-45-4]; $3.95 paper [0-919364-46-2]

Games, crafts and materials for creative fun in childhood. *Middle to older.*

HOBBIES AND CRAFTS

Abrahamson, Una; Crafts Canada: the useful arts. Clarke, Irwin, 1974. 191 pages. $10.95 [0-7720-0711-X]

Knitting, rug making, weaving, ceramics, illustrated with photographs that demonstrate Canadian creativity. *Older.*

Buchan, Bryan; Discovering stamps. Illustrated. Scholastic-Tab, 1977 (1973). 91 pages. $1.05 paper.

The history and use of postage stamps combined with tips for collecting them, glossary included, for beginning collectors. *Middle to older.*

Charlton, James E.; Charlton standard catalogue of Canadian coins. Charlton, 1980. Rev. ed. $3.00 paper [0-88968-005-1]

Since 1953 a standard illustrated reference work on Canadian coinage, revised semiannually.

Conoley, Ken; Stamps, their lure and lore. Academic, 1967. 202 pages. $6.95 [0-7747-0091-2]

Not on stamp collecting, but on the fascination of stamps. *Older.*

Conroy, Mary; 300 years of Canada's quilts. Griffin, 1976. 133 pages. $6.95, paper [0-88760-077-8]

This general history of quilting and quilting methods developed in Canada is valuable also for its coverage of social and political history from the earliest settlement. *Older to mature.*

Fales, Douglas; A Kite on the wind. Borealis, 1973. 16 pages. $2.95 paper [0-919594-11-5]

Introduction to different kinds of kites and directions for the construction of one simple kite. *Middle to older.*

Ferrier, Shannon; Kids in the kitchen. Zander, Hans (illus.). Lorimer, 1978. 32 pages. $9.95 cloth [0-88862-225-2]; $4.95 spiral [0-88862-230-9]

An introduction to cooking with natural foods and the metric system for both boys and girls. Amusing line drawings illustrate the instructions. *Middle to older.*

Franklyn, Mary Eliza; Costume guide and suggestions, 1848-1868. Illustrated. Petheric, 1978. 24 pages. $1.25 paper [0-919380-26-3]

Prepared for the Joseph Howe Festival in Halifax this short guide gives enough information to create a costume. *Middle.*

Franklyn, Mary Eliza; Pepper makes me sneeze. Petheric, 1978. 120 pages. $4.95 paper [0-919380-25-5]

Indigo Proboscis gives helpful hints, reminders, bits of local history and food notes in this cookbook featuring Nova Scotia recipes easy for young people to cook. *Older.*

Hinton, Jane and **Oliver, Hugh;** The Art of aluminum foil. General, 1974. 100 pages. $4.95 paper [0-7736-1014-6]

Simple instructions for making masks, reliefs, Christmas decorations, from aluminum foil. *Middle to older.*

Iserhoff, Juliette and **others;** Traditional Indian recipes from Fort George, Quebec. Highway Book Shop, 1971. 55 pages. $2.00 paper [0-88954-000-4]

Recipes in Cree syllabics and English translations for cooking Indian style. *Older.*

Jacobs, Betty E.M.; Growing herbs for the kitchen. Rueter, Gustav (illus.); Gray, 1972. 93 pages. $5.95 [0-88826-034-2]

Growing and using 26 basic culinary herbs. *Older.*

Johnson, Ruth; What to do till the garbage man arrives: a miser's craft manual. (illus.); Gage, 1977. 117 pages. $6.95 cloth [0-7715-9950-1]; $5.95 paper [0-7715-9951-X]

Recycled household materials become toys, games, puppets and decorations in the hands of children and adults alike. *Middle to mature.*

Mika, Nick and **Mika, Helma;** Mosaic of Canada on postage stamps. Mika, 1967. 143 pages. $25.00 [0-919302-04-1] (Historic Series) Hurtig, 1967. $9.95 [0-88830-067-0]

Canadian events, people, industry, art and nature are subjects commemorated on our stamps. *Older.*

Montagnes, James; Charltons Canada stamp & story album. Charlton, 1979. 88 pages. $4.95 paper [0-88968-007-8]

Designed for children this handsome annual has full-colour reproductions of and excellent descriptive notes on Canadian stamps issued since 1947. *Older to mature.*

Papaspyrou, George; The 1980 Charlton stamp guide. Charlton, 1980. 233 pages. $1.50 paper [0-88968-012-4]

The only annual buyer's guide for Canadian stamps with photographs of every issue since 1851 to date. *Older to mature.*

Patrick, Douglas and **Patrick, Mary;** The Stamp bug: an illustrated introduction to stamp collecting. McGraw, 1978. 96 pages. $8.95 [0-07-082779-6]

A well organized guide to starting and maintaining a stamp collection. *Older to mature.*

Percival, Robert and **MacKean, Ray;** The Little boats: inshore fishing craft of Atlantic Canada. Brunswick, 1979. 111 pages. $12.95 paper [0-88790-104-2]

Paintings and photos of meticulous models of the inshore fishing craft of Atlantic Canada evoke sympathy for the painter's and the model maker's wish to leave a permanent record of these "crumbling wrecks" dotting our Eastern coastline. *Older to mature.*

Scargall, Jeanne; Pioneer potpourri: recipes, remedies, memories. Methuen, 1974. 151 pages. $9.95 cloth [0-458-91070-8]; $6.95 paper [0-458-91060-0]

Quaint sayings and household hints enliven this cookbook. *Older to mature.*

Schaffer, Marion; I love my plant!/ J'aime ma plante! Vanderlinden, Kathy (illus.). Kids Can Press, 1979. 28 pages. $2.95 paper [0-919964-23-0]

Simple, useful information about the care of plants in a well-illustrated picture book for the very youngest plant lover. *Younger to middle.*

Seary, Victor; A Postage stamp history of Canada. McGraw, 1972. 168 pages. $6.95 [0-07-077327-0]

Brief overview of Canada, 1851-1971, presented through postage stamps. *Older.*

Surcouf, Lorraine; Growing a green thumb. Greey de Pencier, 1975. 80 pages. $3.95 paper [0-919872-14-X]

A creative home gardening guide clearly written and delightfully illustrated specifically for children. *Middle.*

Vandergun, Alison; Puppets for the classroom, illustrated with photos. Lampoon, 1974. 34 pages. $2.50 paper.

Excellent photographs accompany directions for making paper and other simple puppets. *Older.*

SPORTS

see also
PUBLISHERS' SERIES
Face-off Series
The Olympic Library of Canada
Sports and Recreation Series

Adams, John; Soccer skills for all ages. Coles, 1978. 176 pages. $3.98 paper.

How to form a club and how to play the game - a clear, precise, accurate guide. *Older to mature.*

Bosetti, Rick; Rick Bosetti's baseball book. Personal Library (Wiley), 1980. 96 pages. $5.95 paper [0-920510-09-4]

Dozens of photographs and a simple text demonstrate winning techniques of the game. *Older to mature.*

Brunet, Mario; All about sailing: a handbook for juniors. de la Haye, Rene (illus.) and Cameron, Andrea (tr.); Greey de Pencier, 1975. $4.95 paper [0-919872-13-1]

Illustrated instructions for young beginning sailors ages 7-15. Available in French. *Middle to mature.*

Canada. Department of National Health and Welfare; Get wet. Canadian Government, 1969. 93 pages. $1.50 paper (Fitness and Amateur Sport Directorate)

A guide to selected aquatic activities complements expert instruction. *All ages.*

Cosentino, Frank and **Leyshon, Glynn A.;** Olympic gold: Canada's winners of the summer games. Holt, 1975. 147 pages. $8.95 cloth [0-03-923330-8]; $5.95 paper [0-03-923331-6]

Almost unknown - and unsung - athletes bring honours to Canada in international competition. *Older to mature.*

Cutler, M. (illus.); Hockey masks and the great goalies who wear them. Tundra, 1978. 34 pages. $3.95 paper [0-88776-101-1]

Information about goalies, history of goalie masks, statistics on players, all highlighted by large paintings of masks. *Middle to older.*

Fischler, Stan and **Fischler, Shirley;** The Fischler's ice hockey encyclopedia. Fitzhenry & Whiteside, 1979. Rev. ed. $9.95 paper [0-88902-570-3]

"The most comprehensive alphabetical listing of hockey subjects from players to teams to riots ever attempted." *Older to mature.*

Fisher, Doug and **Wise, S.F.;** Canada's sporting heroes: their lives and times. General, 1974. 338 pages. $14.95 [0-7736-0036-1]

Biographical facts and sports attainments of participants in team sports, winter and water sports, track and field, golf, tennis and others that Canadians enjoy. List of members of Halls of Fame. Well illustrated. *Older to mature.*

Kalchman, Lois; Safety on ice. Totem Books, 1979. 158 pages. $9.95 paper [0-00-216604-6]

A concerned "hockey mother" devoted to making the game safer for young players writes a simple guide to the equipment needed to pursue this end as well as chapters on rules, fitness, nutrition and injuries. *Older.*

Lough, Richard and **Stinson, David;** Aquabics. Fitzhenry & Whiteside, 1973. 77 pages. $2.60 paper [0-88902-002-7]

Recreation and exercises in the water. *Older.*

McFarlane, Brian; Hockey annual '80. Gage, 1979. $7.95 paper [0-7715-9454-2]

Highlights from the past and present that every fan will want to know. *Older.*

McPhee, Harry; Learning to swim. Mitchell, 1970. 50 pages. $3.50.

Beginner's manual includes graphic illustrations. *Middle.*

May, Zita Barbara; Canada's international equestrians. Burns, 219 pages. $14.95 [0-88768-061-5] $8.95 [0-88768-068-2]

Canadian involvement in international competitions from 1840. *Mature.*

Meeker, Howie; Howie Meeker's hockey basics. Prentice, 1973. 139 pages. $4.95 paper [0-13-444257-1]; Special Bauer ed. $1.16 paper [0-13-444265-2]

Meeker, Howie; More hockey basics from Howie Meeker. Prentice, 1975. 128 pages. $4.95 paper [0-13-600700-7]

Skills, techniques and drills carefully described and illustrated. *Middle to older.*

Obodiac, Stan (ed.); The Leafs; the first 50 years. McClelland, 1976. 287 pages. $14.95 [0-7710-9064-1]

Excellent photographs, fascinating statistics and ten chapters by Canadian sports writers. *Older.*

Redmond, Gerry; Soccer practice. Le Bel, 1978. 111 pages. $3.95 paper [0-920008-04-6]

An unpretentious guide to a game fast growing in popularity among people who want to pursue sports that de-emphasize physical size and violence. *Older to mature.*

Roxborough, Henry; Canada at the Olympics. McGraw, 1976. 2nd ed. $8.95 [0-07-082328-6]

Canada's role in international competition as background to her role as host country to the Olympics in 1976. *Older.*

Spencer, David; The New professional hockey almanac. Illustrated. Pagurian, 1978. 192 pages. $4.95 paper [0-88932-087-X]

Statistics, rules, history and some photographs. *Older to mature.*

Sullivan, Jack; The Grey Cup story: the dramatic history of football's most coveted award. Pagurian, 1974. Rev. ed. 222 pages. $8.95 [0-919364-67-5]. *Older to mature.*

Thom, Douglas; The Hockey bibliography: ice hockey worldwide. OISE, 1978. 153 pages. $7.50 paper [0-7744-0166-4] (OISE Bibliography Series)

A comprehensive listing of books, articles and periodicals, not annotated. *Mature.*

Watt, Tom; How to play hockey. Berger, Bob (illus.); Doubleday, 1971. 176 pages. $4.95 cloth (1971) [0-385-03073-8]; $2.95 paper (1974).

A well illustrated, comprehensive guide for young players and their coaches. *Middle to mature.*

Wayne, Bennett (ed); Hockey hotshots, illustrated. Garrard (Thomas Nelson), 1977. 167 pages. $7.65 [0-8116-4917-2] (A Target Book).

Basic biographical material records the achievements of seven famous hockey players of the past, including Howie Morenz, Bobby Hull, Maurice Richard. *Older.*

Zebroff, Kareen and **Zebroff, Peter;** Yoga with your children, Linkert, Lo (illus.); Fforbez, 1973. 127 pages. $7.95 cloth [0-88976-007-1]; $4.95 paper [0-88976-002-0]

Introduction to hatha yoga for parents and children, stressing its physical rather than its meditative side. *Older to mature.*

OUTDOOR LIFE

Assiniwi, Bernard; Survival in the bush. Copp, 1972. $4.50 [0-7730-4004-8]

Practical advice on how to build a shelter, how to start a fire, how to identify and use edible plants - the Indian way. *Middle to mature.*

Baldwin, Ned; Skiing cross country, illustrated. McGraw, 1977. 174 pages. $6.95 paper [0-07-082490-8]

Techniques, equipment, outdoor survival presented in a straightforward style. *Older.*

Berglund, Berndt; Wilderness survival: a complete handbook and guide for survival in the North American wilds. Modern Canadian Library, 1972. 175 pages. $6.95 cloth [0-919364-34-9]; $3.95 paper [0-919364-35-7]

Aimed at hikers, hunters, snowmobilers and pilots this guide book covers shelter, heat, food, first aid. *Older to mature.*

Bickle, Ian (ed.); Outdoors west; wildlife adventure stories. Western Producer Prairie, 1979. 152 pages. $7.95 paper [0-88833-016-2]

Compilation of articles originally appearing in *Fish and Game Sportsman* that highlight the danger and excitement in the Canadian outdoor sports scene. *Older.*

Blackstock, Brian and **Latimer, John;** Camp counselor's handbook. Gage, 1975. 120 pages. $7.95 cloth [07715-9924-2]

Activities and routines, first aid and special problems, children's characteristics and needs, and other essentials to guide counsellors in their responsibilities. *Mature.*

Canada. Dept. of Indian Affairs and Northern Development; Northern survival. Canadian Government. 1972. 93 pages. $2.75 paper.

Survival techniques in the wilderness include providing heat, shelter, food, first aid. Emphasizes Arctic conditions. *Mature.*

Knap, Jerome; The Complete outdoorsman's handbook: a guide to outdoor living and wilderness survival. Pagurian, 1974. $8.95 cloth [0-919364-62-4]; 1976. $4.95 paper [0-88932-041-1]

Basic skills for outdoor survival include axmanship, cooking, skiing, first aid and foraging. This book encourages an outdoor ethic that ensures man's harmony with nature. *Mature.*

Monk, Carl and **Knap, Jerome;** A Complete guide to canoeing in North America; a manual on technique and equipment and the best canoeing routes in North America. Wiley, 1976. 192 pages. $8.95 cloth [0-88932-023-3]; $3.95 paper [0-919364-98-5] *Mature.*

Nickels, Nick: Canoe Canada. Van Nostrand, 1976. 278 pages. $9.95 paper [0-442-299303]

Both novice and expert will find useful information in this accurate, up-to-date book. *Older to mature.*

Nowell, Iris; Cross-country skiing in Ontario. Greey de Pencier, 1974. 2nd rev. ed. 77 pages. $2.50 paper [0-919872-48-4]

The best places to go and what to expect when you get there. *Older to mature.*

Ruck, Wolfgang E.; Canoeing and kayaking. McGraw, 1974. $6.95 [0-07-077761-6] *Mature.*

Smith, Ken (ed.); The Canadian bicycle book. Davies, Will (illus.); Heath, 1972. 128 pages. $3.95 [0-669-80564-5]

History and practical advice on purchasing and repairing bicycles. Lavishly illustrated. *Older to mature.*

YOUTH ORGANIZATIONS

Boy Scouts of Canada; Canadian scout handbook. Boy Scouts, 1973. $5.95 cloth; $1.95 paper. *Older.*

Boy Scouts of Canada; The Cub book. Boy Scouts, 1971. $1.85 paper. *Middle.*

Crocker, Dorothy; The Guide handbook. O'Young, Leoung (illus.) and Fox, Helen (illus.). Girl Guides, 1977. 377 pages. $3.00 paper [0-919220-00-2]

The official handbook for girls of ages 10 to 14 involved in the Girl Guide program which includes boating, first aid, bird watching among other activities. *Older to mature.*

Girl Guides of Canada; Brownies around the world. Girl Guides, 1975. Rev. ed. 2 vol. $2.00 each.

A continuing series about Brownies throughout the world. Twenty-four countries are covered in the two volumes. *Middle.*

Gloin, Anne; Like measles: it's catching. Crocker, Barbara; Girl Guides, 1974. 128 pages. $2.00 paper.

Reminiscences about guiding by women who have been involved over the years. *Older to mature.*

Hébert, Jacques; Have them build a tower together. Fischman, Sheila (trans.). McClelland, 1979. 334 pages. $10.95 paper [0-7710-4057-1]

Through Katimavik, a private corporation financed by the federal government, over 4,000 young Canadians have worked as volunteers in over 180 Canadian communities. *Mature.*

Hébert, Jacques; The World is round. Fischman, Sheila (trans.) McClelland, 1976. $4.95 paper [0-7710-4063-6]

Canada World Youth is a unique international program of learning in action about other peoples, cultures and heritages. *Mature.*

LANGUAGE AND LITERATURE

LITERATURE
see also
PUBLISHERS' SERIES
Teachers and Writers Education Project Resource Guides
Themes in Canadian Literature

LANGUAGE

Colter, Rob; Grammar to go. Anansi, 1979. Rev. ed. 160 pages. $3.95 [0-88784-077-9]

"An informal guide to correct usage" lists common errors and confusions and sets the reader straight about such challenges as when to use accept/except, obtuse/abstruse, loath/loathe. *Middle to mature.*

Green, James; A First thesaurus: the word-hunter's companion. Book Society, 1977. 112 pages. $2.95 net [0-7725-5024-7]

This simple treasury of words lists 210 common words with their synonyms. *Middle to mature.*

O'Byrne, Lorainne; What is it? Boston, 1977. 48 pages. $3.00 paper [0-919822-44-4]

Delightful introduction to the craft origins of common sayings, like: strike while the iron is hot, from the smithy. *Middle to older.*

Sherk, Bill; Brave new words. Doubleday, 1979. 174 pages. $12.95 cloth [0-385-15552-2]; $6.95 paper [0-385-15331-7]

"The newest, funniest, and most original dictionary in the world" of words coined by Canadians. *Mature.*

DEBATING

Wall, Clevie; Debate: a guide for Canadian students. Atlantic Institute, 1977. 65 pages. $2.00 paper.

A thorough presentation of all aspects of debating. *Mature.*

ANTHOLOGIES
see also
PUBLISHERS' SERIES
Hiyou Series
Teachers and Writers Education Project Resource Guides
Themes in Canadian Literature
Zap Series

Colombo, John Robert; Colombo's book of Canada. Hurtig, 1978. 176 pages. $18.95 cloth [0-88830-155-3]; $12.95 paper [0-88830-161-8]

The finder of unusual Canadian facts here collects unusual poems, plays, stories, speeches, quotations from our literary past. *Mature.*

Goldberg, Gerry; I am a sensation. Wright, George (designs); McClelland, 158 pages. Text ed. $3.75 paper [0-7710-3373-7]; Trade ed. $4.95 paper [0-7710-3377-X]; Teacher's manual paper free.

Potpourri of poems and pieces, drawings and photos that elaborate universal themes. *Older.*

Gooderham, Kent (ed.); I am an Indian. Dent, 1969. 195 pages. Educational ed. $3.50 net [0-460-92551-2]; Trade ed. $3.50 list [0-460-92550-4]; $3.50 list paper [0-460-92552-0]

Poetry, prose, legends and songs tell us what it means to be an Indian. *Older.*

Major, Kevin; Doryloads. Breakwater, 1974. 204 pages. $4.95 paper [0-919948-04-9]

A collection of prose, poetry and photos from Newfoundland - a get-acquainted sampling. *Older to mature.*

Mersereau, Grace; Singing under ice. Macmillan, 1974. 264 pages. $3.95 paper [0-7705-1178-3]

Short stories, articles, excerpts from longer works, many by well known Canadian writers. *Older.*

Nielsen, Robert F. (ed.); Canadian children's annual. Potlatch, 1975. $6.95 paper [0-919676-01-4]; 1976. $4.95 paper [0-919676-04-9]; 1977. $8.95 cloth [0-919676-08-1]; 1977. $4.95 paper [0-919676-05-7]; 1978. $8.95 cloth [0-919676-10-3]; $4.95 paper [0-919676-09-X]; 1979. $8.95 cloth [0-919676-12-X]; $4.95 paper 1980; $9.95 cloth [0-919676-21-9]; $6.95 paper [0-919676-20-0]

Canadian short stories, puzzles, recipes, essays and comics. All editions still available. *Middle to older.*

CHILDREN AS AUTHORS

Another wordsandwich; stories by kids for kids. Annick Press/Books By Kids, 1979. 94 pages. $4.25 paper [0-91984-07-X]

More stories, poems and drawings by kids, about kids, for kids. *Middle to mature.*

The Children's island, illustrated, P.E.I. Department of Tourism, P.O. Box 2000, Charlottetown, C1A 7N8, 1979. 34 pages. $2.50 paper, plus postage.

An International Year of the Child project encouraged P.E.I. children to draw pictures about Island activities. *Younger.*

Glistening in the sun; an anthology of YC Verse originally published in the Western Producer. Western Producer 1977. 122 pages. $3.25 paper [0-919306-78-0]

Spanning 50 years with 100 poems this anthology reflects the changing outlooks and techniques of the young contributors to Saskatchewan's largest newspaper through the last half century. *Older.*

Hazzard, Russ; My third eye: images of a cold country: an anthology of writings by young Canadian authors. All about us, 1976. $4.95 paper [0-919970-01-X]. *Mature.*

Hildes, Joey; How the pelican got its baggy beak. Peguis, 1974. 32 pages. $4.00 cloth [0-919566-26-X]; $1.95 paper [0-919566-30-8]

Pastel drawings complement the story of a pelican, written and drawn by a 10 year old. *Younger.*

Jason-Hearne, Zama; Zama's book: visions of a six-year old. Intermedia, 1977. 85 pages. $4.95 paper.

Stories, songs, poems and drawings by a precocious little girl. *Younger.*

McClard, Judy (ed.); and **Wall, Naomi** (ed.); Come with us: children speak for themselves. Women's Educational Press, 1978. 117 pages. $5.95 paper [0-88961-045-2]; Teacher's Guide. $1.50 paper [0-88961-053-3]

Children write about where they came from, why they came to Canada, what they have found here, and draw pictures of their experience. *Middle to older.*

MacDonald, Kendall; Patrick the diesel. Peguis, 1974. 24 pages. $3.50 cloth [0-919566-27-8]; $1.25 paper [0-919566-31-6]

A nine-year-old boy writes and draws a cautionary tale about trains. *Younger.*

Me, myself and I. Spector, Norma Haller (illus.). Books for Children (H.B. Fenn), 1979. 55 pages. $4.95 [0-9690083-0-9]

Short, pithy poems by Kingston area children submitted to a contest during The Children's Book Festival. These are the 27 winning verses. *Middle to older.*

Millyard, Anne (ed.); **Wilks, Rick** (ed.); Making waves; stories and poems by kids for kids. Books by Kids, 1976. 78 pages. $3.95 paper [0-919984-02-9]

Stories, poems and pictures by young people, recovered from an imaginary sea-borne bottle, should encourage young readers to express their own thoughts on paper. *Middle to older.*

Nickerson, Betty (comp.); All about us/ Nous autres. Content, 1973. 36 pages. $1.75 paper [0-919636-08-X]

An impressive selection of paintings, poems, stories and letters from young Canadians. *Middle to older.*

Nickerson, Betty (ed.); Girls will be women/Femmes de demain. All about us, 1975. 75 pages. $2.00 paper [0-919970-00-1]

Poems and pieces that reveal the interests and cares of young writers. *Middle to older.*

Nickerson, Betty; Of you and me; a contemporary view of human rights by young Canadians/Nous autres; vue contemporaine des droits de la personne par des jeunes Canadiens. All about us, 1977. 96 pages. $3.95 paper [0-919970-02-8]. *Older.*

Of dogs and cats and things like that . . . Mika, 1979. 96 pages. $5.00 paper [0-919303-29-3]

Children write about themselves and about nature for International Year of the Child. *Middle.*

Tap, Monica; Mr. Brown and his magic mustache. Jablonski-Jones, Martha (illus.). Tree Frog, 1979. 48 pages. $7.95 [0-88967-030-7]

Mr. Brown wiggles his mustache and makes things disappear. *Middle.*

Thinking; poems produced at the poetry workshop. North Vancouver Public Library, 1973. 34 pages. $1.75 paper.

Collages, pictures and prints enhance this collection of children's poems. *Middle to older.*

Wilks, Rick (ed.) and **Millyard, Anne** (ed.); Riding an apple, facing the sun: stories by kids for kids. Annick Press/Books By Kids, 1979. 60 pages. $4.25 paper [0-919984-29-0] (Books By Kids For Kids)

More poems, drawings and stories that reveal intimate thoughts and feelings. *Middle to older.*

Wordsandwich. Books by Kids, 1975. 98 pages. $3.25 paper [0-919984-00-2]

Stories, poems and drawings by kids, about kids, for kids - imaginative, sensitive and well edited. *Middle to older.*

POEMS

Betisse, Ken George and others; Native sons. Highway Bookshop, 1977. 59 pages. $2.50 paper [0-88954-138-8]

Native prison inmates write about the plight of the Native people in a changing, indifferent environment. "We speak because you need to understand." *Mature.*

Brand, Dionne; Earth magic. Crosse, Roy (illus.). Kids Can, 1979. 61 pages. $2.95 paper [0-919964-25-7]

Trinidad evoked in poetic and pencil images brings the author's childhood days to life again. *Older.*

Carroll, Mae; Phillip Neault, pioneer. Adams, Ernest L. (illus.). Upland Peddlers Press, 1977. 40 pages. $8.25 [0-920096-02-6]

A biographical narrative poem records the life of a hardy Northern Ontario pioneer. A modern folktale. *Older to mature.*

Desbarats, Peter; The Night the city sang. Newfeld, Frank (illus.). McClelland, 1977. 24 pages. $5.95 [0-7710-2685-4]

Three rollicking poems that evoke the spirit of Christmas with unsentimental delight. *Middle to older.*

Downie, Mary Alice (ed.) and **Robertson, Barbara** (ed.); The Wind has wings: poems from Canada. Cleaver, Elizabeth (illus.); Oxford, 1978. 95 pages. $5.95 paper [0-19-540287-1]

Striking collages illumine these poems from Canadian sources. *Middle to older.*

Dudek, Louis (ed.); All kinds of everything. Clarke, Irwin, 1973. 150 pages. Educ. ed. $2.40 [0-7720-0584-2]; Teachers ed. $2.25 [0-7720-0596-6]; (1977) $3.95 paper [0-7720-1152-4]

A Canadian poet chooses all kinds of poems to demonstrate his thesis that poetry is "a kind of spontaneous happy life of the mind." *Older to mature.*

DuVernet, Sylvia; Perceptions. Herald Gazette, 1975. 57 pages. $6.00

"Not to be looked at simply, but symbolically to be examined, significantly to be perceived, by the interpreting mind of the reader." *Mature.*

Du Vernet, Sylvia; Tut-Tut. The author, 37 Hortfield Court, Islington M9A 3E5, 1979. 51 pages. $7.50 paper.

The author's familiarity with Tut's tomb and the travelling exhibit contribute to her sensitivity to Tut as an adolescent like her own son. *Mature.*

Evans, R. (ed.); Song to a seagull. McGraw, 1969. 104 pages $7.95 (educ.); $6.95 (retail) [0-7700-3198-6]

Poems and songs with their scores represent some of our lesser known poets and composers. *Older.*

Fry, J.D.; Old Wives' Lake. Wagner, Neil (illus.). Thistledown, 1978. 74 pages. $12.00 cloth [0-920066-18-6]; $5.00 paper [0-920066-17-8]

The night before a hopeless battle, old Cree women keep camp and stoke the fires as their people escape to safety. A dramatic poem. *Mature.*

Grawbarger, Josephine; The Legend of Joseph Driver. Highway Book Shop, 1974. 61 pages. $2.00 paper [0-88954-063-2]

Records the life of an Irish immigrant to the Parry Sound area in unrhymed trochaic verses. *Older.*

Gutteridge, Don; Riel: a poem for voices. Van Nostrand, 1972. 72 pages. $3.50 text.

Powerful poem about Louis Riel, episodic in style and interspersed with excerpts from journals and newspapers. *Older to mature.*

Hogan, Homer (ed.); Listen! Songs and poems of young Canada. Methuen, 1972. 166 pages. $4.25 paper [0-458-90900-9] (University of Guelph Canadian Literature Series)

Modern Canadian songs and poems that speak to young people. *Older.*

Johnson, Pauline; Flint and feather. Musson, 1957 (c1931). 170 pages. $4.95 cloth [0-340-12509-8]; PaperJacks, 1972. $1.50 paper [0-7737-7021-6]

"The Song My Paddle Sings" and all the other poetic celebrations written by a Mohawk princess. *Older.*

Lee, Dennis; Alligator pie. Newfeld, Frank (illus.); Macmillan, 1974. 64 pages. $6.95 [0-7705-1193-7]; (1975) $4.25 paper [0-7705-1369-7]

Silly, funny, surprising poems that grew from a poet's search for a Canadian *Mother Goose.* Marvellous interpretive illustrations. *Younger to middle.*

Lee, Dennis; Garbage delight, Newfeld, Frank (illus.). Macmillan, 1977. 64 pages. $6.95 [0-7705-1566-5]

Poet and artist, prize winners both, treat young readers to new amusements. *Middle.*

Lee, Dennis; Nicholas Knock and other people. Newfeld, Frank (illus.); Macmillan, 1974. 64 pages. $6.95 [0-7705-1194-5]; $4.25 paper [0-7705-1400-6]

Colourful, imaginative lilting verses full of Canadian allusions. For children older than *Alligator Pie's* readers. *Older.*

Lee, Dennis; Wiggle to the laundromat. Pachter, Charlie (illus.); New Press, 1970. 32 pages. $4.95 [0-88770-062-4].

Oversize format with striking pictures and catchy poems, some of which appear in Lee's *Alligator Pie* and *Nicholas Knock. Middle to older.*

Lochhead, Douglas (ed.); **Souster, Raymond** (ed.); 100 poems of nineteenth century Canada. Macmillan, 1974. 218 pages. $7.95 cloth [0-7705-1139-2]; $3.95 paper [0-7705-1140-6]

Includes the nature poets - Carman, Lampman, Scott, Roberts, Crawford - and other representative poets to illuminate the era. *Older to mature.*

Metcalf, John (ed.); The Speaking earth. Van Nostrand, 1976. 128 pages. $3.95 paper [0-442-25318-4]

Wide selection of contemporary poetry. *Middle to older.*

Motheral, Elva A. (ed.) and **Wilson, K.** (ed.); The Poets' record: verses on Canadian history. Peguis, 1975. $7.50 cloth [0-919566-41-3]; $3.25 paper [0-919566-42-1]

An excellent anthology of poems by historical figures like Thomas D'Arcy McGee, about the country's history up to modern times. *Older to mature.*

Musgrave, Susan; Gullband. Ducornet, Erica (illus.) Douglas McIntyre 1974. 50 pages. $7.95. [0-88894-058-0]

A poet stretches children's fantasy-quotient and delights them all the way. *Middle to older.*

Newman, Fran; Sunflakes and snowshine. Boulanger, Claudette (illus.). Scholastic, 1977. 47 pages. $1.45 paper.

Starting with September two cunning poems and two coloured paintings capture children's activities for each month of the school year. *Middle.*

Pittman, Al; Down by Jim Long's stage; rhymes for children and young fish. Hall, Pam (illus.). Breakwater, 1976. 44 pages. $5.95 [0-919948-29-4]

Rollicking rhymes and just-right drawings introduce some Atlantic fish. *Younger to middle.*

Pratt, Edwin J.; Brébeuf and his brethren. Macmillan, 1966 (c1940). 65 pages. $1.75 paper [0-7705-0259-8]

Long narrative poem about the missionary, Brébeuf, and his hardships among the Indians who finally tortured and killed him. *Older.*

Rasmussen, Knud J.V. (ed.); Beyond the high hills. Mary-Rousselière, Guy (illus.); World (Collins), 1976 $8.95 [0-529-03691-6]

Folk verse collected from the Eskimo of Hudson Bay and translated by a Danish explorer. *Older.*

Scott, Frank R. (ed.) and **Smith, A.J.M.** (ed.); The Blasted pine: an anthology of satire, invective and disrespectful verse. Macmillan, 1967. Rev. and enlarged ed. 166 pages. $4.95 paper [0-7705-0280-6]. *Mature.*

Service, Robert W.; The Collected poems of Robert Service. McGraw, 1971 275 pages. $9.95 [0-7700-0041-X]

The spirit of the Canadian North comes alive in these humorous, exuberant, robust poems. *Older to mature.*

Service, Robert W.; The Song of the campfire. Galaburr, Richard (illus.). 1912, 1978. 22 pages. $8.95 [0-396-07623-8]

Vivid silhouettes enhance this evocative ballad of the comforts of a campfire. *Older.*

Straiton, Bill; Selections from The Tiger witch and the winkle pickers. Norris, Len (illus.). Scholastic-Tab, 1976. 61 pages. $1.50 paper.

Swinging nonsense verse especially suited to reading aloud. Whimsical illustrations will delight children. *Middle.*

Stump, Sarain; There is my people sleeping. Gray, 1974. 2nd ed. 158 pages. $2.95 paper [0-88826-056-3]

Line drawings illustrate poems about the meaning of Indian life. *Older.*

Woollatt, Richard and **Souster, Raymond;** Sights and sounds. Macmillan, 1973. 216 pages. Educ. ed. $3.95 paper [0-7705-1004-3]

Mélange of poems - about half are Canadian. *Older.*

PLAYS

Baxter, Vera; Famous people once were kids! and other mini-plays; Canadian history dramatized. Morrison, Donald (illus.). Early Years, 1977. 88 pages. $5.00 paper [0-88787-003-1]

Ten mini-plays about famous Canadians, to be read aloud or for classroom staging. *Middle to older.*

Beissel, Henry; Inook and the sun. Gage, 1980. 80 pages. $5.95 paper [0-7715-9979-X]

A play for masks and marionettes recreates Inuit life and legend. *Older.*

Bolt, Carol and **Peterson, Len;** Cyclone Jack, by Carol Bolt, Billy Bishop & the Red Baron, by Len Peterson, Kalman, Rolf (ed.); Simon & Pierre, 1975. 62 pages. $4.95 paper [0-88924-011-6]

Dramas about Tom Longboat, winner of the 1907 Boston Marathon, and Billy Bishop who shot down 72 German planes in the first world war. *Older.*

Campbell, John Gounod; Fox of a thousand faces. Playwrights Co-op, 1973. 49 pages. $2.50 [0-919834-73-6]

Excellent musical fantasy for children may be performed by adults or older children. *Middle to older.*

Campbell, Paddy; Chinook and Too many kings. Playwrights, 1977. 50 pages. $3.00 paper [0-88754-051-1]

Two plays for production "in-the-round" allow for audience participation. Both are fantasies involving familiar characters. *Older.*

Deverell, John; The Copetown City kite crisis. Playwrights, 1972, 1977. 35 pages. $2.50 [0-919834-11-6]

Serious comedy about a successful kite factory that produces the pollution that causes the crisis. *Older.*

Deverell, Rex; You want me to be grown up, don't I? Playwrights, 1979. 36 pages. $2.50 paper [0-88754-168-2]

Five children discuss and demonstrate the worst thing an adult has done to them - for a real catharsis. *Older.*

Foon, Dennis; Heracles. Talonbooks, 1978. 44 pages. $3.95 paper [0-88922-158-8]

A new reworking of an old Greek myth in which Heracles acquits his 12 labours only to immolate himself. *Older.*

Foon, Dennis; Raft baby. Talonbooks, 1978. 44 pages. $3.95 paper [0-88922-156-1]

A baby's starving parents set her afloat on a raft in the Peace River and she is saved downstream by her uncle, a Blackfoot trapper. *Mature.*

Foon, Dennis; The Windigo and The Last days of Paul Bunyan. Playwrights, 1978. 41 pages. $3.00 paper [0-88754-094-5]

Two well written one act plays: about the Ojibway ice spirit which can overtake and enter a hunter in times of great hunger, and about the greatest logger of them all. *Older.*

Foord, Isabelle; Say hi to Owsley. Playwrights, 1975, 1977. 25 pages. $2.50 paper [0-919834-13-2]

Two Martian spaceships collide and crash on earth causing a time warp with unusual results. *Mature.*

Goulding, Dorothy-Jane; We're doing a play. McGraw, 1970. 85 pages. $5.88 [0-7700-3181-1]

Eight short plays for young children with notes on how to play them. *Middle.*

Grieve, Wally; Animal parade, a children's musical. Waterloo, 1974. 12 pages. $1.25 paper.

A simple and simply delightful musical play that children will enjoy as actors and audience. *Middle.*

Guay, Georgette; The Bling said hello/ You'll never be the same: two plays for young people. Playwrights, 1979. 49 pages. $3.00 paper [0-88754-133-X]

Two science fiction plays using the same characters who face all-too-human dilemmas. *Older.*

Jones, Sandra; Ready steady go. Playwright's Co-op, 1975. 40 pages. $2.50 paper [0-919834-51-5]

"A light, enjoyable escape for children imparting a happy innocence that is very appealing." *Older.*

Kalman, Rolf, (ed.); A Collection of Canadian plays, Volume IV. Simon & Pierre, 1975. 376 pages. $16.75 [0-88924-013-2]

Ten plays for children to enjoy as audience by Eric Nicol, Carol Bolt, Leonard Peterson and other Canadian playwrights. *Older.*

Keller, Betty; Trick doors and other dramatic sketches. November, 1974. 129 pages. $3.50 paper [0-88894-053-X]

Eleven short sketches for two to three players, using simple staging, and suitable for any small theatrical group. *Older to mature.*

Kemp, David; King Grumbletum & the magic pie. Simon & Pierre, 1977. 63 pages. $4.95 [0-88924-007-8]

About a king with a richly deserved belly-ache. The second play is *Professor Fuddle's fantastic fairy-tale machine,* based on an updated *Snow White and the seven dwarfs. Older.*

Kenny, George; October stranger. Chimo, 1978. 77 pages. $3.95 paper [0-920344-04-6]

Based on the author's *Indians Don't Cry,* stories and poems on Native Indian themes, this play was Canada's representative at the Sixth International Theatre Festival in Monaco in 1977. *Older to mature.*

McFarlane, Leslie; Fire in the north. Highway Book Shop, 1973. 36 pages. $1.50 paper [0-88954-009-8]

Radio documentary play of the Haileybury fire which razed 2000 acres and killed 44 inhabitants. *Older.*

McMaster, Beth; Put on the spot/When everybody cares; two children's plays. Simon & Pierre, 1975. 148 pages. $4.95 paper [0-88924-045-0]. *Older.*

Put on the spot is about the animals in a zoo who fight its closure. *When everybody cares* is about a robot in 1990 who fights prejudice successfully.

Marcus, Felicity; George, Gertie and the garbage grabbers. Playwrights Co-op, 1973. 35 pages. $2.50 paper [0-88754-025-2]

A garbage can fantasy that involves the audience in a riotous adventure. *Middle to older.*

Nicol, Eric; Beware the quickly who. Playwrights Co-op, 1973. 48 pages. $2.50 [0-919834-29-9]

Nonsensical fantasy about a boy who is searching for himself while threatened by a monster, the Quickly Who. *Older.*

Nicol, Eric; The Clam made a face; a play for children. New Press, 1972. 36 pages. $1.25 paper [0-88770-693-2]

A play for children by a distinguished Canadian humorist. *Older.*

Peterson, Len; Let's make a world. Playwrights 1973. 42 pages. $2.50 [0-88754-024-4]

Creation, seen in Greek and Viking mythology and by modern science. *Older.*

Reaney, James; Apple butter. Talonbooks, 1978. $3.95 paper [0-88922-152-9] (Theatre for Young People)
Geography match; Talonbooks, 1978. $3.95 paper [0-88922-153-7] (Theatre for Young People)
Ignoramus; Talonbooks, 1978. $3.95 paper [0-88922-155-3] (Theatre for Young People)
Names and nicknames; Talonbooks, 1978. $3.95 paper [0-88922-154-5] (Theatre for Young People)

Four plays with Canadian themes, loosely constructed to allow for improvisation and audience participation. They are "shamelessly patriotic and should be played recklessly and with all the stops pulled out." *Older.*

Reaney, James and **Beckwith, John** (music); All the bees and all the keys. Porcépic, 1976. 48 pages. $9.95 cloth [0-88878-058-3]; $4.95 paper [0-88878-059-1]

Rival musical bands are led by Kenneth who put 24 bees in a bottle and Benjamin who let them out. How the bees repaid Ben's kindness makes for a good story. Beckwith has written appropriate music to expand the reader-listener's imagination. *Mature.*

Robb, Dodi and **Patterson, Pat;** The Dandy lion: a one-act musical play for children. New Press, 1972. 56 pages. $3.95 [0-88770-687-8]

The excitement of the circus comes over the footlights for child audiences. *Middle.*

Robb, Dodi and **Patterson, Pat;** The Popcorn man: a one-act musical play for children. New Press, 1972. 51 pages. $3.95 [0-88770-689-4]

A popcorn man and group of run-aways try to return the kangaroo to the zoo. Scenario and music that children can enjoy most as viewers. *Middle.*

Robb, Dodi and **Patterson, Pat;** Red Riding Hood: a one-act musical play for children. New Press, 1972. 49 pages. $3.95 [0-88770-685-1]

A slapstick version of *Little Red Riding Hood. Middle.*

Schwartz, Ernest J.; Pig tales/ Treasure island. Playwrights, 1979. 74 pages. $3.00 paper [0-88754-180-1]

Audience participation is integral to these two plays, about two pigs who run away to Hoggeywood, and an adaptation of Stevenson's novel. *Older.*

Truss, Jan; Oomeraghi oh and A Very small rebellion. Playwrights Co-op, 1978. 45 pages. $3.00 paper [0-88754-06315]

Two plays, the first a fantasy and the second an historical drama of the Riel rebellion, for reading or performing by older children or adults. *Older.*

Watts, I.N.; A Blizzard leaves no footprints, and three other participation plays for children. Playwrights, 1978. 39 pages. $3.50 paper [0-88754-096-1]

The four plays involve the audience in the action of dramatized Inuit legends, Japanese stories and traditional tales, first produced by Edmonton's Citadel on Wheels/Wings Touring Company. *Middle.*

Watts, I.N.; A Chain of Words. Talonbooks, 1978. 40 pages. $3.95 paper [0-88922-159-6]

These six short plays are based on familiar Japanese folk tales and borrow Kabuki production methods. *Older.*

Watts, Reg; In the blood. Watts, 1977. Rev. 2nd ed. 100 pages. $10.50 cloth [0-920072-03-8]; $5.95 paper [0-920072-01-1]

A B.C. fishing village of the 1870's comes alive in this drama of a storm at sea that the fishermen survive. *Mature.*

HUMOUR

Burke, Stanley; Blood, sweat and bears, Peterson, Roy (illus.). Douglas & McIntyre 1976. 47 pages $5.95 [0-88894-117-X]

In which is explored the only thing that really mattered in the swamp - hockey. *Mature.*

Burke, Stanley and **Peterson, Roy;** The Day of the glorious revolution. James Lorimer, 1974. 43 pages. $5.95 [0-88862-067-5]

Members of Parliament and members of the media change places after the Revolution. *Mature.*

Burke, Stanley and **Peterson, Roy;** Frog fables and beaver tales. James Lorimer, 1973. 43 pages. $5.95 [0-88862-048-9]

Delicious caricatures people an allegory for the Canadian political situation in 1972-73. *Mature.*

Carlson, Natalie Savage; Alphonse that bearded one. Harcourt Brace (Academic), 1954. 78 pages. $8.95 [0-15-202648-7]

A settler of New France sends a bear to take his place in the army. *Middle.*

Carlson, Natalie Savage; The Talking cat. Harper (Fitzhenry & Whiteside), 1952. 92 pages. $9.90 library binding [0-06-021081-8]

Stories of French Canadian village life, told with sly humour and folk flavour. *Middle.*

Haliburton, Thomas Chandler; The Clockmaker. McClelland, 1958 (1871). 164 pages. $1.95 paper [0-7710-9106-0] (New Canadian Library)

The Yankee peddler, Sam Slick, takes advantage of Down East Canadians to sell his wares. *Mature.*

Harron, Don; Charlie Farquharson's histry of Canada. McGraw, 1972, 132 pages. $6.95 [0-07-092530-5]

A Parry Sound farmer leaves the plow to write a hist'ry of his country. *Mature.*

Harron, Don; Charlie Farquharson's jogfree of Canada. Gage, 1976. 130 pages. $7.95 cloth [0-7715-9314-7]; $4.95 paper [0-7215-9931-5]

A Parry Sound farmer's version of a Canadian geography textbook. *Mature.*

Henderson, Gordon; Sandy Mackenzie, why look so glum? Pickersgill, Peter (illus.). Deneau, 1979. 30 pages. $6.95 [0-88879-019-8]

Lear-like whimsical verses and matching humorous drawings sketch memorable profiles of our prime ministers from Sir John A. to Joe Who. *Older.*

Leacock, Stephen; Sunshine sketches of a little town. McClelland, 1958. 275 pages. $12.95 [0-7710-5040-2]; $1.95 paper [0-7710-9115-X] (New Canadian Library)

Affectionate vignettes of a small Ontario town written by a master humorist. *Older and mature.*

MacNutt, W. Stewart and **Werthman, William C.;** Canada in cartoon. Brunswick, 1967. 216 pages. $6.50 [0-88790-006-2]

Satiric pictorial history of the confederation years, 1867-1967. *Mature.*

Mowat, Farley; The Dog who wouldn't be. Little, 1957. 238 pages. $9.00 [0-316-58636-6]

Hilarious adventures of Mutt, a dog who couldn't be convinced he wasn't a person. *Mature.*

Mowat, Farley; Owls in the family. McClelland, 1961. 103 pages. $1.95 paper [0-7710-6647-3]; Text ed. $1.50 paper [0-7710-6625-2]

Misadventures of pet owls, Wol and Weeps, who shared the same family as Mutt, the dog who wouldn't be. *Middle and older.*

Orkin, Mark M.; Canajan eh? Bickerstaff, Isaac (illus.); General, 1973. 127 pages. $8.95 cloth [0-7736-0022-1]; $5.95 paper [0-7736-1025-1]

Fractured English, mangled meanings, picturesque social comment. *Mature.*

Orkin, Mark M.; French Canajan, hé? Bickerstaff, Isaac (illus.); Lester and Orpen, 1975. 127 pages. $8.95 cloth [0-919630-01-4]; $5.95 paper [0-919630-82-0]

More picturesque comment through a French Canadian glass lightly. *Mature.*

FICTION

STORIES
see also
PUBLISHERS' SERIES
Canadian Favourites
Face-off Series
Kids Like Us
Women at Work
ZAP Series

Allan, Norman; Lies my father told me, based on the screenplay by Ted Allan. New American Library, 1975. 124 pages. $1.50 paper

Based on the screenplay by Ted Allan this nostalgic novel brings young David and his grandfather and their horse Ferdeleh into a beautiful, loving relationship. *Older to mature.*

Allen, Robert Thomas; The Violin. Pastic, George (illus.); McGraw, 1976. 79 pages. $8.95 [0-07-082300-6]

A quiet celebration of the music and friendship shared by a young boy and an old man. *Older.*

Barnes, Michael; Cobalt adventure, Highway Book Shop, 1973. 34 pages. $1.50 paper [0-88954-024-1]

Mystery adventure story of two teenage boys in Northern Ontario. *Middle.*

Barton, Carl F.; Robber's roost. Holt, 1972. 142 pages. $6.95 cloth [0-03-923313-8]

Family of children solve several robberies on a British Columbia Gulf of Georgia Island. *Older.*

Bedard, Michael; Woodsedge and other tales. Zych, Stan (illus.). Gardenshore, 1979. 105 pages. $2.95 paper [0-920134-02-5]

Twelve original fairy tale-like stories told in a rather florid style. *Older.*

Bice, Clare; A Dog for Davie's Hill. Macmillan, 1956. 120 pages. $5.50 cloth [0-7705-0009-9]; $2.95 paper [0-7705-0939-8]

A boy in the Scottish Highlands trains his dog and places first in the August sheep dog trials. *Middle to older.*

Bice, Clare; Hurricane treasure. Macmillan, 1966. 190 pages. $3.95 paper [0-7705-1505-3]

Mystery of two boys in Nova Scotia during a hurricane. *Older.*

Bjornson, Magnus; Dan Patch and other stories of pioneering in the west. Daniel, Alan (illus.); Scholastic, 1975. 110 pages. $1.05 paper.

Six humorous stories about prairie life 1913-1924 reveal the struggles of hard working people trying to wrest a living from an inhospitable land. *Older.*

Blades, Ann; A Boy of Taché. Tundra (Collins), 1973. 23 pages. $5.95 [0-88776-023-6]

Charlie goes into the British Columbia wilderness with his Indian grandparents and finds that only his skill can save his grandfather's life. Glowing varicoloured drawings. *Middle.*

Bleeks, Bill; No way back. Scholastic-Tab, 1978. 116 pages. $1.15 paper.

Susan searches for her runaway sister and finds her own identity. *Older.*

Bradford, Karleen; A Year for growing. Hilder, Charles (illus.). Scholastic-Tab, 1977. 137 pages. $1.05 paper.

Robbie Wicks clashes with his grandfather over their different approaches to conservation. *Middle.*

Burnford, Sheila; Bel Ria. McClelland, 1977. 204 pages. $10.00 [0-7710-1785-5]

The author of *The Incredible journey* writes about a little circus dog's experiences in England during the second world war. *Older to mature.*

Burnford, Sheila; The Incredible journey. PaperJacks, 1973. 145 pages. $1.50 paper [0-7737-7040-2]

Two dogs and a cat endure hardships on a 250 mile trek through the wilderness to reach their home. *Older.*

Callaghan, Morley; Luke Baldwin's vow. Poulton, Michael (illus.); Macmillan, 1974 (1948). 187 pages. $6.95 [0-7705-1164-3]; Scholastic-Tab, 1975. $1.75 paper.

Reissue of a famous novelist's story for children about a dog and a boy whose father's death begins a dialectical exploration of the young man's maturing process. *Older.*

Carrier, Roch; The Hockey sweater and other stories. Fischman, Sheila (trans.). Anansi, 1979. 160 pages. $6.95 paper [0-88784-078-7]

These wry recollections of Quebec village life in the forties reveal the formative influences on a boy growing up in that gentle, protective atmosphere. *Mature.*

Chetin, Helen; The Lady of the strawberries. King, Anita (illus.). Peter Martin, 1978. 89 pages. $7.95 [0-88778-183-7]

Ten year old Jessica finds difficulties in accepting her parents' divorce and transfers her affections to "The Lady of the Strawberries" when her mother leaves the family farm. *Older.*

Childerhose, R.J.; Hockey fever in Goganne Falls. Macmillan, 1973. 169 pages. $5.95 [0-7705-1042-6]

Boys in a small Saskatchewan town develop a winning hockey team, in a warm humorous story imbued with community feeling. *Older.*

Clemson, Donovan; Lost mine. Macmillan, 1967. 176 pages. $5.95 cloth [0-7705-0047-1]; $2.95 paper (1972) [0-7705-0938-X]

Action-packed prospecting trip satisfies young Paul's dreams of adventure. *Older.*

Connor, Ralph (pseud.); Glengarry school days, McClelland, 1975 (c1902). 340 pages. $2.95 paper [0-7710-9218-0]; Educ. ed. $2.50 (New Canadian Library).

Rural school days 100 years ago had a warmth and humour we can still appreciate. *Older.*

Cook, Lyn; The Bells of Finland Street. Macmillan, 1978. 197 pages. $4.95 [0-7705-1702-1]

A young figure skater in Sudbury learns to love Canada but wants to preserve her Finnish traditions too. *Middle to older.*

Cook, Lyn; Jady and the general. Macmillan, 1955. 242 pages. $6.50 [0-7705-0055-2]

Life on a Niagara peach farm has its adventures for young Jady. *Middle.*

Cook, Lyn; Pegeen and the pilgrim. Macmillan, 1973. 248 pages. $2.95 paper. [0-7705-0986-X]

Stratford's Shakespearean Festival encourages Pegeen's daydreams about becoming an actress. *Older.*

Cook, Lyn; The Road to Kip's Cove. Macmillan, 1961. 222 pages. $6.50 [0-7705-0061-7]

Kip has an exciting time the summer his parents renovate an old pioneer school on the Bay of Quinte. *Middle to older.*

Cook, Lyn; Samantha's secret room. Macmillan, 1978. 210 pages. $6.50 [0-7705-0062-5]; Scholastic-Tab, 1979 $1.75 paper.

Samantha looks for a secret room which belonged to her namesake a hundred years earlier. Set in Penetanguishene, Ontario. *Older.*

Craig, John; The Last canoe. Peter Martin, 1979. 128 pages. $11.95 [0-88778-196-9]
A small band of Indians plans to upset federal authorities by paddling a canoe across the Atlantic to petition the Queen in protest against the expropriation of their land. *Mature.*

Craig, John; No word for good-bye. PMA, 1969. 194 pages. $3.95 paper [0-88778-093-8]
Two boys, Ojibway and white, spend their fifteenth summer in the discovery of friendship. *Older.*

Craig, John; Zach. Coward McCann (Longman), 1972. 254 pages. $8.95 [0-698-20187-6]
An Indian, a black youth and a young girl come together in a mutual search for their own identities. *Mature.*

Craig, John; The wormburners. Scholastic-Tab, 1975. 159 pages. $1.05 paper.
A team of long distance runners from the inner city organize a fund-raising marathon. Exciting and easy to read sports story. *Middle.*

Craven, Margaret; I heard the owl call my name. Clarke, Irwin, 1967. 138 pages. $5.50 [0-7720-0049-2]; $1.40 Educ. ed. [0-7720-0617-2]
A dying priest learns to understand the Kwakiutl Indians in his British Columbia parish. *Older.*

Crawford, Isabella Valancy; Fairy tales of Isabella Valancy Crawford. Petrone, Penny (ed.); and Ross Swan (illus.). Borealis, 1977. 158 pages. $9.95 [0-919594-53-0]
Six poetic tales of fairies by a late nineteenth century author and poet, published in large format paperback. *Older to mature.*

Cutler, Ebbitt; I once knew an Indian woman. Johnson, Bruce (illus.); Tundra (Collins), 1974. 61 pages. $1.95 paper [0-88776-068-6]
An Indian woman lives her life with loyalty, integrity and humanity. *Older.*

Davies, Peter; Fly away Paul. Crown (General), 1974. 213 pages. $7.95 [0-517-514370] PaperJacks 1976. $1.95 paper [0-7737-7136-0]
A compelling story about a teenager who lives in a Home after his deserted mother suffers a breakdown. *Older to mature.*

Dowell, Jack; The Look-off bear: stories of the outdoors. McGraw, 1974. 150 pages. $7.95 [0-07-077630-X]
The joys of camping, hunting and fishing are expressed in these anecdotes and yarns. *Mature.*

Doyle, Brian; Hey Dad! Groundwood (Douglas & McIntyre), 1978. 121 pages. $9.95 cloth [0-88899-005-7]; $3.95 paper [0-88899-004-9]
Megan takes an unwanted holiday across Canada by car and grows toward a mature understanding of her family. *Older.*

Doyle, Brian; You can pick me up at Peggy's Cove. Groundwood, 1980. 120 pages. $8.95 cloth [0-88899-003-0] $4.95 paper [0-88899-001-4]
This sequel to *Hey, dad!* finds Ryan spending summer holidays at Peggy's Cove because his father has "run away from home." *Older.*

D'Oyley, Enid; Between sea and sky. Huie, Albert (illus.). Williams-Wallace Productions, 1979. 144 pages. $12.95 cloth [0-88795-002-7]; $5.95 paper [0-88795-003-5]
A Jamaican-Canadian family go on a summer holiday to their grandparent's home in Jamaica. Susan and Jackie were born in Canada and find their mother's nostalgic memories helpful in establishing their black identity. *Mature.*

Duncan, Frances; Kap-Sung Ferris. Burns, 1977. 126 pages. $4.95 paper [0-88768-074-7]
Two teenaged girls suffer identity crises but overcome their problems through mutual help and friendship. *Older.*

Eckert, Allan; Incident at Hawk's Hill. Little, 1971. 173 pages. $7.95. [0-316-20866-3]
Ben, a boy of six, gets lost on the prairies and survives with the help of a badger. *Middle to older.*

Ellis, Mel; Cariboo crossing. Holt, 1971. 183 pages. $6.35 [0-03-086227-2]

Two young men open up a wilderness area to sports fishermen - and come to regret it. *Older to mature.*

Engel, Marion; My name is not Odessa Yarker. Gal, Laszlo (illus.). Kids Can, 1977. 32 pages. $6.95 cloth [0-919964-70-2]; $2.95 paper [0-919964-13-3]

Geraldine's brother announces her change of name to Odessa, over the public address system at school! *Middle.*

Evans, Hubert; Mist on the river. New, William H. (intro.); McClelland, 1973 (c 1954) 282 pages. $2.95 paper [0-7710-9186-9] (New Canadian Library).

A convincing story of the alienation of a young Indian in the white world. *Older to mature.*

Grey Owl (pseud.); A Book of Grey Owl: pages from the writings of Wa-Sha-Quon-Asin. Reynolds, E.E. (ed.); Macmillan, 1941. 2nd ed. 272 pages. $5.50 paper [0-7705-1373-5].

Selections from all of the writings of Wa-Sha-Quon-Asin. *Mature.*

Grey Owl (pseud.); The Men of the last frontier. Macmillan, 1976. 253 pages. $5.50 paper [0-7705-1393-X] (Laurentian Library)

Written to arouse public interest in conservation. *Older to mature.*

Grey Owl (pseud.); Sajo and the beaver people. Macmillan, 1935. 187 pages. $4.50 paper [0-7705-1105-8]

Two Ojibway children and two beaver kittens - orphans all - live exciting lives together in Northern Quebec. *Older to mature.*

Grey Owl (pseud.); Tales of an empty cabin. Macmillan, 1975 (c1936). 335 pages. $5.50 paper [0-7705-1299-2] (Laurentian Library)

Short stories of the Canadian North. *Mature.*

Guillot, René; A Boy and five huskies. Thompson, Ralph (illus.). Pantheon (Random), 1957. 185 pages. $5.39 lib. ed. [0-394-90972-0]

Eric and his dog team meet severe hardships in the Arctic wilderness when he tries to save his fugitive uncle from the Mounties. For *Lost in the Barrens* fans. *Older.*

Harris, Christie; Mystery at the edge of two worlds. Crockett, Lou (illus.). McClelland, 1978. 175 pages. $8.95 [0-7710-3977-8]

Gangling Lark and her new summer friend Andy investigate the theft of valuable argillite Indian artifacts in this well-told story of suspense. *Older.*

Hiebert, Susan; Alphonse has an accident. Cobiness, Eddy (illus.); Peguis, 1974. 31 pages. $4.00 [0-919566-29-4]

A Cree Indian boy plays with matches and is taken 400 miles to a Winnipeg hospital for burns. Sympathetically told. *Middle.*

Hinds, Margery; Makpa: the story of an Eskimo-Canadian boy. McGraw, 1971. 142 pages. $5.95 [0-7700-0342-7]

An 11-year-old boy living on Baffin Island kills a polar bear and buys a snowmobile with the proceeds. *Middle to older.*

Holling, Holling C.; Paddle-to-the-sea. Houghton (Thos. Allen), 1941. $5.95 [0-395-15082-5]

An Indian boy's carved wooden canoe dropped in a Northern Ontario river finds its way through the Great Lakes to the Atlantic. Classic illustrations follow the route. *Middle.*

Houston, James; Akavak: an Eskimo journey. Academic, 1968. 79 pages. $6.95 [0-15-201729-1]

A boy accompanies his grandfather on a last long northern trek. *Middle.*

Houston, James; Frozen fire. McClelland, 1977. 149 pages. $6.95 [0-7710-4249-3] Penguin, 1979. $2.50 paper. [0-14-03-1233-1]

Matthew's father goes missing so he and his Eskimo friend Kayak brave the Arctic winter in secret to search for him. *Older.*

Houston, James; River runners: a tale of hardship and bravery. Illustrated. McClelland, 1979. 142 pages. $9.95 [0-7710-4282-5]

The Naskapi boy Pashak and Scottish Andrew find challenges enough when they set up a fur trading outpost far inland from Fort Chimo. Another well-written modern adventure story by an award-winning author. *Older to mature.*

Houston, James; The White archer. Academic, 1967. 95 pages. $7.75 [0-15-295851-7]

An Eskimo boy seeks revenge against his family's Indian assassins. Starkly told. *Middle.*

Houston, James; Wolf Run: a Caribou Eskimo tale. Academic, 1971. 64 pages. $7.75 [0-15-299104-2]

In time of famine an Eskimo boy leaves his family shelter to seek food. *Middle.*

Hughes, Monica; The Ghost dance caper. Nelson, 1978. 122 pages. $7.95 [0-241-10021-6]

A half-Indian boy learns about his Indian heritage from his grandfather who helps him to find his totem. *Older.*

Hyde, Dayton O.; Strange companion; a story of survival. Clarke, Irwin, 1975. 152 pages. $6.95.

A plane crash summons up the strengths of young David and old Archie to survive - and also to save a rare whooping crane's egg. *Older.*

Kellerhals-Stewart, Heather; She shoots she scores! Women's Educational Press, 1975. 54 pages. $0.95 paper [0-88961-024-X]

Hilary joins a boys' hockey team and succeeds as a good player despite sexist ridicule. *Middle.*

Kenny, George; Indians don't cry. Angeconeb, Allen (illus.). Chimo, 1977. 78 pages. $3.25 paper [0-920344-00-3]

Sensitive, perceptive poems and short stories about the Indian experience reach hidden depths of humanity. *Older to mature.*

Korman, Gordon; Beware the fish! Scholastic-Tab, 1980. 176 pages. $1.25 paper.

A prolific teenager writes another humorous story about Bruno and Boots. This time the R.C.M.P. investigate their shenanigans. *Older.*

Korman, Gordon; Go jump in the pool. Scholastic-Tab, 1979. 185 pages. $1.25 paper [0-590-71014-1]

Bruno and Boots return to terrorize Headmaster Sturgeon in this sequel to *This can't be happening at MacDonald Hall* when they attempt to raise $25,000 for a swimming pool. *Older.*

Korman, Gordon; This can't be happening at MacDonald Hall. Mohammed, Affie (illus.). Scholastic-Tab, 1978. 124 pages. $1.25 paper.

Roommates at a southern Ontario boarding school with a penchant for practical jokes cause havoc when they are assigned to different dormitories. *Older.*

Kronby, Madeline; A Secret in my pocket. Vojtech, Anna (illus.). McClelland, 1977. 32 pages. $4.95 [0-88869-001-0] (A Magook Publication)

A French-English mix of language in an engaging story about Michelle's friend-in-her-pocket, a frog, and his successor. *Middle.*

Langford, Cameron; The Winter of the fisher. Macmillan, 1971. 222 pages. $8.50 [0-7705-1117-1]

The realistic relationship between a fisher, a white trapper, and an Ojibway who empathizes with the animal's world. *Older to mature.*

Lawrence, R.D.; The North runner. Holt, 1979. 287 pages. $8.95 [0-03-041551-9]

A record of the friendship between a man and a part-wolf sled dog brings new insights to man's relationship to the natural world. *Mature.*

Leclerc, Felix; Allegro. McClelland, 1974. 125 pages. $2.25 paper. (New Canadian Library) [0-7710-9190-7]

Fables about the *habitants* - virtuous, innocent, hard-working and religious people - translated from the French. *Older to mature.*

Leitch, Aelaide; The Blue roan. Macmillan, 1971. 185 pages. $6.50 [0-7705-1116-3]

Thirteen-year-old Roddy begins to grow up when he discovers that his birthday horse is going to foal and needs his special care. *Older.*

Lippincott, J.W.; Wilderness champion, McClelland, 1969. 195 pages. $1.95 paper [0-7710-5311-8]

Johnny looks for his lost pup who is running with a pack of wolves. *Older.*

Little, Jean; From Anna. Harper (Fitzhenry & Whiteside), 1977. 2nd ed. 201 pages. $1.75 school net paper [0-88902-373-5] (The Contemporary Scene)

Everyone thinks Anna is awkward until a sympathetic teacher and new glasses prove otherwise. *Older.*

Little, Jean; Home from far. Little, 1965. 145 pages. $6.75 [0-316-52792-0]

The tragedy of a twin brother's death seems too much for Jenny but a change for the whole family helps her to adjust to their loss. *Middle to older.*

Little, Jean; Kate. Harper (Fitzhenry & Whiteside), 1971. 162 pages. $9.90 L.B.; $2.75 paper [0-06-023913-1]

Kate struggles to come to terms with her mixed heritage. *Older.*

Little, Jean; Listen for the singing. Dutton (Clarke Irwin), 1977. 215 pages. $9.95 [0-525-33705-9]

This sequel to *From Anna* involves Anna and her German immigrant family in difficulties in wartime Canada. *Older.*

Little, Jean; Look through my window. Harper (Fitzhenry & Whiteside), 1970. 258 pages. $9.90 L.B; $3.95 paper, library binding [0-06-023924-7]

The arrival of four cousins upsets Emily's quiet, orderly life as an only child. *Middle to older.*

Little, Jean; Mine for keeps. Little, 1962. 186 pages. $6.75 [0-316-52793-9]

Fitting into regular school is not easy for Sally who has cerebral palsy. *Middle to older.*

Little, Jean; One to grow on. Little, 1969. 140 pages. $5.95 [0-316-52796-3]

Janie has trouble telling the truth but her grandmother helps her work out her problem. *Middle to older.*

Little, Jean; Spring begins in March. Little, 1966. 156 pages. $6.75 [0-316-52785-8]

Meg thinks having her own room will solve her problems but her family feel she must learn to get along with others. *Middle to older.*

Little, Jean; Stand in the wind. Arnold, Emily; Harper (Fitzhenry & Whiteside), 1975. 248 pages. $9.90 L.B. [0-06-023903-4]

Sisters can be sisters who are also friends. *Older.*

Little, Jean; Take wing. Little, 1968. 176 pages. $7.95.

About a girl caught between her shyness and her determination to protect her handicapped brother. *Older.*

Lunn, Janet; Double spell. PMA, 1968. 134 pages. $6.95 [0-88778-023-7]

Twins buy an antique doll that involves them in mystery and suspense. Also appeared in the U.S.A. as *Twin spell. Middle to older.*

Mackay, Claire; Exit Barney McGee. Simpson, David (illus.). Scholastic-Tab, 1979. 146 pages. $1.25 paper [0-590-71002-8]

When his mother remarries and has a baby Barney feels unwanted and goes off to find his father. *Older.*

Mackenzie, Jean; River of stars. McClelland, 1971. 160 pages. $6.95 [0-7710-5812-8]

A West Coast Indian boy takes his injured father's place on his fishing boat and learns about the ways of the white man. *Older to mature.*

Major, Kevin; Hold fast. Clarke, Irwin, 1978. 170 pages. $7.95 [0-7720-1175-3]

Michael survives the break-up of his family life and works through it to find his own identity in this realistic novel of Newfoundland. *Mature.*

Markoosie; Harpoon of the hunter. McGill-Queen's, 1974. 81 pages. $2.95 paper [0-7735-0232-7]; Deluxe ed. $40.00

Canada's first Eskimo novelist writes a starkly simple story of the struggle for survival in Canada's North. Also in French. *Older.*

Marquis, Helen; The Longest day of the year. PaperJacks, 1974. 116 pages. $1.25 paper [0-7737-7056-9]

Three children are trapped in their prairie home by a blizzard the day before Christmas when their parents are away. *Middle.*

Mitchell, William O.; Jake and the kid. Macmillan, 1974. 184 pages. $2.95 paper [0-7705-0962-2] (Laurentian Library)

Jake stands in for the kid's soldier father and helps him grow up on a farm out West during the Second World War. *Older to mature.*

Montgomery, Lucy M.; Anne of Avonlea. McGraw, 1968. 367 pages. $1.50 paper [0-7700-0005-3]

Anne teaches school at Avonlea until she goes to college at the age of 18. Second in the *Anne* series. *Older to mature.*

Montgomery, Lucy M.; Anne of Green Gables. McGraw, 1942. 329 pages. $5.95 cloth [0-7700-0006-1]; $1.50 paper (1968) [0-7700-0008-8]

The first of eight books on the blithe-spirited redhead of Prince Edward Island. *Older to mature.*

Montgomery, Lucy M.; Anne of Ingleside. McClelland, 1939. 323 pages. $2.95 paper [0-7710-6154-4] (Canadian Favourites Series)

Anne's own children, Jem, Shirley, Walter and the twins, Nan and Di grow up together in lovely Prince Edward Island. Sixth in the *Anne* series. *Older to mature.*

Montgomery, Lucy M.; Anne of the Island. McGraw, 1942. 326 pages. $5.95 cloth [0-7700-0009-6]; $1.50 paper (1968) [0-7700-0011-8]

Anne graduates from college at Redmond, teaches at Valley Road, and promises to wait for Gilbert to finish medical school so they can marry. Third in the *Anne* series. *Older to mature.*

Montgomery, Lucy M.; Anne of Windy Poplars. McClelland, 1973 (1936). 301 pages. $2.95 paper [0-7710-6175-7] (Canadian Favourites Series)

Anne teaches school in Summerside, P.E.I. for two years, and wins over the most difficult school board. Fourth in the *Anne* series. *Older to mature.*

Montgomery, Lucy M.; Anne's house of dreams. McClelland, 1972 (1922). 291 pages. $2.95 paper [0-7710-6196-X] (Canadian Favourites Series)

Dr. Gilbert Blythe and his wife Anne begin life together at Four Winds Harbour. Fifth in the *Anne* series. *Older to mature.*

Montgomery, Lucy M.; Blue castle. McClelland, 1926. 263 pages. $2.95 paper [0-7710-6217-6] (Canadian Favourites Series)

Set in Muskoka, Ontario. *Older to mature.*

Montgomery, Lucy M.; Chronicles of Avonlea. McGraw, 1943. 306 pages. $5.95 [0-7700-0043-6]

Short stories. *Older to mature.*

Montgomery, Lucy M.; The Doctor's sweetheart: and other stories. McLay, Catherine (comp.); McGraw, 1979. 190 pages. $7.95 [0-07-082790-7]

These 14 previously-uncollected stories are among 500 written by the author of *Anne of Green Gables* and appeared in popular magazines at the turn of the century. Lovers of Anne will respond to these stories of love. *Mature.*

Montgomery, Lucy M.; Emily climbs. McClelland, 1974 (c1924). 312 pages. $2.95 paper [0-7710-6299-1] (Canadian Favourites Series)

Emily goes to high school in Shrewsbury after she promises Aunt Elizabeth that she will write "no word that was not strictly true." Second in the Emily Starr trilogy. *Older to mature.*

Montgomery, Lucy M.; Emily of New Moon. McClelland, 1925. 351 pages. $2.95 paper [0-7710-6238-9] (Canadian Favourites Series)

First of three *Emily* books - in which Emily prepares to be an author. *Older to mature.*

Montgomery, Lucy M.; Emily's quest. McClelland, 1972 (1927). 262 pages. $2.95 paper [0-7710-6280-X] (Canadian Favourites Series)

Graduation from high school brings many changes into Emily's life, yet her love for Teddy Kent does not change - and all ends happily in this third book in the Emily Starr trilogy. *Older to mature.*

Montgomery, Lucy M.; Further chronicles of Avonlea. McGraw, 1953. 301 pages. $5.95 [0-7700-0071-1]

Short stories. *Older to mature.*

Montgomery, Lucy M.; The Golden road. McGraw, 1967 (c1910). 369 pages. $8.95 [0-7700-0077-0]

The Story Girl entertains her friends with her inventive, imaginative bent for telling an appropriate tale. *Older to mature.*

Montgomery, Lucy M.; Jane of Lantern Hill. McClelland, 1977 (1937). 297 pages. $2.95 paper [0-7710-6300-8] (Canadian Favourites Series)

Jane spends joyful summers with her father in Prince Edward Island and dreary winters with her grandmother and mother in Toronto. *Older to mature.*

Montgomery, Lucy M.; Kilmeny of the orchard. McGraw, 1944 (1910). 256 pages. $8.95 [0-7700-0103-3]

Kilmeny speaks through the music of her violin, then recovers her voice to save her true love. *Older to mature.*

Montgomery, Lucy M.; Magic for Marigold. McClelland, 1977 (1929). 328 pages. $2.95 [0-7710-6322-9] (Canadian Favourites Series)

Marigold and her great-grandmother share the old woman's memories of the past on the last night of her life. *Older to mature.*

Montgomery, Lucy M.; Mistress Pat; a novel of Silver Bush. McClelland, 1977 (1935). 338 pages. $2.95 paper [0-7710-6343-1] (Canadian Favourites Series)

This sequel to ***Pat of Silver Bush*** finds Jingle, now an architect, and Pat ready to be married. *Older to mature.*

Montgomery, Lucy M.; Pat of Silver Bush. McClelland, 329 pages. $2.79 paper [0-7710-6364-4]

Pat Gardiner and Jingle Gordon grow up together in Prince Edward Island. *Older to mature.*

Montgomery, Lucy M.; Rainbow Valley. McClelland, 1923. $2.95 paper [0-7710-6385-7] (Canadian Favourites Series)

About the children who played in Rainbow Valley and how they acquired a mother. Seventh in the *Anne* series. *Older to mature.*

Montgomery, Lucy M.; Rilla of Ingleside. McClelland, 1920. 285 pages. $2.95 paper [0-7710-6406-3] (Canadian Favourites Series)

Rilla, youngest of the Ingleside children, grows up in the era of the First World War. Eighth in the *Anne* series. *Older to mature.*

Montgomery, Lucy M.; The Road to yesterday. McGraw, 1974. 251 pages. $7.95 [0-07-077721-7]

Posthumously published collection of 14 stories about the characters who lived around the Blythe family home in Avonlea. *Older to mature.*

Montgomery, Lucy M.; The Story girl. McGraw, 1944. 365 pages. $5.95 [0-7700-0196-3]

Felix and Beverley return to the Island and meet their cousin whose storytelling abilities have earned her the nickname The Story Girl. *Older to mature.*

Montgomery, Lucy M.; Tangled web. McClelland, 1931. 324 pages. $2.95 paper [0-7710-6427-6] (Canadian Favourites Series)

Various adventures of the Penhallow clan including the affair of Aunt Becky's jug. *Older to mature.*

Moore, Tom; Good-bye momma. Breakwater, 1976. 70 pages. $7.95 cloth [0-919948-19-7]; $3.95 paper [0-919948-18-9]

A young boy's mother dies and his world collapses; then he refuses to accept his father's new wife. *Older to mature.*

Moore, Tom; Tom cods, kids and Confederation. Savory, Rosemary (illus.). Jesperson Press, 1979. 65 pages. $2.95 paper [0-920502-10-5]

Unity with Canada was a big issue in pre-1949 Newfoundland; even children participated in the confederation controversy. Here young John's family contends with conflicting loyalties. *Middle.*

Morgan, Marjorie C.; Packy: the little elephant who came to the cold. Savage, Harry (illus.); Le Bel, 1973. 78 pages. $5.95 cloth [0-920008-00-3]; $2.95 paper.

Based on the true story of a baby elephant's dilemma when she comes to Al Oeming's Game Farm in Alberta. *Middle.*

Motiar, Ahmed; I am not dumb. Highway Book Shop, 1979. 37 pages. $2.25 paper [0-88954-213-9]

This sympathetic portrayal will help to demystify the problems encountered by the learning disabled child. *Younger to older.*

Mowat, Farley; The Black joke. McClelland. 177 pages. $7.95 cloth [0-7710-6649-X]; $2.95 paper.

Two plucky Newfoundland boys outsmart rum runners in this 1930's pirate story. *Older to mature.*

Mowat, Farley; The Curse of the Viking grave. McClelland, 1966. 243 pages. $5.95 cloth [0-7710-6642-2]; $2.95 paper.

Eskimo, Indian and white friends find Viking relics in this sequel to *Lost in the Barrens. Older to mature.*

Mowat, Farley: Lost in the Barrens. McClelland, 1956. 244 pages. $5.75 cloth [0-316-58638-2]; $2.95 paper [0-7710-6615-5]; Text ed. $1.75 paper.

A city boy and an Indian are forced to test their survival skills in the Canadian North. *Older to mature.*

Munsterhjelm, Erik; A Dog named Wolf. Macmillan, 1972. 137 pages. $2.95 paper [0-7705-1210-0]

Wolf's sire was a wolf but his domestic ancestry calls on him to befriend a human. An excellent dog story. *Older to mature.*

Newton-White, Muriel E.; The Adventures of the sparrow family. Highway Book Shop, 1974. 29 pages. $1.50 paper [0-88954-032-2]

Michel Moineau and Susie Sparrow raise a bilingual family in this unique story. *Younger.*

O'Kelly, Barbara and **Allinson, Beverley;** All aboard: a cross-Canada adventure. Greey de Pencier, 1979. 96 pages. $6.95 paper [0-919-872-44-1]

Kate travels from her grandmother's house in Woody Point, Newfoundland to her father's in Vancouver all the way by train. Her 400-mile trip is recorded in stunningly apposite photographs. *Middle to older.*

Palmer, C. Everard; Big Doc Bitteroot. Deutsch (Collins), 1968. 158 pages. $8.50 [0-672-51359-5]

Doc tricks the people in a Jamaican village into buying his miraculous tonic. The author now lives in Ontario. *Mature.*

Paperny, Myra; The Wooden people; Stampnick, Ken (illus.). Little, 1976. 1st ed. 168 pages. $6.95 [0-316-69040-6]

Staging marionette plays makes life in a small Alberta town in 1927 bearable for the Stein children who still yearn for their old home in the Okanagan Valley. *Older.*

Radu, Kenneth; The Bird no one noticed; Radu, Diane L. (illus.); Borealis, 1975. 29 pages. $4.95 paper [0-919594-43-3]

An allegory bearing Native Indian overtones tells the story of a dull, brown bird's quest for beauty. *Middle.*

Read, Elfreida; Brothers by choice. Farrar, Straus & Giroux (McGraw-Hill Ryerson), 1974. 153 pages. $8.50 [0-374-30996-5]

A boy searches for his adopted brother who thinks his parents do not love him. *Older.*

Richardson, Grace; Douglas. Harper (Fitzhenry & Whiteside), 1966. 230 pages. $11.00 library binding [0-06-025011-9]

A teenaged boy travels the road to maturity. *Mature.*

Rivkin, Ann; The Time to choose, Mohammed, Affie (illus.). Scholastic, 1976. 161 pages. $1.05 paper.

Cindy joins a travelling theatre group for the summer on the West Coast and enjoys her adventures. *Older to mature.*

Roberts, Charles G.D.; Eyes of the wilderness and other stories. Carter, Brian (illus.). McGraw, 1980. 123 pages. $8.95 [0-07-077829-X]

Five stories by the originator of the animal biography in a new edition sympathetically illustrated. *Older to mature.*

Roberts, Charles G.D.; The Heart of the ancient wood. McClelland, 1974 (1902). $2.95 paper [0-7710-9210-5] (New Canadian Library)

Miranda is befriended by the forest animals and loved by a hardy woodsman. *Mature.*

Roberts, Charles G.D.; King of beasts. Gold, Joseph (ed.); McGraw, 1967. 240 pages. $5.95 [0-7000-0104-1]

Fourteen stories of animals and birds native to Canada, selected from the author's out-of-print books. *Middle to mature.*

Roberts, Charles G.D.; The Last barrier and other stories. McClelland, 1958. $1.95 [0-7710-9107-9] (New Canadian Library)

A selection of stories from *The Kindred of the wild, Earth's enigmas,* and *The Haunters of the silences. Older to mature.*

Roberts, Charles G.D.; Kings in exile. McGraw, 1947. $5.95 [0-7700-0106-8]

Stories of the sufferings of wild animals in captivity. *Middle to mature.*

Roberts, Charles G.D.; Neighbours unknown. Macmillan, 1924. $1.25 [0-7705-0685-2] (St. Martin's Classics Series)

An early (1911) collection of animal stories. *Older to mature.*

Roberts, Charles G.D.; Red Fox. Schoenherr, John (illus.). Houghton, 1972. $4.95 [0-395-13735-7]; Dell, 1973. $0.95 paper [440-07207-095]; McGraw, 1948. $5.95 [0-7700-0163-7]

Roberts's only full-length animal biography tells "the story of Red Fox's adventurous career in the Ringwaak wilds and of his final triumph over the enemies of his kind." *Middle to older.*

Roberts, Charles G.D.; Seven bears. MacDougall, Ken (illus.). Scholastic-Tab, 1977. 124 pages. $1.25 paper.

Selections from *Thirteen Bears* that show Roberts at his best as an animal biographer. *Middle to Mature.*

Robinson, Robert R.; On the rocks. Scholastic-Tab, 1979. 142 pages. $1.56 paper [0-590-71017-6]

Alcoholic parents and their attendant problems pose real difficulties for 16-year-old Greg, a mature and competent hero. *Older to mature.*

Roy, Gabrielle; Children of my heart. Brown, Alan (tr.); McClelland, 1979. 111 pages. $12.95 [0-7710-7838-2]

Roy communicates an infinite tenderness of feeling for the fragile humanity of the heroine's young pupils and of her own young self; she understands the influences that beggar the human spirit and suffers with the children of her heart. *Mature.*

Rolfe, Sheila; Sasquatch adventure. Hancock House, 1975. $2.95 paper [0-919654-17-7]

Suspense and humour are blended in the adventures of a boy and girl kidnapped by a band of sasquatch. *Middle to older.*

St. Pierre, Paul; Boss of the Namko Drive. McGraw, 1965. 115 pages. $5.95 [0-7700-0027-4]; $3.65 School ed. (1968) [0-7700-3024-6]

When his father gets hurt, 15-year-old Delore becomes the boss of a 200-mile cattle drive. Fine realistic writing. *Older to mature.*

St. Pierre, Paul; Breaking Smith's quarterhorse. McGraw, 1966. 164 pages. $5.95 [0-7700-0029-0]; School ed. (1969) $3.15 paper [0-7700-3193-5]

Epitomizes the realities of ranch life in British Columbia. Adapted from a television script. *Older to mature.*

Seton, Ernest T.; Animal heroes: being the histories of a cat, a dog, a pigeon, a lynx, two wolves and a reindeer, and elucidation of the same. Norwood Editions, P.O. Box 38, Norwood, Pa. 19074. $20.00 [0-685-735-17-6]

Middle to mature.

Seton, Ernest T.; King of the grizzlies. Künstler, Mort (illus.). Scholastic-Tab, 1975 (1970). 95 pages. $0.95 paper.

A slightly edited version of *Biography of a grizzly. Middle to mature.*

Seton, Ernest Thompson; Selected stories of Ernest Thompson Seton. Morley, Patricia (ed.). U of O., 1977. 168 pages. $6.00 paper [0-7766-4339-8]

Five stories from *Wild Animals I Have Known* and three with Canadian settings from his later writing. *Older to mature.*

Seton, Ernest T.; Two little savages. Dover (General Publishing); 416 pages. $4.75 paper [0-8446-2909-X]

Woodcraft and woodlore are part of this Canadian classic about two boys who play at being Indians. *Middle to older.*

Seton, Ernest T.; Wild animals I have known. McClelland, 1977 (1898). 304 pages. $3.50 paper [0-7710-9254-7] (New Canadian Library)

Collection of true animal tales illustrated with the author's sympathetic pen-and-ink drawings. *Middle to mature.*

Sherwood, Roland H.; Maritime mysteries; haunting tales from Atlantic Canada. Lancelot, 1976. 112 pages. $3.50 paper [0-88999-056-5]

Entertaining and sometimes spine-chilling tales with a Maritime quality. *Mature.*

Shipley, Nan; Return to the river. Peguis, 1976. 186 pages. $4.00 paper [0-919566-51-0]

Nona Hawk of Roaring Rapids Reserve contends with insuperable odds when she tries to make a life for herself in Winnipeg. *Mature.*

Siamon, Sharon; Strange Lake adventure. Simpson, David (illus.). Gage, 1979. 128 pages. $2.40 paper [0-7715-5982-8]

The three Savela children live in Northern Ontario where helping an old prospector file his mining claim involves adventures on snowmobiles and snowshoes. *Middle to older.*

Stevenson, William; The Bushbabies. Houghton (Thos. Allen), 1965. 278 pages. $11.75 [0-395-07116-X]

Jackie and her African friend Tembo have exciting adventures while returning a bushbaby to his home. *Older.*

Stren, Patti; There's a rainbow in my closet. Harper (Fitzhenry), 1979. 136 pages. $11.75 [0-06-026082-3]

Emma feels abandoned by her mother who goes on holiday in Europe and leaves her in charge of her grandmother who becomes "the first person to really understand my drawings." Fey drawings right in the text. *Older to mature.*

Swede, George; The Case of the moonlit gold dust. Jones, Danielle (illus.). Three Trees (Firefly), 1979. 36 pages. $2.95 paper [0-88823-023-0]

In an easy-to-read mystery Sherlock, a bloodhound, and Watson, a cat, solve a gold smuggling case. *Middle.*

Tennant, Veronica; On stage, please. Briansky, Rita (illus.). McClelland, 1977. 176 pages. $6.95 [0-7710-8453-6]

Principal ballerina with the National Ballet of Canada writes an informative but entertaining story about 10-year-old Jennifer's pursuit of a career in dance. *Older.*

Troendle, Yves; Journey to the sun; a novel based on the myths of the Iroquoian Indians. MacLean, Julia (illus.). Oolichan, 1977. 169 pages. $8.95 cloth [0-88982-008-2]; $4.95 paper [0-88982-006-6]

More a selection of stories than a novel, this will appeal to children with some background in Native folklore. *Older to mature.*

Truss, Jan; A Very small rebellion; essay by Jack Chambers. Mielward, Peter (illus.). LeBel, 1977. $6.95 [0-920008-02-X]

Prairie Métis children discover the tragic role played by Louis Riel in the 1885 rebellion against John A. Macdonald's government as their own "small rebellion" challenges white hostility, unchanged since Riel's day. The accompanying historical essay delineates Riel's life and times. *Middle to older.*

Walker, David; Pirate rock. Collins, 1969. 190 pages. $3.75 [0-00-222088-1]; $0.95 paper.

Exciting contemporary adventure story set near the New Brunswick–Maine border. *Older.*

Walker, Diana; The Hundred thousand dollar farm. Abelard, 1977. 182 pages. $8.75 [0-200-00170-1]

A close-knit family lives on a farm in Prince Edward Island and gets a chance to sell it. *Older.*

Walker, Diana; Mother wants a horse. Crowell (Fitzhenry and Whiteside), 1978. 186 pages. $8.95 [0-200-00181-7]

This sequel to ***The Year of the horse*** finds the 16-year-old heroine opening a riding school. *Older.*

Walker, Diana; The Year of the horse. Abelard (Fitzhenry & Whiteside), 1975. 177 pages. $8.50 [0-200-00151-5] $1.95 paper [0-685-96147-8]

Mystery, love, humour, adolescent adjustments and horses of course in an appealing story for horse story buffs. *Older.*

Wallace, Ian; The Christmas tree house. Kids Can, 1976. 48 pages. $2.95 paper [0-919964-10-9]

Frightening Don Valley Rose makes Christmas an extraordinary event for two Cabbagetown children. Haunting illustrations by the author. *Younger to middle.*

Weir, Joan; Career girl. Tree Frog, 1979. 141 pages. $5.95 cloth [0-89967-032-3]; $3.95 paper [0-89967-027-7]

Patti wants to be a prima ballerina and works hard to achieve that aim. *Middle to older.*

Weir, Joan S.; Three day challenge, Daniels, Alan (illus.). Scholastic, 1976. 190 pages. $1.05 paper.

An 18-year-old Western girl competes for a place on the Canadian Equestrian Team. *Older.*

Wilkins, M.G.; The Unwanted adventure of Harold Greenhouse. Condy, Roy (illus.). Scholastic-Tab, 1977. 72 pages. $1.35 paper.

Harold is mistaken for a millionaire's son and kidnapped. *Middle to older.*

Wilson, Eric; Murder on the Canadian. Clarke, Irwin, 1976. 108 pages. $5.95 [0-370-11013-7]

A typical mystery story format that finds a junior detective involved in a killing on the Canadian National Railway's transcontinental train, the Canadian. *Older.*

Wilson, Eric; Susie Q. Scholastic, 1978. 162 pages. $1.50 paper.

A teenager chooses to have an abortion to prevent "the hopeless future of an unwanted child" and the resentment of a trapped husband, in this realistic moral tale. *Mature.*

Wilson, Eric; Vancouver nightmare. Clarke, Irwin, 1978. 100 pages. $7.95 [0-7720-1234-2]

Sequel to *Murder on the Canadian* features Tom helping to apprehend a drug ring. *Older.*

Wilkinson, Douglas; Sons of the Arctic. Clarke, Irwin, 1965. 179 pages. $3.75 [0-7720-0030-1]

The Arctic adventures of three Eskimo boys include combat with a polar bear and surviving a blinding snowstorm. *Older.*

Wood, Kerry; Samson's long ride. Collins, 1968. 77 pages. $3.95.

Ten-year-old Samson Beaver leaves mission school and travels 400 miles to find his beloved family. *Middle.*

Young, Scott; A Boy at the Leafs' camp. Little, 1963. 256 pages. $4.95 [0-316-97701-2]

A young boy unexpectedly tries out at the Leafs' hockey camp. *Middle to older.*

Young, Scott; Scrubs on skates. Little, 1952. 218 pages. $3.95 [0-316-97704-7]

A school develops a hockey team and school spirit too. A hockey classic. *Middle to older.*

FANTASY

Aubry, Claude; The Christmas wolf. Kane, Alice E. (trans); McClelland, 1965. 42 pages. $4.95 [0-7710-0962-3]

A starving wolf and a miracle on Christmas Eve restore our faith in humanity. *Middle.*

Bailey, Paul; Charlie meets the Goomby: The land of Urd; Wladyka, Dan (illus.) McClelland, 1977. 32 pages. $4.95 [0-88869-003-7] (A Magook Publication)

The monster Goomby threatens to eat Charlie who goes to the land of Urd to restore peace and understanding. *Middle.*

Bodger, Joan; Clever-Lazy: the girl who invented herself. Atheneum (McClelland), 1979. 201 pages. $11.25 [0-689-30674-1]

A baker and her husband ask the Goddess for a daughter, clever enough to be lazy and lazy enough to be clever, and the Goddess complies. A satisfying story in traditional fairytale style by a storyteller who enjoys her craft. *Older to mature.*

Clark, Catherine Anthony; The Diamond feather. Macmillan, 1962. 224 pages. $6.50 [0-7705-0044-7]

Magic adventures of two children searching for the family of an old prospector. *Middle to older.*

Clark, Catherine, Anthony; The Hunter and the medicine man. Macmillan, 1966. 183 pages. $2.95 paper (1972) [0-7705-0927-4]

Fantasy about breaking a medicine man's spell in Rocky Mountain country. *Middle to older.*

Clifton, N. Roy; The City beyond the gates. Broadhurst, Christopher (illus.) and Graham, Jennifer (illus.); Scholastic-Tab, 1979. Rev. ed. 118 pages. $1.25 paper.

In this allegory for children, Janey-Anne explores a horrifying gadget-ridden world. *Middle to older.*

Cook, Lyn; The Magical Miss Mittens. Macmillan, 1974. 233 pages. $2.95 paper [0-7705-1209-7]

A time fantasy in which three children meet Shakespeare, Socrates and other historical personalities. *Older.*

Cutt, W. Towrie; Message from Arkmae. Collins, 1972. 95 pages. $3.95 [0-00-184512-8]

The message that man is fouling his last refuge, the sea, is delivered to two Orkney Island boys by the leader of a seal herd. *Older.*

Cutt, W. Towrie; Seven for the sea. Collins, 1973. 96 pages. $3.95 [0-00-211749-5]

The interweaving of legend and reality is well handled in this fantasy set in the Orkney Islands. *Older.*

Engel, Marian; Adventure at Moon Bay Towers. Clarke, Irwin, 1974. 34 pages. $5.75 [0-7720-0717-9]

A fantasy involving two city children who become caretakers of a lakeside cottage complete with pet alligator. *Younger to middle.*

Garcia, Claire Watson; The Peanut plan. Kids Can, 1979. Rev. ed. 66 pages. $2.25 paper [0-919964-00-1]

A young squirrel learns about nutrition and ecology and survival from her grandmother. Lovingly illustrated by the author. *Younger to middle.*

Harris, Christie; Secret in the stlalakum wild. Tait, Douglas (illus.); McClelland, 1972. 186 pages. $5.95 cloth [0-7710-4014-8]; $3.95 paper (1975) [0-7710-4013-X]

Indian forest spirits liven this British Columbia fantasy. *Older.*

Harris, Christie; Sky man on the totem pole? McClelland, 1975. 167 pages. $7.95 [0-7710-4027-X]

Fantasy combining West Coast Indians and space men who visit earth to find the secret of ecological balance. *Older.*

Laurence, Margaret; Jason's quest, Torell, Staffan (illus.); McClelland, 1970. 211 pages. $5.95 [0-7710-4730-4]

A young mole accompanied by an owl and two cats seeks a cure for the wearying invisible sickness suffered by the inhabitants of Molanium. *Middle to older.*

Laurence, Margaret; The Olden days coat. Wood, Muriel (illus.). McClelland, 1979. 35 pages. $7.95 [0-7710-4744-4]

Sal puts on the olden days coat she finds in her grandmother's trunk and suddenly she finds herself 60 years back in time. Sympathetic illustrations in full colour. *Middle.*

Nichols, Ruth; The Marrow of the world. Hyman, Trina Schart (illus.); Macmillan, 1977. 168 pages $4.50 paper [0-7705-1540-1]

Philip and Linda are drawn into a dramatic struggle for survival in the strange world under Georgian Bay waters. An award winning quest fantasy. *Middle to older.*

Nichols, Ruth; A Walk out of the world. Academic, 1969. 192 pages. $8.95.

Judith and Tobit plunge through time into another world threatened by an evil sorcerer. *Middle to older.*

Piper, Eileen; The Magician's trap. Daniel, Alan (illus.). Scholastic-Tab, 1976. $1.35 paper.

A prince, under the spell of a wicked magician, is saved by a blind girl in a fantasy for young and middle readers. Strikingly illustrated. *Middle.*

Richler, Mordecai; Jacob two-two meets the hooded fang. Wegner, Fritz (illus.); McClelland, 1975. 84 pages. $6.95 [0-7710-7482-4]

Fantastical adventures of a boy too young, too little, too misunderstood. A recording featuring Christopher Plummer is available: Caedmon TC 1525. $7.95 disc; $8.50 cassette. *Middle to older.*

Riley, Louise; Train for Tiger Lily. Macmillan, 1954. 186 pages. $5.95 [0-7705-0932-0]

An unscheduled stop on a train journey west leads to magic adventure. *Middle.*

Roberts, Theodore Goodridge; The Red feathers. McClelland, 1976 (c 1907). 325 pages. $3.50 paper [0-7710-9227-X] (New Canadian Library)

The loss of two little feathers precipitates titanic struggles for the use of power between Wise-as-a-She Wolf and Bright Robe, culture hero and shaman, among the now extinct Beothuks of Newfoundland. This story is myth making of a very high level. *Older to mature.*

Sauer, Julia L.; Fog Magic. Ward, Lynd (illus.) Archway (PaperJacks) 1977. 107 pages. $1.25 [0-671-29817-8]

Greta loved the fog that enveloped her little Nova Scotia fishing village and when she was ten she walked into another world that existed only in the fog bank. *Older.*

Young, Chip; Foxy Grandpa. Palleck, Tye (illus.); Clarke, Irwin, 1971. 58 pages. $2.50 [0-7720-0522-2]

A lively fantasy about the Wild Canadians, a hockey team with old grandpa groundhog as the star player. *Younger to middle.*

Young, Chip; The Wild Canadians. Clarke, Irwin, 1975. 44 pages. $5.95. [0-7720-10316]

Hockey's bush league champs continue their fantastic adventures. *Younger to middle.*

SCIENCE FICTION

Gotlieb, Phyllis; Sunburst. Fitzhenry & Whiteside, 1977. 3rd ed. $1.95 school net paper [0-88902-039-6] (The Contemporary Scene)

Thirty years after a thermo-nuclear explosion sealed off an American town a group of the incarcerated children escape. *Older to mature.*

Hargreaves, Henry Allen; North by 2000: a collection of Canadian science fiction. PMA, 1975. 160 pages. $8.95 cloth [0-88778-119-5]; $3.95 paper [0-88778-128-4]

Six short science fictions for dedicated sci-fi buffs. *Mature.*

Hill, Douglas; Galactic warlord. Gollancz (Clarke Irwin) 1979. 127 pages. $11.95 [0-575-02663-4]

Keill Randor is dying from the effects of radiation, but his final mission is to find the destroyers of his home, the planet Moros. *Older.*

Hughes, Monica; Beyond the dark river. Thomas Nelson, 1979. 152 pages. $13.95 [0-17-6007-69-5]

Benjamin seeks help for his Hutterite Colony's ailing children from a young Indian healer, Daughter-of-She-Who-Came-After in the year 2025AD, 45 years after the atomic holocaust destroyed the closest city. A way-out science-fiction fantasy. *Older to mature.*

Hughes, Monica; Crisis on Conshelf Ten. Copp, 1975. 144 pages. $4.25 [0-7730-1042-4]

The first child born on the moon, Kepler Masterman, journeys to Earth with his father, the moon's governor, but cannot adjust to Earth's gravity and lives in an undersea lab with friends. *Older to mature.*

Hughes, Monica; Earthdark. Hamish Hamilton (Thomas Nelson), 1977. 122 pages. $7.95 [0-241-89544-8]

In this sequel to *Crisis on Conshelf Ten* Kepler Masterman returns to the moon and rebels against its rigid life style by leaving the base for a forbidden ride on the lunar surface with dire results. *Older to mature.*

Hughes, Monica; The Tomorrow city. Hamish Hamilton (Thomas Nelson), 1978. 137 pages. $10.50 [0-241-89887-0]

A computer designed to serve community needs is programmed for the utmost efficiency in keeping the city clean and neat. Finally C-Three controls the whole population and Caro and David have to do something about it. *Older to mature.*

Lyngseth, Joan; Martin's starwars. Collier, Steven (illus.). Borealis, 1978. 69 pages. $6.95 paper [0-919594-89-1]

Martin puts on the space suit his parents gave him for Christmas and embarks on adventures from science fiction. *Older.*

HISTORICAL FICTION
see also
PUBLISHERS' SERIES
Buckskin Books
Northern Lights

Allan, Iris; The Boy in buckskins. Western Producer, 1978 (c1959) 169 pages. $4.95 paper [0-919306-53-5]

Fictional biography of John McDougall, a young explorer who travelled west from Norway House from 1860 to 1872 when he was ordained a Methodist minister. *Older.*

Allan, Iris; White Sioux: Major Walsh of the Mounted Police. Gray, 1969. 209 pages. $6.95 [0-88826-021-0]

Northwest Mounted Police participate in the settlement of the West in the 1870's. *Older.*

Andersen, Doris I.; Blood brothers. Macmillan, 1967. 136 pages. $5.50 [0-7705-0000-5]

Bella Coola Indian and Norwegian-American boys become friends in late 19th century British Columbia. *Middle to older.*

Andersen, Doris I.; Slave of the Haida. Macmillan, 1978. 176 pages $4.95 paper [0-7705-1699-8].

A compelling story about slavery's implications for a young Salish boy captured by Haida warriors. Also available in French as *Esclave des Haïdas. Middle to older.*

Aubry, Claude; Agouhanna. Doubleday, 1972. 89 pages. $4.50 [0-385-04786-X]; PaperJacks, 1973. $0.95 paper [0-7737-7051-8]; McGraw, 1974. $6.95 trade [0-07-077682-2] educ. ed. $4.95
An Iroquois boy repelled by violence and a warlike young girl who admires him people a tale set in Canada before the white men came. *Middle to older.*

Barnhouse, D.P.; Quest of the Golden Gannet. Breakwater, 1979. 97 pages. $4.95 paper [0-919948-60-X]

Tod and his great-uncle, skipper Jabez Evans, join the crew of a Yankee Trader carrying contraband and bound for Newfoundland where they risk encounters with the fearful Devon Captains. *Older.*

Burton, Hester; Tim at the fur fort. Ambrus, Victor (illus.). Hamish Hamilton (Thomas Nelson), 1978. 88 pages. $3.75 [0-241-89571-5] (Antelope Books)

Tim embarks from England in hopes of fame and fortune in the vast, unexplored Hudson's Bay Company territory in British North America. *Middle.*

Clark, Joan; The Hand of Robin Squires. Taylor, William (illus.) and Cserepy, Mary (illus.). Clarke, Irwin, 1977. 145 pages. $6.95 [0-7720-1091-9]

Pirates and buried treasure figure in an exciting adventure based on Nova Scotia's Oak Island mystery. *Older.*

Cline, Beverly F. Louisa Clark's annual 1841/1842; Louisa Clark's annual 1843. MacDonald, Robert (design). Porcépic, 1976. 3 vols. Vol. 1 1841 (1976). $2.95 paper [0-88878-0958]; Vol. 2 1842 (1977). $2.95 paper [0-88878-133-4]; Vol. 3 1843 (1978). $2.95 paper [0-88878-099-0] 64 pages each.

Fictionalized annuals relate the events and way of life in Goderich, Ontario at the mid-19th century. *Mature.*

Clutton-Brock, Elizabeth; Woman of the paddle song. Copp, 1972. 176 pages. $1.95 [0-7730-4003-X]

The half-Indian half-Scots wife of the explorer David Thompson tells the story of his employ in the Northwest Company and his mapping of North America from Hudson Bay to the mouth of the Columbia River as shared by her and their 13 children. *Mature.*

Cook, Lyn; Rebel on the trail. Macmillan, 1953. 247 pages. $6.50 [0-7705-0060-9]

A brother and sister become involved with Mackenzie in the 1837 Rebellion. *Older.*

Cook, Lyn; The Secret of Willow Castle. Macmillan, 1966. 235 pages. $6.50 [0-7705-0063-3]

About Napanee in the 19th century and a girl who is related to John A. Macdonald. *Older.*

Cooper, Gordon; Hester's summer. Oxford, 1974. 137 pages. $8.75 [0-19-271361-2]

This sequel to *A Second springtime* follows Hester through her nurse's training. *Older.*

Cooper, Gordon; A Second springtime. Oxford, 1973. 161 pages. $9.75 [0-19-271351-5]
Chronicles the first year Hester spends with her adoptive family in Nova Scotia after leaving a British orphanage in 1873. *Older.*

Corriveau, Monique; The Wapiti. L'Heureux, J.M. (trans.); Macmillan, 1968. 188 pages. $5.50 cloth [0-7705-0064-1]; $2.95 paper [0-7705-1007-8]
A French orphan's trials and troubles in New France. Translated from the French. *Older.*

Cutt, W. Towrie; Carry my bones northwest. Collins, 1973. 144 pages. $4.95 [0-00-184119-X]
Willie goes to live with his grandparents in the Orkney Islands after his father and Indian mother are killed in an Indian massacre at a Hudson's Bay post in 1794. *Older.*

Cutt, W. Towrie; On the trail of Long Tom. Collins, 1970. 95 pages. $4.95 [0-00-184006-1]
The story of a half-breed youth's involvement in the North West Rebellion of 1885. *Older.*

Downie, Mary Alice and **Downie, John:** Honor bound. Oxford, 1971. 192 pages $8.50 [0-19-540192-1]
A Loyalist family flees to Kingston at the close of the American War of Independence. *Older.*

Dunham, Mabel; Trail of the Conestoga. McClelland, 1970 (1942). 340 pages. $4.50 paper [0-7710-2955-1]
An ancestor writes about the Mennonite trek to the Grand River area of Ontario. *Mature.*

Eaton, Sara; Lady of the backwoods. McClelland, 1969. 175 pages. $7.95 [0-7710-3015-0]
Fictional biography of a pioneer author and naturalist, Catherine Parr Traill. *Older.*

Faulknor, Cliff; The Smoke horse. McClelland, 1968. 187 pages. $4.50 cloth; $2.97 paper [0-7710-3108-4]
A Piegan Blackfoot tribe needs horses and hunts for wild ones. *Middle.*

Faulknor, Cliff; The White calf. Tailfeathers, Gerald (illus.); Scholastic-Tab, 1973. 180 pages $1.05 paper.
Mystery and humour combine in the story of a young Blackfoot boy growing up in the 1800's. *Middle to older.*

Feather, Jean Hayes; Sawtooth Harbour boy. Calvert, L. (illus.): Nelson, 1973. 128 pages $2.20 paper [0-176-32913-7]
Billy's outport life was happy but without frills in 1920's Newfoundland. *Middle.*

Franchere, Ruth; Stampede North. Collier-Macmillan, 1969. 218 pages. $5.95.
About the Klondike Gold Rush in 1897. *Older.*

Fraser, William Douglas; Nor'east for Louisburg, illustrated with photographs. Consolidated Amethyst, 1978. 228 pages. $5.95 paper [0-920474-01-2]
Profusely illustrated with maps and photographs, an adventure story of 30 years (1745-1775) in Jonathan Steele's life while he was involved in the siege of Louisburg by the Americans. *Mature.*

Freeman, Bill; First spring on the Grand Banks, illustrated. Lorimer, 1978. 171 pages. $9.95 cloth [0-88862-220-1]; $4.95 paper [0-88862-22-X]
In this sequel to *Shantymen of Cache Lake* and *The Last voyage of the Scotian* Meg and John Baines join their friend Canso in deep sea chases, shipwreck and adventure on the Grand Banks of Newfoundland. *Older.*

Freeman, Bill; The Last voyage of the Scotian, illustrated. Lorimer, 1976. 178 pages. $9.95 cloth. [0-88862-113-2]; $3.95 paper [0-88862-112-4]
This sequel to *Shantymen of Cache Lake* is an exciting adventure and "a magnificent picture of conditions on the sailing ships of the 19th century." *Older.*

Freeman, Bill; Shantymen of Cache Lake. Lorimer, 1976. 166 pages. $9.95 cloth [0-88862-091-8]; $3.95 paper [0-88862-090-X]; School ed. $3.95 paper [0-88862-101-9]

Two young people whose father tried to organize a trade union among the lumber workers go to work at the Ottawa Valley lumber camp where he was murdered. *Older.*

Freeman, Madeline Austin; A Horse for Running Buffalo. Daniel, Alan (illus.); Van Nostrand, 1972. 88 pages. $1.95 paper [0-442-22440-0]; Scholastic-Tab, 1975. $1.00 paper.

A Blackfoot Indian boy is devoted to his horse. Beautiful charcoal drawings and factual epilogue. *Middle.*

Fryer, Mary Beacock; Escape; adventures of a Loyalist family. Clarke, Stephen (illus.) Dent, 1976. 152 pages. $4.95 paper [0-460-91410-3]

The 10 members of the Loyalist Seaman family escape to Canada when they are hounded as dissident Americans after the American Revolution, in 1789. *Older.*

German, Tony; River race. PMA Books, 1979. 158 pages. $9.95 cloth [0-88778-194-2]; $4.95 paper [0-88778-195-0]

This sequel to *Tom Penny* follows Tom from his uncle's shanty on the Gatineau down the Ottawa to the Quebec market with a winter's haul of square cut timbers. Adventures all the way! *Older to mature.*

German, Tony; Tom Penny. PMA, 1977. 180 pages. $8.95 cloth [0-88778-171-3]; $4.95 paper [0-88778-172-1]

In an exciting story full of incredible adventures Tom Penny proves his worth as a hardy Upper Canadian pioneer when he is left an orphan in 1829. *Older to mature.*

Greene, Marion; Canal boy. Macmillan, 1959. 152 pages. $1.95 [0-7705-0123-0]

Working on the Rideau Canal in 1820, Sean stands accused of stealing Colonel By's pistols - but is vindicated. *Older.*

Harris, Christie; Raven's cry. Reid, Bill (illus.); McClelland, 1966. 193 pages. $4.38 Library ed. [0-7710-4034-2]; $2.79 paper [0-7710-4033-4]

A descendant of Haida chiefs decorates an inspired book about the tragic destruction of the Haida people by white fur traders. *Older.*

Hayes, John F.; A Land divided. Copp, 1951. 285 pages. $4.25 paper.

Problems arise for Michael's family because his mother is Acadian and his father an English army officer. *Older.*

Hémon, Louis; Maria Chapdelaine. Blake, W.H. (trans.) and MacDonald, Thoreau (illus.); Macmillan, 1973. 162 pages $7.95 cloth [0-7705-0012-9]; $2.50 paper (1973) [0-7705-1041-8] (Laurentian Library)

A simple story about French Canadian farmlife at the turn of the century. *Older.*

Herapath, Theodora; Journey into danger. Wheeler, William (illus.). Scholastic-Tab, (1966) 1974. 135 pages. $1.05 paper.

Rob de Soren, young visitor from France, misses the last boat out of Quebec before the freeze and spends the winter in Fort Toronto where Intendant Bigot sends him in November, 1751. *Older.*

Hoople, Elizabeth L.; Medicine maid. Mika, 1977. 182 pages. $12.00 cloth [0-919303-17-X]; $8.00 paper [0-919303-17-X]

Mary Whitmore survived an Indian attack on her home but had to live with the Delawares for seven years whence she found her way back to her Pennsylvania mother's family in 1787. *Older to mature.*

Houston, James; Eagle mask. Academic, 1966. 64 pages. $7.25.

Two Kwakiutl princes suffer initiation rites to assume their traditional tribal responsibilities. *Middle.*

Hughes, Monica; Gold-fever trail: a Klondike adventure. Peacock, Patricia (illus.); Le Bel, 1974. 92 pages. $5.95 cloth [0-920008-01-1]; $2.95 paper.

Two children go to Dawson City in search of their missing father during the Gold Rush. *Middle.*

Kilian, Crawford; The Last Vikings. Clarke, Irwin, 1975. 24 pages. $1.25 paper [0-7720-0726-8]; $1.15 ed.

A day in the life of Olaf a Viking boy, whose fatherless family joins an Eskimo group to face the harsh Greenland winter of 1354 together. *Younger to middle.*

Kirby, William; The Golden dog: a romance of old Quebec. McClelland, 1969. 321 pages. $2.95 paper [0-7710-9165-6] (New Canadian Library)

Intendant Bigot's regime in New France 1855 included treachery, intrigue and murder. *Mature.*

Kouhi, Elizabeth; Jamie of Thunder Bay. Borealis, 1978. 72 pages. $4.95 paper [0-919594-78-6]

Young Jamie joins the Northwest Company at old Fort William and lives a life of adventure among the Indians and fur traders and finally becomes a voyageur himself. *Middle.*

Lunn, Janet; Larger than life. Press Porcepic, 1979. 78 pages. $4.95 paper [0-88878-097-4]

Ten artfully sketched "true stories of Canadian heroes" include Crowfoot, Paul Kane and Madeleine de Verchères. *Middle to older.*

Macdonald, Zillah and **Macdonald, Colin;** Prisoner in Louisbourg. Macmillan, 1966 (reissue). 231 pages. $2.95 paper (1972) [0-7705-0929-0]

An action packed novel of an American boy who took part in the siege of Louisburg on Cape Breton Island in the 18th century. *Mature.*

McFarlane, Leslie; The Last of the great picnics. McClelland, 1965, 1974. 99 pages. $2.79 paper [0-7710-5784-9]

Short, humorous tale of two children and a memorable Dominion Day celebration with Sir John A. Macdonald. *Middle.*

McNamee, James; Them damn Canadians hanged Louis Riel! Macmillan, c1971, 1976. 133 pages. $3.95 paper [0-7705-1506-1]

Eccentric Uncle Joe and his 12-year-old nephew travel the West on business during the Riel Rebellion. *Older.*

Peck, Robert Newton; Eagle fur. Knopf (Random), 1978. 236 pages. $10.50 [0-394-42785-8]

Abbot Coe comes to Canada as an indentured servant to the factor of the Hudson's Bay Company and learns about the fur trade business. *Mature.*

Phelan, Josephine; The Boy who ran away. Macmillan, 1954. 152 pages. $1.95 [0-7705-0234-2]

Asher Mundy ran off to the Canadian West to become an apprentice artist like Paul Kane. *Middle.*

Reaney, James; The Boy with an R in his hand. Rampen, Leo (illus.). Porcupine's Quill, 1980, (c 1965). 102 pages. $5.95 paper [0-88984-031-8]

A reprinting of the 1965 edition, using the same plates, of "a tale of the type-riot at William Lyon Mackenzie's printing office in 1826." Excellent historical recreation. *Older.*

Reekie, Isabel M.; Journey to Red River. Holt, 1973. 199 pages. $6.95 [0-03-923317-0]

A fictionalized history of Selkirk's Red River Settlement built in 1812. *Middle.*

Reekie, Isabel M.; Red, horse of the west. Holt, 1972. 100 pages. $6.95 cloth [0-03-923581-5]

A boy's search for his stolen horse, set against the background of Manitoba in 1885 - the time of the Riel Rebellion. *Middle.*

Sharp, Edith Lambert. Nkwala. McClelland, 1979. (1958). $3.95 paper [0-7710-8124-3]

A Salish Indian boy finds his totem and leads his people to a better hunting ground in this authentic and sympathetic recreation of Native life before the white incursion. *Middle to older.*

Shipley, Nan; The Blonde voyageur. Burns, 1971. 122 pages. $5.25 [0-88768-026-7]

Compelling story of the first white woman to live in the Canadian West. *Mature.*

Slater, Patrick (pseud.); The Yellow briar. Macmillan, 1970 (c1933). 196 pages. $3.50 paper [0-7705-0284-9]; $4.50 quality paperback [0-7705-1100-7]; $2.95 Laurentian Library paperback [0-7705-0962-2]

Paddy, a nine-year-old Irish orphan grows up in Ontario in the 1840's. *Older to mature.*

Smucker, Barbara Claassen; Days of terror. Clarke Irwin, 1979. 156 pages. $8.95 [0-7720-1280-6]

A Russian Mennonite family emigrates to a Western Canadian farm in the wake of the Revolution of 1917. *Older to mature.*

Smucker, Barbara; Underground to Canada. McNeely, Tom (illus.) Clarke, Irwin, 1977. 157 pages. $7.95 [0-7720-1111-7] Penguin, 1979. $1.95 paper [0-14-03-1122-X]

Julilly and Liza escape the degradations of slavery via the Underground Railway from Mississippi to Canada before the American Civil War. *Older.*

Stirling, Lilla; Gretchen of Grand Pré. Lancelot, 1974. 2nd ed. 34 pages. $1.50 paper [0-88999-019-0]

Vignettes of early pioneer life in the Maritimes. *Middle.*

Stirling, Lilla; The Stowaway piper. Werth, Kurt (illus.). Formac, 1978. 128 pages. $3.95 paper [0-88780-024-6]

In a story full of humour and suspense Young Dougal Macdonald stows away on a ship leaving Scotland for Canada. *Older.*

Swayze, Fred; Fire over Huronia. McClelland, 1968. 144 pages. $6.50 [0-7710-8360-2]

The destruction of the mission at Fort Ste. Marie is told in this exciting novel. *Middle.*

Turner, D. Harold; To hang a rebel. Smith, Merle (illus.). Gage, 1977. 218 pages. $9.95 [0-7715-9368-6]

The Upper Canada Rebellion and William Lyon Mackenzie are convincingly recreated through the involvement of Doug Lachlan in the stirring events of 1837. *Older to mature.*

Williams, Bert; Sword of Egypt. Gal, Laszlo (illus.). Scholastic-Tab, 1977. 129 pages. $1.15 paper.

A fast paced recreation of ancient Egyptian history through the adventures of young Aahmes. *Older.*

Wood, Kerry; The Boy and the buffalo. Wood, 1963. 120 pages. $2.95. Macmillan, 1963. $3.95 [0-7705-0030-7] (Buckskin Books)

Adopted by a buffalo herd, a young Plains Indian boy survives one cold prairie winter before finding his family. *Middle.*

Wood, Kerry; The Medicine man. Wood, 1969. 91 pages. $3.00.

One day in the life of a Cree camp 200 years ago, and especially about the medicine man's role. *Middle to older.*

Young, Chip; The Little hen of Huronia. Duchesne, Christiane (illus.); Clarke, Irwin, 1971. 32 pages. $3.95 [0-7720-1099-4]

A hen helps to save the settlers from starving in this historical tale about the 17th century Huron mission. *Younger to middle.*

Yong, Delbert A.; Last voyage of the Unicorn. Clarke, Irwin, 1969. 182 pages. $6.95 [0-7720-0094-8]

A Danish attempt to find the Northwest Passage in 1619, seen through the eyes of a 15-year-old pilot in training. *Older to mature.*

SHORT STORY COLLECTIONS

Boswell, William; Lamont, Betty and Martyn, John (eds.); Crossroads: Canadian stories, poems and songs. Van Nostrand, 1979. 2 vols. Vol. 1, 144 pages. $6.95 paper [0-442-29772-6]; Vol. II, 175 pages. $6.95 paper [0-442-29773-4]

Poems, legends, songs and short stories by Canadians from a wide range of regional and ethnic backgrounds. Bio-bibliographies of the authors are included. *Mature.*

McEvoy, Bernard; Stories from across Canada. McClelland, 1966. 110 pages. $5.95 [0-7710-5768-7]

Mowat, Haig-Brown and Burnford among others share their view of Canadian life with young readers. *Older to mature.*

MacNeil, James and **Sorestad, Glen;** Tigers of the snow. Nelson, 1972. 213 pages. $3.25 net limp [0-176-33043-7]

Eighteen modern Canadian stories in a variety of styles and subjects, uniformly excellent. *Older to mature.*

Stevens, John and **Smith, Roger J.** (ed.); Canadian stories of action and adventure. Macmillan, 1978. 218 pages. $4.00 paper [0-7705-1688-2]

Eighteen previously published stories and excerpts of novels by Alice Munro, Ernest Buckler, Farley Mowat and other distinguished Canadian writers. *Mature.*

Tait, George E. (ed.); Famous Canadian stories. McClelland, 1953. 310 pages. $6.50 cloth [0-7710-8400-5]; Text ed. $4.25 [0-7710-8421-8]; $3.95 paper.

Three to five page stories about important people and events in Canada's history. *Older.*

Whitaker, Muriel (ed.); Great Canadian animal stories. Van Kampen, Vlasta (illus.). Hurtig, 1978. 232 pages. $12.95 [0-88830-165-0]

Seton and Roberts initiated a new literary genre, the animal biography. Included here are 16 stories representative of Canada's best, beautifully illustrated. *Older to mature.*

GEOGRAPHY AND TRAVEL

GEOGRAPHY
see also
PUBLISHERS' SERIES
Studies in Canadian Geography
Wild Rivers

Fuller, William A. and **Holmes, John C.**; The Life of the Far North. McGraw, 1972. 232 pages. $7.25 [0-07-022614-8] (Our Living World of Nature Series)

Fine colour photographs, informative text, diagrams and maps of the Far North by two professional ecologists. *Middle to older.*

Hills, Theo L. and **Hills, Sarah Jane**; Canada. Fideler, 1974. 224 pages $8.70 paper [0-88296-090-3]

A volume in the Canada and Latin America Series gives general information about Canadians and their way of life. *Older.*

Lambie, Beatrice; The Mackenzie; river to the top of the world. Garrard (Nelson), 1967. 94 pages. $4.50 library binding [0-8116-6369-8]

Well researched, accurate social history of one of our mightiest rivers. *Middle.*

Putnam, D.F. and **Putnam R.G.;** Canada: a regional analysis. Dent, 1970. $8.45 [0-460-90391-8]

Excellent physical and social geography of Canada with special emphasis on demography and urban development. *Older to mature.*

Robinson, J. Lewis; Resources of the Canadian Shield. Methuen, 1969. 136 pages. $3.65 paper [0-458-90420-1]

Readable regional economic geography based on the natural resources of the Canadian Shield. *Older.*

Summers, William F.; Geography of Newfoundland. Copp, 1972. Rev. ed. 182 pages. $8.25 [0-7730-1800-X]

Physical and social geography for children. Textbook format. *Middle to older.*

Washington, John and others; Focus on Canada. Hammond, Frank (illus.). McGraw, 1978. 314 pages. $13.82 [0-07-082309-X] (Concepts in Geography)

This textbook deals with the physiography, economy, regional diversities and global influences relating to modern Canada. *Older to mature.*

DESCRIPTION AND TRAVEL

see also

PUBLISHERS' SERIES

The Canada Series

Oxford Canadian Pictorial Series

Addison, Ottelyn: Early days in Algonquin Park. McGraw, 1974. 144 pages. $9.95 cloth [0-07-077786-1]; $5.95 paper [0-07-077791-8]

Illustrated history of Ontario's provincial park by a naturalist who spent childhood summers there. *Older to mature.*

Baird, David M.; Banff national park; how nature carved its splendour, illustrated. Hurtig, 1977. Rev. ed. 237 pages. $9.95 cloth [0-88830-132-4]; $5.95 paper [0-88830-133-2]

This guide book also has geographical and historical information with illustrations and maps. *Older to mature.*

Brooks, Bill; The Colour of Ontario. Hounslow, 1977. 48 pages. $9.95 [0-88882-007-0]

Pictorial and descriptive survey of colourful Ontario approached through six geographical areas that show the province's disparate geography. *Middle to mature.*

Bruce, Harry; Nova Scotia. Joyce, Fred (illus.) and McGowan, Gordon (illus.); Hounslow Press, 1975. $9.95 [0-88882-006-2]

Short descriptive captions accompany outstanding photographs of an Atlantic province. *All ages.*

Clery, Val; Canada in colour. Brooks, Bill (illus.); Hounslow Press, 1972. 77 pages $8.95 cloth [0-88882-000-3]; $4.95 paper [0-88882-008-9]

Photographs of Canada, the vast and beautiful country, linked by a brief text. *All ages.*

Clery, Val (ed.); Seasons of Canada. Brooks, Bill (illus.). Hounslow Press, 1979. 96 pages $14.95 [0-88882-041-0]

Short introductions to a visual feast of the seasons across Canada. *All ages.*

Czolowski, Ted; British Columbia; western splendour, illustrated. Xanadu Publications, 306 West 25th Street, North Vancouver, B.C. V7N 2G1, 1977. 128 pages. $9.95

A maximum of glossy photographs and a minimum of information serve as introductory material for the browser. *All ages.*

Dobbs, Kildare; Canada. Varley, Peter (illus.); Macmillan, 1969. 2nd rev. ed. $10.50 cloth [0-7705-0297-0]; $5.95 paper [0-7705-0296-2]

Beautiful pictures of a majestic country, with brief captions. *All ages.*

Earle, Stafford; The Basic Jamaica book. E.C.I., 1977. 71 pages. $3.50 paper [0-920448-00-3]

A short well written introduction to the history and geography as well as contemporary society of the Island. *Mature.*

Earn, Josephine; Looking at Canada. Black (Lippincott), 1976. 64 pages. (Looking at Other Countries). $6.75 [0-397-31704-2]

Concise, accurate text and true-colour photos in an attractive format introduce Canada to the uninitiated. *Middle.*

Greene, Lorne Edmond; The Beauty of Canada. Octopus, 1978. 96 pages. $9.95 [0-7064-0794-6]

This expanded picture book boasting of Canada's scenic beauty is up to date and full of colour photos. *All ages.*

Harrington, Lyn; Covered bridges of central and eastern Canada. Harrington, Richard (illus.) McGraw, 1976. 88 pages. $10.95. [0-07-082406-1]

Well researched survey of these survivors from another age provides much hard to find information along with excellent photographic coverage. *Older.*

Harrington, Lyn; Ontario. Scholars' Choice, 1975. 96 pages. $5.67 [0-516-04071-5] (The Enchantment of Canada)

General history and geography written in a lively style. *Middle.*

Harrington, Lyn; The Polar regions. Nelson, 1973. 186 pages. $9.75 [0-8407-6338-7]

Contemporary view of the Arctic and Antarctic. *Older.*

Harrington, Richard; Richard Harrington's Yukon. Alaska Northwest Pub. (U.S.A.), 1974. 103 pages. $7.95 paper. [0-88240-043-6]

A book of photographs illustrating the unique character of the Yukon. *All ages.*

Harrison, Ted. Children of the Yukon, illustrated. Tundra, 1977. 24 pages. $7.95 [0-88776-092-9]

Captivating captioned paintings of Yukon scenes that reveal the unique lives of Northern children. *Middle.*

Hunsberger, David L. (photos); Hertel, James (photos); Lattner, Koni (photos); and Fretz, J. Winfield (text). People apart: portrait of a Mennonite world in Waterloo County, Ontario. Sand Hills, 1978. 111 pages. $19.95 [0-920446-03-5]

Expressive captioned photographs interpret the Old Order Mennonite way of life still pursued in Waterloo County, Ontario. *Older to mature.*

Kane, Robert S.; Canada A to Z. Doubleday, 1976, (1964). Rev. ed. 346 pages. $9.95 cloth [0-385-09947-9] $4.50 paper [0-385-09948-7]

An American sees Canada as a tourist attraction, but gives succinct historical and geographical information on the provinces, regions and cities. *Older to mature.*

Macdonald, R.H.; Four seasons west. Western Producer, 1975. 116 pages. $25.00 [0-919306-55-1]

"A photographic odyssey of the three Prairie Provinces. *All ages.*

MacLennan, Hugh; Seven rivers of Canada. Macmillan,1977. 170 pages. $7.95 cloth [0-7705-0785-9]; $4.95 paper (1971) [0-7705-1562-2] (Laurentian Library)

Historical, geographical and personal descriptions of seven great Canadian rivers. *Older to mature.*

Mason, Philip; Colorful Niagara Falls. Travelpic,1977. $2.25 paper [0-919840-03-5]. *All ages.*

Mason, Philip; Niagara and the daredevils. Travelpic, 1976. $0.89 paper [0-919840-02-7]. *All ages.*

Mason, Philip; Old Fort Henry and Upper Canada Village. Travelpic,1977. $2.25 paper [0-919840-04-3]. *All ages.*

May, Julian; The Arctic . . . top of the world. Creative Education Society (Dent), 1972. 48 pages. $5.80 [0-87191-957-8]

Photographs and succinct text on every page show how Canada and her Arctic neighbours respond to their snowbound environment. *Middle.*

Northern regions: or, A relation of uncle Richard's voyages for the discovery of a North-West Passage, and an account of the overland journies of other enterprizing travellers. Johnson Reprint (Clarke, Irwin), 1970 (1825). 315 pages. $29.95

A typical 19th century travelogue about the New World for the amusement and instruction of young people includes the journals of four explorers edited for children. *Mature.*

Nowlan, Alden. Campobello, the outer island, illustrated with photographs. Clarke, Irwin, 1975. 132 pages. $8.95 [0-7720-1009-6]; $3.95 paper [0-7720-1022-7]

Located near the Bay of Fundy, this small island is the site of the world's only international park, established in 1964 at the former summer residence of the Roosevelts. Good historical survey. *Mature.*

Pratson, Frederick; A Guide to Atlantic Canada. Chatham (Beaverbooks), 1973. 160 pages. $5.25 paper [0-85699-073-6]

This excellent travel guide includes brief accounts on the history, geography, resources, industries. *Older.*

Russell, Andy; The Rockies. Hurtig, 1975. 160 pages. $20.00 [0-88830-094-8]
Vibrant colour photographs and a lyrical text celebrate the beauty of the Rockies' natural wonders. *Older.*

Snyder, Peter Etril and Herrfort, A.K.; Mennonite country: Waterloo County drawings by Peter Etril Snyder. Sand Hills, 1978. 86 pages. $19.95 [0-920446-04-3] (Waterloo County Collection)
Two Old Order Mennonites share their sketches and thoughts on the ways of the plain folk as they continue their simple age-old life style in Waterloo County, Ontario. *Older to mature.*

Staebler, Edna; Cape Breton harbour. Anthes, Tom (illus.); McClelland, 1972. 176 pages. $8.95 cloth [0-7710-8288-6]; $3.95 paper [0-7710-8289-4]
Personal experiences of three weeks spent in a remote fishing village. *Older.*

Staebler, Edna; Sauerkraut and enterprise. McClelland, 1969. $2.95 paper [0-7710-8290-8]
A week long visit with a 169-year-old Waterloo County Amish family who live much as the pioneers did, without modern conveniences. *Older.*

Stewart, Daryl; Point Pelee, Canada's deep south, illustrated. Burns, 1977. 112 pages. $6.95 paper [0-88768-073-9]
A guide to the birds, animals, fish and insects which frequent this unique Canadian environment. *Older to mature.*

Tanobe, Miyuki; Québec je t'aime/ I love you. Tundra, 1976. 48 pages. $10.95 [0-912766-42-5]
"A Japanese artist's hymn to Quebec in painting and descriptive prose." Bilingual text complements 22 beautiful full colour paintings. *Middle.*

Traill, Catharine Parr; The Young emigrants; or, Pictures of Canada. Calculated to amuse and instruct the minds of youth, Johnson Reprint (Clarke, Irwin) 1969 (1826). 168 pages. $9.50.
"Many of the scenes and events were communicated to the writer by a family who emigrated to America in 1821." Traill wrote the book before she came to Canada, and it seems to be the only known contemporary account on Upper Canada written for children. *Older to mature.*

Watson, Jane Werner; Canada, giant nation of the north. (illus.). Garrard (Thos. Nelson), 1968. 111 pages. $8.05.
Highlights of Canadian history and geography. *Middle.*

Wilson, K.; Manitoba: profile of a province. Mullins, Linda (illus.); Peguis, 1975. 120 pages. $4.00 paper [0-909566-44-8]
Excellent survey of Manitoba history, government, and social and economic life. *Middle to older.*

Wilson, Roger (ed.); The Land that never melts; Auyuittuq National Park. PMA, 1976. 212 pages. $5.95 paper [0-88778-144-6]
The history and description of Canada's most northern national park, with excellent colour photographs. *Mature.*

CITIES AND TOWNS

Armitage, Andrew; Owen Sound: the day the Governor-General came to town and other stories. Boston, 1979. 88 pages. $6.95 paper [0-919822-84-3]
Articles selected from the Owen Sound *Sun Times* about small town life to 1917 reflect a genuine nostalgia for the old days. *Mature.*

Barnes, Michael; The Town that stands on gold. Highway Book Shop, 1978. 192 pages. $5.95 paper [0-88954-093-4]
This modest historical account of Kirkland Lake reveals the dreams, the vicissitudes, the persistence and the hard work that were the pioneers' lot. *Middle to mature.*

Carroll, James A. and **Milberry, Larry.** Canadian communities. Ginn, 1975. 224 pages. $8.10 [0-7702-0022-2]; (Ginn World Studies)
Communities as diverse as Lunenburg and Inuvik are used to illustrate the concept of community in Canada. *Middle.*

Blair, Gladys and **Blackburn, Clyde;** Towns and villages of the national capital region/Villes et villages de la région de la capitale nationale. Shaw, R.P. (illus.). The National Capital Commission, n.d. 56 pages. $3.00 paper.

Short historical accounts of the people and places around Ottawa. *Older.*

Clarke, Sheila; Linton, Marilyn and **Scargall, Jeanne;** Toronto is for kids, Ireland, James (illus.). Greey de Pencier, 1976. 208 pages. $4.95 paper. [0-919872-21-2]

A glorious compendium of scenes and activities guaranteed to interest and involve most youngsters. *Middle to older.*

Corkum, Nadja: How Canada got its capital. Hesse, Emma (illus.); McClelland, 1975. 64 pages. $4.95 paper [0-7710-2285-9]

Ottawa's development from forest camp to settlement, village, town and great city. Realistic drawings illumine the text. *Middle.*

Filey, Michael; Passengers must not ride on fenders. Musson, 1974. 154 pages. $10.95.

A delightful nostalgic look at points of interest, past and present, emphasizes the streetcar's place in Toronto's development. *Older.*

Filey, Michael; A Toronto album: glimpses of the city that was. U.T.P., 1970. 120 pages. $10.00 [0-8020-1737-1]

Photographic journal records the evolution of Toronto from 1860 to 1950. *Middle to older.*

Hart, Patricia W.; Pioneering in North York. General, 1968. 324 pages. $3.98 paper. Available from: North York Historical Society, Gibson House, 5168 Yonge St., Willowdale M2N 5P6.

Development and growth from pioneer village to metropolitan borough. *Mature.*

Hull, Raymond; Soules, Gordon and **Soules, Christine;** Vancouver's past. Soules, 1974. 96 pages. $9.95 cloth [0-919574-02-5]

Brief overview of the city's history and development. *Mature.*

Jenson, Latham B.; Vanishing Halifax. Petheric, 1968. 86 pages. $3.95 [0-919380-02-6]

Georgian and Victorian buildings attest to Halifax's long history. *Older.*

Lamont, Graham; Toronto and York County; a case study. Dent, 1970. 120 pages. $3.75 net [0-460-95268-4]

Geographical study emphasizing the nature of urban changes and resulting problems. *Mature.*

Major, Henriette and **Sainte-Marie, Paule;** Hello Montreal/Bonjour Montréal. Heritage, 1975. 96 pages. $2.50 paper [0-7773-4005-4]

A bilingual children's guide to the sights of Montreal - Old and new. *Middle to older.*

Mika, Nick and **Mika, Helma;** Historic Belleville. Mika, 1977. 2nd ed. 159 pages. $25.00 [0-919303-16-1]

A complete account of centennial celebrations, a brief history, and reproductions of drawings and post-cards produced over the years honour Belleville's 100 years as a city. *Older to mature.*

Morgan, Roland; Vancouver then and now, illustrated. Bodima, Box 48913, Bentall Centre 3, Vancouver L7X 1A8, 1977. 125 pages. $6.95 paper [0-88875-000-5]

Pairs of captioned photographs show the same scene in the present and in the past, documenting the changing city. *All ages.*

Murray, Kristin and **Shute, Allan;** Kidmonton: every kid's guide to Edmonton, illustrated. Tree Frog Press, 1978. 224 pages. $3.95 paper [0-88967-054-4]

The what, where and when of activities and information about Edmonton — every kid's guide to Edmonton. *Older to mature.*

National Capital Commission; A Child's capital, a guide to Canada's capital for children/Ta capitale, un guide de la capitale du Canada pour les enfants. National Capital Commission, 1977. 46 pages. Free, paper. *Middle to older.*

National Capital Commission; The Guide to Canada's capital/Le guide de la capitale du Canada. Publishing Centre, Supplies and Services Canada, 1974. 205 pages. $1.50 paper. *Older.*

Nova Scotia Association of Architects; Exploring Halifax and the south shore of Nova Scotia. Greey de Pencier, 1976. 127 pages. $3.50 paper [0-919872-23-9]

Points of interest and historic perspectives. *Older.*

Robertson, John Ross; Old Toronto: a selection of excerpts from Landmarks of Toronto. Kyte, E.C. (ed.); Macmillan, 1954. $4.95 [0-7705-0243-1] (Pioneer Books)

Excerpts from *Landmarks of Toronto* that document historic sights of the city that was. *Older to mature.*

Rowe, Percy. Niagara falls and falls. Simon & Schuster (PaperJacks) 1976. 173 pages. $1.95 paper [0-671-80376-X]

The falls, the daredevils, the two cities and the frontier - in historical and modern perspective. *Older.*

Shipley, Nan; Churchill, Manitoba: Canada's northern gateway. Burns, 1974. 124 pages. $3.75 paper [0-88768-046-1]

Short introduction to the history, ecology, industry, native peoples and future of a far northern town. *Older to mature.*

Spelt, Jacob and **Kerr, Donald;** Toronto. Collier-Macmillan, 1973. 183 pages. $5.95 [0-02-976610-9] (Canadian Cities Series)

The physical, sociological and economic factors that have influenced Toronto from 1780 to the present. *Mature.*

Stafford, Ellen; Stratford: around and about. Fanfare, 1972. 122 pages. $2.95 paper.

A description and history with some emphasis on the Shakespearean Festival. *Older.*

Stein, Sherry and **Shapiro, Howard;** Kidding around Montreal: an excursion guide; where to go and what to do with children. Collier Macmillan, 1976. 97 pages. $2.50 paper [0-02-976710-5]. *Middle to older.*

Toronto Chapter of Architects: Exploring Toronto. Slaight, Annabel (ed.); Greey de Pencier, 1977. Rev. ed. 132 pages. $3.95 paper [0-919872-01-8]

Unusual guidebook that includes walks through notable sections of the city, chosen by 15 members of the Toronto Chapter of Architects. *Older.*

Wood, Daniel and **Davis, Chuck;** Kids! Kids! Kids! and Vancouver, Walters, Bee (illus.). Fforbez, 1975. 316 pages. $3.95 paper [0-88976-020-9]

A thousand things to do and places to go in Greater Vancouver and the Fraser Valley. A valuable guidebook. *All ages.*

MAPS

The Atlas of Canada and the world. Raintree, 1979. 96 pages. $39.95 [0-89810-001-1]

This superlative atlas includes accurate coloured maps, Canadian emphasis, an index to 35,000 locations, tables, and illustrations. *Middle to mature.*

Cluett, Gordon (ed.); **Scrimger, Nicki** (ed.) and **Smith, James K.** (ed.); The Gage junior atlas of Canada. Loates, James (illus.). Gage, 1978. 132 pages, $11.95 [0-7715-9446-1]

This metric atlas includes an important introduction on how to read a map as well as some geography, a glossary and a gazetteer. *Middle to mature.*

Dewdney, Selwyn; The Map that grew. Oxford, 1960. 32 pages. $3.95 [0-19-540023-2]

Fictionalized introduction to map-reading for young children. *Middle.*

Kerr, D.G.G.; Historical atlas of Canada. Nelson, 1975. 3rd rev. ed. 120 pages. $11.95 cloth [0-176-00409-2]; $5.95 paper [0-176-00408-4]. *Mature.*

The New Canadian Oxford atlas, illustrated. Oxford, 1977. 172 pages. $6.95 paper [0-19-540263-4]

Handsome maps and 20 pages of statistics make this an essential purchase at the price. *Middle to mature.*

BIOGRAPHY

BIOGRAPHY
see also
PUBLISHERS' SERIES
Canadian Biographical Studies
Canadian Lives
The Canadians
Canadians All Series
Prime Ministers of Canada
Superpeople Series
Women in Canadian Life

Andrew, Robert and **Mason, Trisha;** We are their children: ethnic portraits of British Columbia. Commcept, 1977. 162 pages. $8.75 paper [0-88829-003-9]

Doukhobors, Japanese, East Indians and Swedes were among the early settlers of B.C.; these are true stories about individual immigrants. *Mature.*

Armstrong, Audrey; The Blacksmith of Fallbrook: the story of Walter Cameron - blacksmith, woodcarver, raconteur. Musson, 1979. 96 pages. $6.95 paper [0-7737-1050-2]

An octogenarian blacksmith recalls village life as it centred on his blacksmith shop. Oral history for older and mature readers. *Older to mature.*

Barker, George; Forty years a chief. Rempel, Judith Anne (illus.). Peguis, 1979. 102 pages. $8.50 cloth [0-919566-68-5] $4.00 paper [0-919566-69-3]

An exemplary Native chief won the franchise for his people, helped to get registered traplines in Manitoba, and helped to organize the Manitoba Indian Brotherhood. *Older to mature.*

Barkhouse, Joyce; George Dawson: the little giant. Clarke, Irwin, 1975. 138 pages. $7.50 [0-7720-0734-9]

Sympathetic, well written biography of a Canadian hero who overcame physical difficulties to become Director of the Geological Survey of Canada in 1895. *Older.*

Blakely, Phyllis Ruth; Nova Scotia's two remarkable giants. Lancelot, 1970. $1.50 paper [0-88999-002-6]

An amusing and informative account of Anna Swan and Angus McAskill who toured the world in circuses. *Older.*

Campbell, Maria; Halfbreed. McClelland, 1973. 157 pages. $8.95 cloth [0-7710-8330-0]; $3.95 paper [0-7710-8331-9]

A half-white half-Indian girl lives in poverty and degradation and overcomes them to tell her story. *Older to mature.*

Carmichael, May; Child of the pioneers. Mole, Elsie Hadden (illus.). Highway Bookshop, 1977. 80 pages. $2.50 paper [0-88954-109-4]

Reminiscences of an immigrant from Glasgow who came to Canada as a child when her family bought a bush farm near North Bay. *Mature.*

Carr, Emily; The Book of Small. Clarke, Irwin, 1966 (c1942). $2.95 [0-7720-0223-1] (Clarke Irwin Canadian Paperbacks)

One of Canada's foremost painters writes about her childhood in Victoria, British Columbia. *Older.*

Carter, Charles Ambrose and **Bailey, Thomas Melville;** The Diary of Sophia MacNab. Bailey, Janet I. (illus.); Bailey, 1974. 2nd Rev. ed. 88 pages. $3.00 paper [0-919874-00-2]

A 13-year-old records her family's daily life from January to July, 1846 at Dundurn Castle, near Hamilton, Ontario. *Middle to older.*

Caswell, Maryanne; Pioneer girl. McGraw, 1964. unpaged $3.95 paper [0-07-082969-1]

The lively letters of a 14-year-old to her grandmother evoke pioneer experience in Saskatchewan in 1885. *Older.*

Conner, Daniel and **Miller, Lorraine;** Master Mariner: Captain James Cook and the peoples of the Pacific. Douglas and McIntyre, 1978. 164 pages. $18.95 [0-88894-191-9]

Captain Cook was a superb navigator who charted the St. Lawrence River, navigated the Canadian West Coast and a great part of the Pacific and advanced the science of naval nutrition. *Mature.*

Dickson, Lovat; Grey Owl: man of the wilderness. Macmillan, 1976. 173 pages. $4.95 paper [0-7705-1372-7]

A detailed and sensitive appreciation of a complex man who eschewed civilized life in England for the dangers and attractions of Canada's northern wilderness. *Older to mature.*

Donaldson, Gordon; Fifteen men. Doubleday, 1975. Rev. ed. 265 pages. $6.95 cloth; $3.50 paper; Educ. ed. $1.67 paper net.

Entertaining and witty look at our prime ministers from Macdonald to Trudeau. *Older.*

Doucet, Clive; My grandfather's Cape Breton. McGraw, 1980. 213 pages. $12.95 [0-07-077870-1]

A teenager spends an idyllic summer with his septuagenarian grandfather whose "peaceful sense of purpose" inspires this recollection. *Mature.*

Epps, Bernard; The Outlaw of Megantic. McClelland, 1973. 157 pages. $6.95 cloth [0-7710-3101-7]; $2.50 paper [0-7710-3102-5]; $1.50 text.

A Scottish settler in Quebec in the 1880's outmanoeuvres authorities who would try him for crimes he did not commit. *Older.*

Faulknor, Cliff; Turn him loose. Western Producer, 1977. 129 pages. $9.25 cloth [0-919306-81-0]; $4.25 paper [0-919306-82-9]

Canada's Mr. Rodeo had an exciting career in the twenties and thirties, here recaptured for western nostalgia buffs. *Mature.*

Forrester, Helen; Minerva's stepchild. Bodley Head (Clarke, Irwin), 1979. 290 pages. $16.95 [0-370-30197-8]

A second autobiographical work poignantly chronicles the Forrester family's life in the thirties ruined by the Great Depression. *Mature.*

French, Alice; My name is Masak. Peguis, 1976. 110 pages. $9.00 cloth [0-919566-55-31]; $4.00 paper [0-919566-56-1]

An Eskimo girl grows up in the north before World War II - influenced by the Inuit and the white societies which divide her loyalties. *Older to mature.*

Goudie, Elizabeth; Woman of Labrador. Zimmerley, David W. (ed.); PMA, 1973. 166 pages. $10.00 [0-88778-079-2]; $4.95 paper [0-88778-116-0]

A trapper's wife tells a courageous story about her family's hard life in the Twenties. *Mature.*

Gould, Jan; Women of British Columbia. Hancock, 1975. 224 pages. $14.95 [0-919654-42-8]

This companion to *Men of British Columbia* by Derek Pethick includes sections on Native women, pioneers and contemporary contributors to the province's history. *Older to mature.*

Grey Owl (pseud.); Pilgrims of the wild. Macmillan, 1978. 282 pages. $8.50 cloth [0-7705-1168-6]; $5.95 paper [0-7705-1033-7]

A wilderness autobiography by the Englishman who would be an Indian. *Mature.*

Gross, George; Donald Jackson, king of the blades. Queen City, 1977. 156 pages. $10.00 [0-9690508-1-X]

The hard work and sacrifice required to become a champion are seen in the life of this dynamic figure skater. *Older to mature.*

Hamilton, K.A. (ed.); Canada writes: the Writers' Union of Canada members' book. Writers' Union, 1977. 399 pages. $2.50 paper.

Two page entries on union members include photograph and bio-bibliography. *Older to mature.*

Hacker, Carlotta; The Indomitable lady doctors. Clarke, Irwin, 1974. 259 pages. $8.50 [0-7720-0723-3]

A lively account of Canada's pioneer medical women. *Mature.*

Hanson, Christilot: Canadian entry. Clarke, Irwin, 1966. 140 pages. $2.95 paper [0-7720-0519-2] (Clarke Irwin Canadian Paperbacks)

An inspiring autobiography of Canada's Olympic dressage champion. *Older.*

Hill, Kay; Joe Howe: the man who was Nova Scotia. McClelland, 1980. 221 pages. $9.95 [0-7710-4096-2]

A fearless young newspaper editor became a champion of the ordinary people and represented them in the legislature throughout a stormy and distinguished career. *Older to mature.*

Horwood, Harold; Bartlett, the great Canadian explorer, illustrated with photographs. Doubleday, 1977. 194 pages. $8.95 [0-385-09984-3]

A readable account of the life of "Captain Bob" who made over 50 voyages into northern latitudes, gaining fame as a navigator and explorer. *Mature.*

Johnston, Jean; Wilderness women: Canada's forgotten history. PMA, 1973. 241 pages. $10.00 cloth [0-88778-084-9]; $4.95 paper [0-88778-127-6]

About eight little known women who followed the men who settled Canada and contributed to their country's development. *Mature.*

Kurelek, William; Lumberjack. Tundra (Collins), 1974. 41 pages. $8.95 [0-88776-052-X]

A strong, healthy 18-year-old spends the summer in Northern Ontario's logging camps; then his older self recalls it vividly in words and pictures. *Older.*

Kurelek, William; A Prairie boy's summer. Tundra (Collins), 1975. 48 pages. $8.95 [0-88776-058-9]

A companion volume to *A Prairie boy's winter* that evokes the Thirties out West. *Middle.*

Kurelek, William: A Prairie boy's winter. Tundra (Collins), 1973. 40 pages. $8.95 [0-88776-022-8]

A realist painter recalls his Western childhood in evocative captions and paintings that capture the artist's view of himself as a young boy. *Middle.*

Lim, John; At grandmother's house. Tundra, 1977. 32 pages. $9.95 [0-88776-089-9]

Stylized delicate drawings and vivid reminiscences of childhood in Singapore and especially at grandmother's house. *Older.*

Lim, Sing; Westcoast Chinese boy. Tundra, 1979. 64 pages. $12.95 [0-88776-121-6]

Vancouver's Chinatown in the 1920's provided the ideal environment for children to grow unhampered. Appropriate monotypes, humorous sketches, nostalgic vignettes. *Older to mature.*

Livesay, Robert; Footprints in the snow: the heroes and heroines of Canada. Little Brick Schoolhouse, 1978, 206 pages. $8.75 paper.

Very short illustrated profiles on about 100 Canadians of note - Tom Thompson, L.M. Montgomery, Dr. Norman Bethune among others. *Older.*

MacEwan, J. W. Grant; Portraits from the Plains, McGraw, 1971. 287 pages. $9.95 cloth [0-07-092909-2]; $4.95 paper [0-07-077436-6]

Brief biographies of 33 Canadian Indian leaders. *Older.*

MacInnis, Joe; Underwater man. McClelland, 1974. 142 pages. $10.95 [0-7710-5526-9]

A doctor-scientist-diver shares his adventures under the sea. *Mature.*

McKenzie, Ruth; Laura Secord: the lady and the legend. McClelland, 1971. 136 pages. $6.95 cloth [0-7710-5819-5]; $3.95 paper [0-7710-5800-4]

The well-known legend about Laura Secord and a cow is shown to be false, but her place as a heroine is upheld. *Middle.*

Maclean, Hugh; Man of steel: the story of Sir Sandford Fleming. McGraw, 1969. 145 pages. $5.95 [0-7700-0303-6]

Private and public life of Sir Sandford Fleming who linked Canada by rail, developed an electric cable system, and established Standard Time. *Older.*

Maynard, Fredelle Bruser; Raisins and almonds. Doubleday, 1972. 196 pages. $6.50 [0-385-02957-8]; PaperJacks, 1973. 189 pages. $1.50 paper [0-7737-7046-1]

A heartwarming story about growing up in a Jewish family on the Canadian prairies through the hungry Thirties. *Mature.*

Metcalf, Vicky: Journey fantastic. McGraw, 1970. 159 pages. $6.95 [0-7700-0309-5]

An account of the hardships suffered by the first woman travelling overland from Winnipeg to British Columbia. *Older.*

Milner, Philip (ed.); Nova Scotia writes. Formac, 1979. 100 pages. $4.95 paper [0-88780-036X]

A descriptive listing includes biographical information, bibliographies and photographs of 87 living Nova Scotia writers. *Older to mature.*

Miner, Jack; Wild Goose Jack. Simon & Schuster, 1971. $1.25 paper [0-671-78078-6]; PaperJacks, 1977. $1.95 paper [0-7701-0014-7]

World renowned conservationist tells his own story, imparting his humanistic philosophy of life. *Mature.*

Montgomery, Lucy M.; The Alpine path: the story of my career. Fitzhenry & Whiteside, 1974. 96 pages. $6.95 [0-88902-019-1]

Anne of Green Gables's author writes a lighthearted but sincere account of her early years. *Mature.*

Newman, Lena; The John A. Macdonald album: a pictorial history. Tundra (Collins), 1974. 224 pages. $25.00 [0-88776-051-1]

Anecdoctal, profusely illustrated biography based on original source materials, some quoted and photographed here. *Older.*

Norcross, E. Blanche (ed.); Pioneers every one: Canadian women of achievement. Burns, 1978. 159 pages. $6.95 paper [0-88768-082-8]

Sixteen Canadian women of achievement include Pauline Johnson, Agnes MacPhail and Catherine Parr Traill who contributed significantly to the arts, politics, community services and frontier life of our country. *Mature.*

Ondaatje, Christopher and **Swainson, Donald;** The Prime ministers of Canada: from Macdonald to Trudeau. Pagurian, 1975. 191 pages. $8.95 cloth [0-88932-012-8]; $3.95 paper [0-88932-007-1]

Life and times of the Prime Ministers from the first to the present day. *Older.*

Pethick, Derek; Men of British Columbia. Hancock House, 1975. 223 pages. $14.95 [0-919654-41-X]

Illustrated biographical narratives of 40 men of influence from Captain James Cook to W.A.C. Bennett. *Mature.*

Pitseolak, Peter; Peter Pitseolak's escape from death. Eber, Dorothy (trans.) McClelland, 1977. 47 pages. $5.95 paper [0-7710-3030-4]

Realistic drawings and a matter of fact narrative detail a brush with death on an ice pan drifting away from the Cape Dorset shore into the Hudson Straits. *Older.*

Provencher, Paul; Provencher, last of the coureurs de bois. Martin-Sperry, A.D. (trans.). Burns, 1976. 287 pages. $5.95 paper [0-88768-071-2]

An expert hunter, fisherman, trapper and early conservationist recounts his experiences with the Montagnais people and as a commando trainer in World War II. *Mature.*

Raby, Ormond; Radio's first voice: the story of Reginald Fessenden. Macmillan, 1972 (c1970). 159 pages. $1.00 paper [0-7705-0937-1]

On December 23, 1900 Fessenden successfully transmitted sound between two 50 foot towers - and radio was born in Canada. *Older.*

Redsky, James; Great leader of the Ojibway: Mis-Quona-Queb. McClelland, 1972. 127 pages. $7.95 [0-7710-7420-4]; $4.95 paper (1977) [0-7710-7421-2]

Biography of a great chief based on the oral tradition of his people. *Older to mature.*

Ridgway, John; Gino Watkins. Oxford, 1974. 116 pages. $6.95 [0-19-273136-X]

Older children will enjoy this fast-paced adventure of an early Arctic explorer. *Older.*

Robinson, Helen Caister; Joseph Brant: a man for his people. Academic, 1971. 178 pages. $6.50 [0-7747-0052-1]

Famous Indian leader, war chief of the Iroquois and a captain in the British army during the American Revolution. *Older to mature.*

Savage, Candace; Our Nell: a scrapbook biography of Nellie L. McClung. Western Producer Prairie, 1979. 253 pages. $17.95 cloth [0-88833-027-8]; $10.95 paper [0-88833-033-2]

"A scrapbook biography of Nellie L. McClung, perhaps the most celebrated and controversial woman in Canadian public life" - politician, author and feminist reformer, 1873-1951. *Older to mature.*

Seton, Ernest Thompson; The Worlds of Ernest Thompson Seton. Knopf, (Random), 1976. First edition. 204 pages. $31.50 [0-394-49547-0]

A celebration in words and pictures of the talents and versatility of the great naturalist. Highly recommended for all libraries. *Mature.*

Shaw, Charles Aeneas and **Hull, Raymond** (ed.); Tales of a pioneer surveyor. Academic, 1971. 165 pages. $8.95 [0-7747-0097-1]

Biographical account of a young man who surveyed much of the present C.P.R. line between 1872 and 1884. *Older.*

Sheffe, Norman (ed.); Canadian portraits. McGraw, 1973. 183 pages. $3.95 paper [0-07-077379-3]

Pocket biographies of six prominent figures in Canadian history first appeared about 40 years ago. *Older.*

Sittler, Darryl and **McFarlane, Brian;** Sittler at centre. Collier-Macmillan, 1979. 119 pages. $5.95 paper [0-02-976790-3]

A favourite Canadian tells his life story as a hockey player. *Older to mature.*

Sluman, Norma.; Poundmaker. McGraw, 1967. 297 pages. $7.95 [0-7700-0159-9]

Sympathetic life of the famous Cree Chief (1826-86) who tried to reverse the government's decision to sequester Indians on reserves and participated in Riel's North West Rebellion. *Older.*

Stevenson, O.J.; The Talking wire: the story of Alexander Graham Bell. Macmillan, 1947. 207 pages. $1.95 [0-7705-1119-8]

Fictionalized biography of the inventor of the telephone - a Canadian! *Older.*

Stewart, Robert; Sam Steele, lion of the frontier. Doubleday, 1979. 303 pages. $12.95 [0-385-13598-X]

A rousing narrative of a military man involved in the policing of the West in the Red River Rebellion, the North West Rebellion and the Klondike Gold Rush. *Mature.*

Syme, Ronald; Alexander Mackenzie, Canadian explorer. Morrow (Gage), 1964. 96 pages. $8.55 [0-688-310-109]

Records Mackenzie's exploration of the Canadian North using excerpts from his diary to add immediacy. *Middle.*

Syme, Ronald; Cartier, finder of the St. Lawrence, Morrow (Gage), 95 pages. $7.55 L.B. [0-688-31146-6]

A brief introduction to Cartier's life and explorations and a good portrayal of social life and customs of the early 16th century. *Middle.*

Syme, Ronald; Frontenac of New France. Morrow (Gage), 1969. 191 pages. $8.50 [0-688-213-189]

Captures the vitality of the man and the spirit of his times. *Middle.*

Syme, Ronald; Fur trader of the North: the story of Pierre de la Verendrye. Cuffari, Richard (illus.); Morrow (McLeod), 1973. 191 pages. $8.75 [0-688-200-761]

The last of the great French explorers started his career at the age of 40, and established trading posts in the Western States and Canada for King Louis XV. *Middle.*

Syme, Ronald; Henry Hudson. Morrow (Gage), 1955. 190 pages. $8.20 [0-688-313-841]

Saga of Hudson's voyages in search of a Northwest Passage includes excerpts from his diaries. *Middle.*

Syme, Ronald; La Salle of the Mississippi. Morrow (Gage) 1953. 184 pages. $8.50 [0-688-215-912]

La Salle was born in France, but spent an exciting life exploring the New World in the late 17th century. *Middle.*

Syme, Ronald; Vancouver, explorer of the Pacific Coast. Morrow (Gage) 1970. 96 pages. $8.50 [0-688-21807-5]

Graphically describes Vancouver's naval service and Pacific coast explorations, and includes excerpts from his writing. *Middle.*

Takashima, Shizuye; A Child in prison camp. Tundra (Collins), 1971. 75 pages. $7.95 cloth [0-88776-017-1]; $3.95 paper [0-88776-074-0]

With sensitivity and no rancour the artist recalls her childhood in a World War II prison camp in the Canadian Rockies. *Middle to older.*

Tetso, John; Trapping is my life. PMA, 1970. 116 pages. $8.95 cloth [0-88778-039-3]; $3.95 paper [0-88778-153-5]

A Slavey Indian trapper reflects on his life along the traplines near Fort Simpson on the Mackenzie river. *Older.*

This is our work; some Newfoundland women talk about their careers. Newfoundland Status of Women, 1975. 1st ed. 40 pages. $1.25 paper.

Profiles and pictures of 20 Newfoundlanders who enjoy their work. *Middle to older.*

Thompson, Albert Edward, Chief; Chief Peguis and his descendants. Peguis, 1973. 84 pages. $6.00 cloth [0-919566-20-0]; $2.00 paper [0-919566-34-0]

About the "famous chief of a band of Saulteaux Indians who came from Sault Ste. Marie to Red River country in the 1790's." *Older.*

Trueman, Stuart; The Ordeal of John Gyles. McClelland, 1966, 155 pages. $1.95 paper [0-7710-8604-0]

Captured by Maliseet Indians, a boy lived nine years as their slave. *Older.*

Vineberg, Ethel; Grandmother came from Dworitz. Briansky, Rita (illus.); Tundra (Collins), 1978 (1969). 64 pages. $2.95 paper [0-88776-086-4]

An illuminating story, confidentially told and sympathetically illustrated, about a Canadian grandmother's life in the Jewish pale of Russia in the late 19th century. *Middle to older.*

Wilder, Joseph E.; Read all about it: reminiscences of an immigrant newsboy. Peguis, 1978. 99 pages. $8.50 cloth [0-919566-62-6]; $4.50 paper [0-919566-63-4]

Reminiscences of an immigrant newsboy who came to Winnipeg from Rumania in 1904 at the age of eight. *Older to mature.*

Wilson, Helen Dacey; More tales from Barrett's Landing. McClelland, 1967. 127 pages. $4.95 [0-7710-9031-5]

Amiable reminiscences of small town and large family life Down East. *Older to mature.*

HISTORY

ARCHAEOLOGY

see also

PUBLISHERS' SERIES

Canadian Prehistory series

Hayward, Patricia; Early man in Nova Scotia. Halverson, George (illus.) and Claridge, Edward (illus.). The Nova Scotia Museum, 1976 (1973). 36 pages. $1.00 paper.

Archaeological excavations in Debert, Nova Scotia establish that Palaeo Indians first inhabited that area about 11,000 years ago. Simple but authoritative account. *Older.*

McGhee, Robert; The Burial at L'Anse-Amour, illustrated. National Museum of Man, 1976. 24 pages. $2.50 paper [0-660-00019-9]

A strangely moving reconstruction of possible events that might have led to this burial site on the Labrador coast of the Strait of Belle Isle, excavated in 1974. *Older.*

Newlands, David L. and **Breede, Claus;** An introduction to Canadian archaeology. McGraw, 1976. $8.95 paper [0-07-082339-1]

A basic presentation of field and laboratory techniques for beginning diggers who want to uncover Canada's past. Resources for involvement, glossary, bibliography and photographs enhance its value. *Older to mature.*

Rowe, Erna; Giant dinosaurs. Smith, Merle (illus.); Scholastic-Tab, 1977. Rev. ed. 32 pages. $1.75 paper.

Facts about seven dinosaurs simply stated and humorously illustrated. *Younger to middle.*

Russell, Dale A.; A Vanished world/ Le monde disparu. Kish, Eleanor M. (illus.). National Museum of Natural Sciences, 1977. 144 pages. $12.95.

A bilingual account of the dinosaurs of Western Canada beautifully illustrated with paintings and photographs. *Mature.*

Swinton, William; Digging for dinosaurs. Bodley Head (Clarke, Irwin), 1966. 32 pages $6.25 [0-370-00835-9]

Clearly describes dinosaurs and their world, and the way scientists reconstruct skeletons for study. Many excellent drawings included. *Middle.*

NATIVE PEOPLES

see also

PUBLISHERS' SERIES

How They Lived in Canada
Indians of Canada Series
Oracles
PONA Series
ROM North American Indian charts

Ahenakew, Edgar; Voices of the Plains Cree. Buck, Ruth Matheson (ed.); McClelland, 1977. 204 pages. $5.95 [0-7710-8471-4]

A Plains Cree Indian records the thoughts and philosophies of two old men of his people. *Mature.*

Allen, D.; Indians of the Northwest coast. Hancock House, 1977. 31 pages. $2.50 paper [0-919654-82-77]

A brief introduction to the Native peoples of British Columbia, illustrated with colourful photographs. *Older.*

Allen, D.; Totem poles of the Northwest. Hancock, 1977. 32 pages. $2.50 [0-919654-83-5]

Full colour illustrations of notable B.C. totem poles. *All ages.*

Anderson, Daniel and **Anderson, Alda M.;** The Métis people of Canada. Alberta Federation of Métis Settlement Associations, 1977. 128 pages. $5.00.

A considered, straightforward history of the Métis people from the days of the fur trade through the Pemmican wars to the movement for Métis rights. *Mature.*

Ashwell, Reg.; Coast Salish: their art, culture and legends. Hancock House, 1978. 88 pages. $3.50 paper [0-88839-009-2] (Native Culture)

Chapters on tribal origins, food, crafts and religion with pertinent photographs of the West Coast Salish people. *Middle to older.*

Ashwell, Reg.; Indian tribes of the Northwest. Thornton, J.M. (illus.). Hancock House, 1977. 89 pages. $3.50 paper [0-919654-53-3] (Native Culture)

Brief text and outstanding photographs serve as an introduction for children on the various Native tribes. *Middle.*

Bjorklund, Karna L.; The Indians of Northeastern America. Bjorklund, Lorence F. (illus.); Dodd, 1969. 192 pages $6.75 [0-396-05985-6]

Origin, history, legends and customs of Woodland Indians, graphically illustrated. *Older.*

Bleeker, Sonia; The Eskimo; Arctic hunters and trappers. Morrow (Gage), 1959. 160 pages. $8.20 L.B. [0-688-31275-6]

A plain and simple narrative about Eskimo life that includes hunting, making igloos, customs and ceremonies. *Middle to older.*

Brasser, Ted. J.; "Bo'jou, Nejee!": profiles of Canadian Indian art. National Museum of Man, 1976. 204 pages. $14.25. Order from: National Museums of Canada, Marketing Services Division, Ottawa K1A 0M8.

A catalogue of an exhibition of early Canadian Indian artifacts, appropriately illustrated with exquisite photographs. *Older to mature.*

Calf Robe, Benjamin Augustine; Siksika, a Blackfoot legacy. Good Medicine, 1979. 107 pages. $12.95 cloth [0-920698-30-1]; $7.95 paper [0-920698-32-8]

The son of a Blackfoot warrior and chief looks back over the past 90 years to recall legends, ceremonies, history and philosophy of his people. *Mature.*

Clark, A. McFadyen; The Athapaskans: strangers of the North. National Museums, 1974. 208 pages. $8.95 paper [0-660-00034-2]

Mainly a catalogue of photographs in the National Museum of Man and in the Royal Scottish Museum dealing with the material culture of the Indians of Alaska and Northwestern Canada. *Older to mature.*

The Canadian Indian: Quebec and the Atlantic Provinces. Information Canada, 1973. 88 pages. $1.50 paper.

Illustrated booklet in English and French texts of 44 pages each which briefly describes the Native people and their old and modern way of life in our eastern provinces. *Older.*

The Canadian Indian; Yukon and Northwest Territories. Information Canada, 1973. 132 pages. $1.50 paper.

Illustrated booklet in English and French texts of 56 pages each briefly describes the old and modern way of life of our northern Indians. *Older.*

Clutesi, George; Potlatch. Gray, 1973. 2nd ed. 188 pages. $2.95 paper [0-88826-046-6]

A native participant poetically describes a traditional ceremony of the Northwest Coast Indians. *Older to mature.*

Dempsey, Hugh A.; Indian tribes of Alberta. Glenbow-Alberta Institute, 1978. 88 pages. $3.50 paper [0-919224-00-8]

Students, particularly in Western Alberta, will find this a concise and objective illustrated review of the history of ten Indian tribes native to that province. No index. *Older to mature.*

Dewdney, Selwyn; They shared to survive. Arbuckle, Franklin (illus.); Macmillian, 1975. 220 pages. $10.95 cloth [0-7705-1320-4]; $6.95 paper [0-7705-1349-2]

How Native peoples of Canada lived in harmony with nature. Graphic line drawings. *Older to mature.*

Embree, Jesse; Let us live: the Native peoples of Canada. Dent, 1977. 64 pages. $3.75 paper [0-460-93588-7]

A short introduction to Indian and Inuit life today and in Canadian history, well illustrated with photographs. *Middle to older.*

Erickson, Sheila; Notice: this is an Indian reserve. Gooderham, Kent (ed.) and Stevenson, Fred (photogr.); Griffin, 1972. 83 pages. $4.50 paper [0-88760-033-6]

Photographic essays combine with poems to portray the everyday life of Canada's Native peoples. *Older.*

Eskimo life of yesterday. Hancock House, 1977. 48 pages. $2.95 paper [0-919654-73-8]

A simple and classic view of Eskimo life at the turn of the century. *Older.*

Fisher, Olive M. and **Tyner, Clara L.;** Totem, tipi and tumpline. Dent, 1955. 264 pages. $4.95 paper [0-460-9528-0-3]

Stories, plays, information on Indian life from diverse sources. Line drawings enhance the text. *Middle.*

George, Dan, Chief: My heart soars. Hirnschall, Helmut (illus.); Hancock House, 1974. 95 pages. $300.00 limited edition; $9.95 cloth [0-919654-15-0]

A famous representative of his people expresses Indian beliefs with simplicity and dignity. Sympathetically illustrated. *Older.*

Hawkins, Elizabeth; Indian weaving, knitting, basketry of the Northwest. Hancock House, 1978. 32 pages. $3.00 paper [0-88839-006-8] (Native Culture).

Excellent photographs with descriptions of traditional and modern arts include masks, totems, jewellery, weaving and knitting. *All ages.*

Herbert, Wally; Eskimos. Collins, 1976. First ed. 128 pages. $10.95. [0-00-100177-9] (International Library)

A thorough coverage from pre-history to the white invasion of the Inuit people who are "physically, socially and temperamentally geared to living in a harsh environment." *Mature.*

Hirnschall, Helmut; The Song of creation. Plainsman, 1979. 89 pages. $19.95 [0-920882-06-4]

Creation myths from the Native peoples of North America, sensitively captured in sympathetic paintings and retellings. *Middle to mature.*

Houston, James and **King, B. Anthony;** Ojibwa summer. Academic 1973. 96 pages. $14.50 cloth; $6.95 paper.

Visual description of the Ojibwa people. *Older.*

Jenness, Diamond; The Indians of Canada. 7th ed. U.T.P., 1977. 432 pages. $10.00 paper [0-8020-6326-8]

First published in 1932 this is the definitive work on Canada's Native peoples by a pioneer in anthropology. *Mature.*

Jenness, Eileen; The Indian tribes of Canada. McGraw, 1966. 123 pages. $3.95 paper [0-7700-6010-2] (Ryerson Paperback Series)

A comprehensive discussion of the societal responses to their environment made by the Native peoples of Canada. Detailed line drawings enhance the narrative. *Older.*

Josie, Edith; Here are the news. Clarke, Irwin, 1966. 135 pages. $3.95 [0-7720-0065-4]

The Whitehorse Star carried Mrs. Josie's unique reports from Old Crow, Yukon Territory from 1963 to 1966. *Older to mature.*

Kaiper, Dan and **Kaiper, Nan;** Tlingit: their art, culture and legends. Hancock House, 1978. 95 pages. $4.00 paper [0-88839-010-6]

An introduction to the social life and legends of the Northern Pacific Coast Tlingit people. *Older.*

Kidd, Kenneth E.; Canadians of long ago. Academic, 1951. $3.50 text [0-7747-1047-0]; $4.50 trade.

Outline history of Indian life before European immigration. Distinctive line drawings. *Middle to older.*

Kurelek, William; The Last of the Arctic. Pagurian, 1978. 94 pages. $19.95 [0-07-082421-5]

With simple text and vivid illustrations, the author depicts the Inuit way of life before it was changed by the influence of white civilization. *Older.*

Maclean, Hope; Indians, an introduction to Canada's Native people. C.A.S.N.P., 1976. 81 pages. $2.00, loose sheets.

Canadian Indian history from the Canadian Indian viewpoint. *Older.*

Marsh, Winifred Petchey; People of the Willow: the Padlimiut tribe of the Caribou Eskimo; Oxford, 1976. 63 pages. $9.95. [0-19-540271-5]

Delicate watercolour sketches make an intimate detailed record of Inuit life about 40 years ago. *Older.*

Pelletier, Gaby (ed.); Traditions decorative Micmac & Matiseet decorative traditions. Simpson, Don (illus.). New Brunswick Museum, 1978. Bilingual ed. 63 pages. $3.95 paper [0-919326-02-1]

Arts and crafts of the Indians of the Maritimes in catalogue form. *Mature.*

Pitseolak, Peter and **Eber, Dorothy;** People from our side: an Inuit record of Seekooseelak - the land of the people of Cape Dorset, Baffin Island. Hanson, Ann (tr.); Hurtig, 1975. 159 pages. $8.95 paper [0-88830-089-1]

An Inuit record of the land and people of Cape Dorset with stunning photographs by Peter Pitseolak. *Older to mature.*

Power, Ann Hervey; Eskimos of Canada. Collier-Macmillan, 1971. 44 pages. $2.70 text [0-02-970250-X] (Canadian History Program)

History, anthropology and archeology of the Inuit. *Middle.*

Powers, William K.; Indians of the Northern Plains. Putnam (Academic), 1969. 256 pages. $5.50 paper [0-399-50277-7]

Sympathetically discusses the homes, religion, language, tribal relations and other societal factors. *Older.*

Quimby, George; Indian life on the upper Great Lakes, 11,000 B.C. to A.D. 1800. University of Chicago (U.S.A.), 1971. 182 pages. $3.95 paper [0-226-70044-5]

Valuable, rather scholarly account of the prehistory of the Upper Great Lakes. *Mature.*

Sealey, D. Bruce (ed.) and **Kirkness, Verna J.** (ed.); Indians without tipis: a resource book by Indians and Metis. Book Society, 1974. 2nd. ed. $4.95 paper [0-7725-5030-1]

Canadian Indian history seen through the eyes of a "defeated and despised race" in 18 essays that elaborate their cultural alienation. *Mature.*

Sealey, D. Bruce and **Lussier, Antoine S.;** The Métis, Canada's forgotten people. Manitoba Métis Federation. (1975), 1977. 200 pages. $9.00 [0-919213-39-1]

A comprehensive, straightforward history of the Métis in Canada, including a careful documentation of the Riel Rebellion 1885. *Older to mature.*

Sendey, John; The Nootkan Indian. Alberni Valley Museum, 1977. 72 pages. $5.95 paper [0-919213-55-3]

Sketches, engravings and drawings, many from historical sources, make a pictorial essay on the Nootka Indians. *Older to mature.*

Smoke tanning; traditional Indian method of preparing animal hides. Saskatchewan Indian Arts Advisory Committee and Department of Indian Affairs and Northern Development, 1974. 18 pages. $3.50 paper.

Coloured photo-essay shows in detail the various steps in the smoke tanning of big game hides. *Middle.*

Stewart, Hilary; Indian fishing: early methods on the Northwest coast. Douglas & McIntyre, 1977. 188 pages. $18.95 [0-88894-120-X]

Fishing is placed within the whole context of Indian culture through pictures, drawings and a readable text. *Older.*

Stories from Pangnirtung, Arnaktauyak, Germain (illus.). Hurtig, 1976. 100 pages. $5.95 [0-88830-109-X]

Recollections by Inuit elders of their battle for survival provide a capsule history of a brave and resourceful people. *Older to mature.*

Such, Peter; Vanished peoples: the Archaic, Dorset and Beothuk peoples of Newfoundland. N.C. Press, 1977. 94 pages. $12.95 cloth [0-919600-84-0]; $6.95 paper [0-919600-83-2]

A readable account of the extinct Beothuks, early inhabitants of Newfoundland. Many maps, drawings and photographs are included. *Older.*

Surtees, Ursula. Lak-la-hai-ee; volume 1: Interior Salish food preparation; volume 2: Building a winter dwelling; Lamont, Gwen (illus.). Lamont-Surtees, Finlay Printing, Kelowna, BC, 1974-75. 16/24 pages. $1.50 paper, each.

Excellent booklets on Salish Indian life, told and illustrated simply. *Middle.*

Symington, D. Fraser; The Canadian Indian: the illustrated history of the great tribes of Canada. McClelland, 1969. 272 pages. $25.00 [0-7710-8373-4]

An illustrated cultural history of the 50 Canadian Indian tribes through 300 years. *Older to mature.*

Symons, R.D. and **Updike, Lee R.;** The First people: an artist's reconstruction of five native Canadian cultures. Western Producer Prairie, 1978. 147 pages. $14.95 cloth [0-919306-95-0]; $8.95 paper [0-919306-92-6]

Profusely illustrated two-page spreads on cultural aspects of the Native peoples of the Eastern Woodlands, subarctic, Arctic, West Coast and Plains. *Middle to older.*

Tait, George E.; The Unknown people. Scholastic-Tab, 1974. 127 pages. $8.70.

Brief information about many Indian tribes, some Canadian. *Middle.*

Taylor, J. Garth; The Canadian Eskimos. ROM, 1971. 16 pages. $1.00 paper [0-88854-043-4]

A concise general introduction to the culture, technology and history of the Inuit. *Middle to older.*

Updike, Lee R.; Our people; Indians of the Plains. Western Producer, 1974. 12 pages. $2.00 paper.

Plains Indian life before European immigration depicted in 12 captioned drawings. *Middle.*

Waubageshig (comp.); The Only good Indian: essays by Canadian Indians. New Press, 1970. 188 pages. $8.50 cloth [0-8870-015-2]; $3.50 paper [0-88770-016-0]; $3.95 paper [0-88770-168-X]

Mature readers will appreciate these contemporary writings by Canadian Indians. *Mature.*

Williams, Sophia and **Williams, Saul;** Weagamow notebook, illustrated. Amethyst, 1978. 46 pages. $2.95 paper [0-920474-02-0]

The diary and drawings of two Ojibway children who record their trip to the family's trapline winter camp capture a way of life fast disappearing. *Middle.*

CANADIAN HISTORY
see also
PUBLISHERS' SERIES
Adventures in Canadian History
All About Series
Canada: Origins and Options
Canada's Heritage in Pictures
Canada's Illustrated Heritage
Canadian Biographical Studies
Canadian History through the Press Series
Canadian Illustrated Library
Canadian Jackdaws
Canadian Lives
Canadiana Scrapbook
The Canadians
Credit Valley Series
Documents in Canadian History
The 5W Series
Footprints in Time
The Gage Canadian Studies Series
Ginn Studies in Canadian History
Great Stories of Canada
Growth of a Nation Series
History of Canadian Cities
Oracles
Prime Ministers of Canada
Toronto Public Library Board Local History Handbooks
We Built Canada

Adamson, Anthony (text and drawings); and Willard, John (photos); The Gaiety of Gables. McClelland, 1974. $17.95 [0-7710-0058-8]

A beautiful photographic record of the 18th and 19th century "gingerbread" evident in the gables of our houses. *Older to mature.*

Anderson, Allen and **Tomlinson, Betty;** Greetings from Canada: an album of unique Canadian postcards from the Edwardian era 1900-1916; (illus.). Macmillan, 1978. 88 pages. $29.95 cloth [0-7705-1736-6]; $14.95 paper [0-7705-1721-8]

An album of unique Canadian postcards from the Edwardian era, 1900-1916, elaborate school days, the Klondike: winter sports among other subjects. *Middle to older.*

Arthur, Eric and **Witney, Dudley;** The Barn; a vanishing landmark in North America. McClelland, 1972. 256 pages. $35.00 [0-7710-0951-8]; Deluxe ed. $60.00 net.

A distinguished architect collected photographic examples of "a vanishing landmark" and comments on them. *Older to mature.*

Barclay, Isabel; The Story of Canada. Gagnon, Cécile (illus.); Pagurian, 1974. 96 pages. $3.95 paper [0-919364-77-2]

Simple narrative illustrated with stylized drawings introduces Canadian history. *Younger.*

Barnes, Michael; Gold in the Porcupine! Highway Book Shop, 1975. 85 pages. $2.50 paper [0-88954-080-2]

Brief readable history of the Northern Ontario people and places involved in gold mining since the early 1900's. *Middle.*

Bedore, Bernie; The Shanty, being part 1 of The Big pine. Mufferaw, 1975 (1963). 84 pages. $9.00.

About the colourful early lumbering days in the Ottawa Valley - with photos of lumbermen at work, their stories, songs and poetry. *Older to mature.*

A 45 rpm disc, *Tall tales of Joe Mufferaw* (Mufferaw, $1.25) complements the book with two songs and a story.

Berton, Pierre; Klondike. McClelland, 1972. Rev. ed. 472 pages. $12.95 [0-7710-1283-7]; Gift ed. $15.00 [0-7710-1282-9]

Excellent history of the Klondike Gold Rush. *Mature.*

Bowman, Robert Turnbull; Dateline: Canada. Holt, 1973. 2nd rev. ed. 374 pages. $4.95 paper [0-03-925262-0]

Daily calendar of historical events with a full page account of one event for each day. *Older.*

Brown, Cassie and **Horwood, Harold;** Death on the ice. Doubleday, 1972, 1978. 270 pages. $8.95 cloth [0-385-05037-2]; $3.50 paper [0-385-05037-2]

Recreates the great Newfoundland sealing disaster of 1914 when 254 sealers died, the victims of greed, carelessness and misunderstanding. *Mature.*

Brown, Roger David; Sentinels from the past. Lancelot, 1977. 124 pages. $3.95 [0-88999-072-7]

This useful survey of Nova Scotian forts includes Louisburg and those in the Annapolis Basin and the Isthmus of Chignecto. *Middle to older.*

Bruce, Jean. The Last best west. Fitzhenry, 1976. 177 pages. $15.00 cloth [0-88902-401-4]; $7.95 paper [0-88902-402-2]

A pictorial history of the development of Western cities and industries by the European, British and American immigrants who flocked to Canada 1896-1914. *Older to mature.*

Campbell, Lyall (ed.); Captain Cook and the Nootka. CommCept, 1978. 45 pages. $4.00 paper [0-88829-042-X]

A detailed research report on the visit of this famous explorer to the Nootka settlements on Vancouver Island in 1778. *Mature.*

Campbell, Susan; Fort William; living and working at the post, (illus.). Ontario Government Bookstore, 1976. 123 pages. $2.50 paper.

Contemporary records and pictures recreate life at Old Fort William built circa 1816-17 at the mouth of the Kaministiquia River in Thunder Bay. Excellent documentation. *Older to mature.*

Canadian National Exhibition. Centennial Committee; Once upon a century: 100 year history of the Ex. J. H. Robinson Publishing, 1255 Yonge Street, Suite 105, Toronto M4T 1W6 1978. 143 pages. $4.00 paper.

Profusely illustrated history of the world's largest annual exhibition. *Older to mature.*

Careless, J.M.S.; Canada: a story of challenge. Macmillan, 1970. 3rd ed. 449 pages. Text ed. $4.95 [0-7705-0432-9]; $4.95 paper [0-7705-1253-4] (Laurentian Library)
The historical record to 1962 written with lively scholarship. *Older to mature.*

Cashman, Tony; A Picture history of Alberta, illustrated. Hurtig, 1979. 215 pages. $15.95 [0-88830-157-X]
Some 400 photographs from the archives of the Glenbow-Alberta Institute arranged into 26 topics with lengthy captions recall Alberta's early days. *Older to mature.*

Chafe, J.W.; Extraordinary tales from Manitoba's history. McClelland, 1973. 180 pages. $7.95 [0-7710-1951-3]
Strange vignettes, a sidelight on the history of a province. *Older to mature.*

Clemson, Donovan; Living with logs: log buildings and rail fences of B.C. Hancock House, 1974. 93 pages. $4.95 paper [0-919654-10-X]
Illustrated retrospective on the use of logs in buildings and fences in the interior of British Columbia. *Older to mature.*

Collard, Eileen; Clothing in English Canada circa 1867 to 1907. The author, 1975. 72 pages. $13.50 paper [0-9690552-0-X]
Profusely illustrated with patterns and photographs this outline of the clothing worn by adults gives an invaluable record of the period. *Older.*

Collard, Eileen. From toddler to teens: an outline of children's clothing circa 1780 to 1930. The author, 1973. 61 pages. $6.50 paper.
What the well dressed child wore in Canada through 150 years. *Older.*

Coombe, Geraldine; Muskoka past and present, illustrated. McGraw, 1976. 248 pages. $12.50 cloth. [0-07-082333-2]; $8.95 paper [0-07-082365-0]
Detailed history of Ontario's vacation playground. *Mature.*

The Corrective Collective; Never done: three centuries of women's work in Canada. Women's Educational Press, 1974. 150 pages. $3.75 paper; $4.50 School ed.
Beautifully designed book on the lives of our unsung pioneer heroines. *Older to mature.*

Coucill, Irma; Founders and guardians, illustrated. Wiley, 1978. 169 pages. [0-471-99801-X]
Pencil portraits and biographical sketches of the Fathers of Confederation and Canada's governors-general and prime ministers 1867-1977. *Middle to older.*

Craig, John; The Noronic is burning. PaperJacks, 1977. 117 pages. $1.95 [0-7701-0010-4]
Recaptures the disastrous fire that destroyed the Noronic and killed 118 people while the ship was moored in Toronto harbour September 16, 1949. *Mature.*

Creighton, Donald; The Story of Canada. Macmillan, 1971. Rev. ed. 319 pages $9.50 cloth [0-7705-0072-2]; $4.95 paper [0-7705-1360-3] (Laurentian Library)
Concise account of Canada's history up to the end of the 1960's. *Mature.*

Crooker, William; The Oak Island quest, illustrated. Lancelot, 1978. 194 pages. $4.95 [0-88999-078-6]
History of the 200 years of treasure hunting on Oak Island "for an ancient artifact concealed by a past civilization." *Mature.*

Dickie, Donalda J.; My first history of Canada. Dent, 1970 (c1958). 204 pages. Text $2.50 [0-460-93567-4] Trade: $4.50 [0-460-93566-6]
Short chapters on the people and events that made Canadian history. *Middle to older.*

Donaldson, Gordon; Battle for a continent: Quebec 1759. Doubleday, 1973. 241 pages. $9.95 [0-385-05819-5]
Lively, popular account of the conquest of Canada 1758-1760. *Older.*

Douglas, W.A.B.; Gunfire on the lakes; the naval war of 1812-1814 on the Great Lakes and Lake Champlain/ Cannonnades sur les lacs; la guerre navale de 1812-1814 sur les Grands Lacs et le lac Champlain. National Museums, 1977. 33 pages. $2.50 paper.
Bilingual account. *Older to mature.*

Eaton's 1901 catalogue. Musson, 1970. 248 pages. $4.98 paper [0-7737-1004-3]

Nostalgia from a past age. *All ages.*

Einarsson, Magnus; Everyman's heritage: an album of Canadian folk life. National Museum of Man, 1978. 201 pages. $12.50 cloth [0-660-00101-2]; $8.50 paper [0-660-00124-1]

A fascinating family album of the people who settled Canada; a photographic essay with brief connecting bilingual text; a multicultural celebration. *Mature.*

Filey, Mike; Trillium and Toronto Island. PMA, 1976. 96 pages. $12.00 cloth, $5.95 paper [0-88778-141]; [0-88778-142-X]

Another in Filey's well-illustrated series on Toronto history. From the earliest houseboat (1843) to the restoration of the ferry boat Trillium (1975) this is fascinating reading. *Middle to older.*

Gillard, William H. and **Tooke, Thomas;** The Niagara escarpment: from Tobermory to Niagara Falls. U.T.P., 1974. 137 pages. $12.50 cloth [0-8020-2090-9]; $4.50 paper [0-8020-6214-8]

An informal history and tour of "the backbone of Ontario," illustrated with over 80 photographs. *Mature.*

Gray, James H.; Boomtime: peopling the Canadian prairies. Western Producer, 1979. 148 pages. $24.95 cloth [0-88833-020-0]; $14.95 paper [0-88833-024-3]

Peopling the Canadian Prairies was a deliberate project of the post-confederation government and brought over a million Europeans to their new homeland before the first world war. Excellent contemporary photographs. *Mature.*

Great stories from the Canadian frontier. Antonson, 1979. 166 pages. $6.95 paper [0-919900-35-6]

Random historical events recalled by 21 Canadian writers lend a popular approach to Canadian history. *Mature.*

Greenough, John Joseph; The Halifax Citadel 1825-60; a narrative and structural history. Canadian government, 1977. 199 pages. $6.00 paper (Canadian Historic Sites/ Lieux historiques)

Well-researched, well-illustrated and detailed history of the fort and its architecture. *Mature.*

Guillet, Edwin C.; The Story of Canadian roads. U.T.P., 1966. 246 pages. $15.00 [0-8020-1414-3]

Emphasizes the importance of roads in Canadian social and economic development, from portage trail to Trans Canada Highway. *Mature.*

Hall, Roger and **Dodds, Gordon;** A Picture history of Ontario. Hurtig, 1978. 224 pages. $15.95 [0-88830-163-4]

Ontario from the late 18th century to the end of World War II presented in 400 pictures well captioned and briefly introduced. *Older to mature.*

Hanlon, Michael (ed.); Page one. Gage, 1978. 140 pages. $7.95 paper [0-7715-9461-5]

The front pages of The Toronto Star, Canada's largest newspaper records 85 years of Canadian and world history. *Older.*

Hannon, Leslie F.; The Discoverers. McClelland, 1971. 256 pages. $22.50 [0-7710-3867-4]

Outstanding illustrations and maps accompany biographies of Cabot, Cartier, Champlain and Cook. *Mature.*

Hannon, Leslie F.; Forts of Canada. McClelland, 1969. 288 pages. $27.50 [0-7710-3866-6]

Well-documented and illustrated history of various forts, posts and bastions. *Mature.*

Harrison, Pamela; The First original authentic unexpurgated great Canadian quiz book, illustrated. John Wiley, 1977. 187 pages. $4.95 paper [0-88932-066-7]

"1001 incredible questions, facts, and answers about Canadian history" that prove that Canada's history is far from dull grey. *Middle to mature.*

A Harvest yet to reap; a history of Prairie women, illustrated. Women's Educational Press, 1976. 240 pages. $20.00 cloth. [0-88961-030-4]; $8.95 paper [0-88061-029-0]

This is a heart-rending chronicle of the hardships endured by women who settled the Prairies; it documents the "courage, creativity, hope, good humour and even occasional joy" in the lives of our incredible foremothers. *Older to mature.*

Hodgetts, A.B. and **Barns, J.D.;** Decisive decades: a history of the twentieth century for Canadians. Nelson, 1973. 512 pages. 2nd rev. ed. $6.75 net [0-17-632928-5]

Another textbook that places Canada in the perspective of world events. *Older to mature.*

Innis, Harold Adams; The Fur trade in Canada: an introduction to Canadian economic history. U.T.P., 1956. Rev. ed. 463 pages. $15.00 cloth [0-8020-4029-2]; $7.50 paper [0-8020-6001-3]

Definitive work on the subject. *Mature.*

Jefferys, C.W. and **McLean, T.W.;** The Picture gallery of Canadian history. Vol. 1 - Beginning to 1783; Vol. 2 - 1763 to 1830; Vol. 3 - 1830 to 1900. McGraw, 1942-50. Vol. 1 $4.95 paper [0-07-077702-0]; Vol. 2 $4.95 paper [0-07-077703-9]; Vol. 3 $4.95 paper [0-07-077704-7]; $17.50 cloth (single volume) [0-07-077705-5]

Illustrations of historical events, maps, portraits, artifacts make an important pictorial record of Canada's development. *Middle to Mature.*

Jones, Mary Fallis; The Confederation generation, illustrated. Royal Ontario Museum, 1978. 128 pages. $10.95 cloth [0-88854-212-7]; $5.95 paper [0-88854-220-8]

A social and material history of the 1860's through the 1880's as seen through the eyes of "respectable" and "prosperous" English speaking urban central Canadians. *Mature.*

Keywan, Zonia and **Coles, Martin;** Greater than kings: Ukrainian pioneer settlement in Canada. Harvest, 1977. 168 pages. $16.95 [0-88772-177-X]

This social history documents the importance of the Ukrainian contribution to Western Canadian development especially in cultivating 40% of Canada's wheat growing land. *Mature.*

Laxer, Robert M. (ed.); Bilingual tensions in Canada. O.I.S.E., 1979. $6.00 paper [0-7744-0183-4] (Curriculum series: 41)

This joint project of the Canada Studies Foundation and the Ontario Institute for Studies in Education presents an overview of the 200 year old conflict over the bilingualism necessary for Canadian unity. *Mature.*

Leefe, John; The Atlantic privateers. Petheric, 1978. 57 pages. $2.95 paper [0-919380-27-1]

Privateers who operated under government licences (1749-1850) during times of war captured vessels belonging to the enemy. *Older.*

Lorimer, James; The Ex: a picture history of the Canadian National Exhibition. Lorimer, 1973. 135 pages. $7.95 [0-88862-054-3]

Contrasts the C.N.E. of the past and the present, and tells what may be in store for the future. *Older to mature.*

Lower, Joseph Arthur; Canada: an outline history. McGraw, 1973. 2nd ed. 248 pages. $3.95 paper [0-07-092968-8] (Ryerson Paperback Series)

A distinguished Canadian scholar writes an introductory history of his country. *Mature.*

McGill, Jean S.; Northern adventure: the exploration of Great Bear Lake 1900. Highway Book Shop, 1974. 58 pages. $2.00 paper [0-88954-065-9]

Gripping, true adventure of James Bell's exploration of the Great Bear Lake country in 1899. *Older.*

MacLean, Harrison John; The Fate of the Griffon. Griffin, 1974. 118 pages. $8.95 [0-88760-069-7]

La Salle's ship, built in 1679 above Niagara Falls, was proved a naval carcass in 1955 after it was found off the Bruce Peninsula near Tobermory, Ontario. *Older to mature.*

Metson, Graham and **MacMechan, Archibald;** The Halifax explosion: December 6, 1917. McGraw, 1978. 173 pages. $19.95 cloth [0-07-082797-4]; $8.95 paper [0-07-082798-2]

MacMechan's complete text of the Halifax Disaster, and documents and pictures bring the Explosion to vivid reality. *Older to mature.*

Mika, Nick and Helma; United Empire Loyalists, pioneers of Upper Canada, illustrated. Mika, 1976. 256 pages. $25.00 [0-919303-09-9]

This comprehensive and well-researched treatment of the United Empire Loyalists is an important contribution to Canada's early social history. *Mature.*

Morgan, Murray; One man's gold rush. Douglas & McIntyre, 1973. 213 pages. $9.95 cloth; $5.95 paper [0-88894-019-X]

Fascinating pictorial documentary of the Klondike gold rush. *Older.*

Morse, Eric W.; Fur trade routes of Canada; then and now. University of Toronto Press, 1979 (c.1969), $5.00 paper [0-8020-6384-5] (Canadian University Paperbooks)

Well-researched history, economics and geography of the fur trade and a guide for the modern canoeist retracing the routes of the voyageurs. *Mature.*

Morton, W.L. and **L.F. Hannon;** This land, these people, an illustrated history of Canada. Gage, 1977. 248 pages. $29.95 [0-7715-9332-5]

Coherent, overall account of Canada's development as a nation appositely illustrated with full page reproductions. *Mature.*

Moyer, William G.; This unique heritage: the story of Waterloo County. CHYM Radio, 1971. 143 pages. $4.50 cloth; $2.95 paper.

Story of Waterloo County interestingly presented in a number of brief historical sketches. *Mature.*

Neatby, Leslie H.; Link between the oceans. Academic, 1960. 139 pages. $3.95 [0-7747-0057-2] (Canadian Pageant Series)

The search for Sir John Franklin's lost expedition for the discovery of the Northwest Passage. *Older.*

O'Connor, D'Arcy; The Money pit: the story of Oak Island and the world's greatest treasure hunt. Coward McCann (Longman), 1978. 256 pages. $11.75 [698-10877-9]

Countless theories about buried treasure on Nova Scotia's Oak Island have cost millions of dollars and led to the loss of six lives in futile search of it. *Mature.*

Ontario. Ministry of Culture and Recreation; Historical sketches of Ontario. The Ministry, 1979. 111 pages. $2.00 paper [0-7743-1610-1]

The Ontario Heritage Foundation issues historical plaques to commemorate people, places and events. For example in 1976 there were 36 plaques erected. *Older to mature.*

Ontario. Ministry of Culture and Recreation. Heritage Administration Branch; Ontario historic sites, museums, galleries and plaques. The Ministry, 1977. 92 pages. $0.50 paper.

Arranged geographically by district, county or regional municipality, all museums and galleries, provincial plaques and national historic sites and markers in Ontario are listed. *Older to mature.*

Owen, I.M. and **Toye, William;** A Picture history of Canada. Hutton, Clarke (illus.); Oxford, 1968. 2nd ed. 62 pages. $5.50 [0-19-540070-4]

Colourfully illustrated with simple narrative for children. *Middle.*

Paterson, T.W. (ed.); Canadian treasure trails. Stagecoach, 1976, 119 pages. $2.95 [0-88983-001-0]

True stories of lost mines and buried treasure from across Canada. *Older.*

Patton, Jan; The Exodus of the Japanese. McClelland, 1973. 47 pages. $1.95 paper [0-7710-1376-0]

Poignant description of the expulsion of Japanese-Canadians from British Columbia. *Older.*

Patton, Jan; How the Depression hit the West. McClelland, 1973. 47 pages. $1.95 paper [0-7710-1375-2]

Absorbing picture of the Great Depression in Canada and how it touched ordinary people. *Older.*

Patton, Jan; The Sinking of the "I'm Alone". McClelland, 1973. 47 pages. $1.95 [0-7710-1377-9]

Rumrunning from Canada to the United States during Prohibition, and the illegal sinking of a Canadian vessel by the U.S. Coast Guard. *Older.*

Peel, Bruce; Early printing in the Red River Settlement: 1859-1870: and its effect on the Riel Rebellion. Peguis, 1974. 56 pages. $5.00 paper [0-919566-28-6]

Facsimiles of broadsides, proclamations and newspapers that might have influenced public opinion and politics in Riel's time. *Mature.*

Pitcher, Rosemary; Chateau Frontenac. McGraw, 1971. 104 pages. $5.95 [0-7700-0347-8]

History, guests and architecture of an imposing hotel opened in Quebec City in 1893. *Older.*

Rasky, Frank; Explorers of the North. McGraw, 1976. Vol. 1, The Polar voyagers. $17.95 [0-07-082405-3]; 1977, Vol. 2, The North Pole or bust. $17.95 [0-07-082548-3]

Two colourful volumes of exploration in the Canadian North. *Mature.*

Rasky, Frank; The Taming of the Canadian west. McClelland, 1968. 270 pages. Trade ed. $22.50; Text ed. $17.50 [0-7710-7301-1]

Vivid descriptions of life and exploration in the Prairies and British Columbia. *Mature.*

Reid, J.H.Stewart, McNaught, Kenneth W. and **Crowe, Harry S.;** A Sourcebook of Canadian history. Academic, 1964. Text ed. $14.95 [0-7747-3051-X]

An invaluable compilation of original source materials connected with decisive Canadian events. *Mature.*

Russell, Paul; The Great Canadian quiz book. Gage, 1977. 170 pages. $4.95 paper [0-7715-9391-0]

Questions and answers about 100 topics - sports, history, politics, people - reveal some crucial, some trivial, but interesting facts about Canada. *Older to mature.*

Saywell, John T.; Canada: past & present. Clarke, Irwin, 1975. 64 pages. $3.50 paper [0-7720-1001-X]

Colourful resumé of Canadian history, well illustrated. *Middle to older.*

Schull, Joseph; The Nation makers. Macmillan, 1967. 133 pages. $2.95 paper (1973) [0-7705-1099-X]

Exciting capsule history of the four years before Confederation involving the men who fought to forge the nation, and culminating in the enactment of the British North America Act by Queen Victoria on March 29, 1867. *Older.*

Scott, Irene G.; The Trek of the overlanders. Burns, 1968. 36 pages. $1.25 [0-88768-034-8]

Based on an episode in the life of Catharine Schubert who participated in an overland march from Fort Garry to the Cariboo gold fields in 1862. *Older.*

Stanton, James B. (ed.); Ho for the Klondike. Hancock House, 1974. 62 pages. $2.95 paper [0-919654-11-8]

A collection of photos, chronologically arranged plus a brief text document the Klondike gold rush. *Older.*

Stewart, Roderick and **McLean, Neil;** Forming a nation; the story of Canada and Canadians, illustrated. Gage, 1977. 313 pages. Book I $7.95 [0-7715-8519-5]; Book II $7.95 [0-7715-8521-7]

An attractive illustrated two volume text leads readers chronologically through Canadian history to 1945. Index. *Older to mature.*

Swettenham, John; Canada and the First World War. McGraw, 1973. 160 pages. $5.95 paper [0-07-092978-5]

Engrossing text and numerous photographs make a stirring record of Canada's part in the First World War. *Mature.*

Tait, George E.; One dominion. McGraw, 1973. Nova Scotia ed. 429 pages. $7.45 [0-07-092974-2]

Maps, diagrams, time charts, summaries, biographical sketches enhance the history of 19th century Canada. *Middle to older.*

Toronto Island School Students; A History of the Toronto Islands. Toronto Island School, 1972. 64 pages. $2.00 paper [0-88910-099-3]

A brief account of the habitation of the islands forming Toronto's harbour - the farm, airport, homes, yacht clubs and ferries. Attractive illustrated format. *Middle to older.*

Toye, William; Cartier discovers the St. Lawrence. Gal, Laszlo (illus.); Oxford, 1970. 32 pages. $6.95 [0-19-540172-7]

Based on material from the author's *The St. Lawrence,* handsomely illustrated. *Middle.*

PIONEER LIFE
see also
PUBLISHERS' SERIES
All About Series
Growth of a Nation Series

Abrahamson, Una; God bless our home: domestic life in 19th century Canada. Burns, 1966. 233 pages. $12.50 [0-88768-022-4]

Fascinating look at Canada's age of elegance, the height of the Colonial period. *Mature.*

Armstrong, Audrey I.; Harness in the parlour: a book of early Canadian fact & folklore. Musson, 1974. 90 pages. $4.95 paper [0-7737-1005-1]

Informal history of the customs, beliefs and attitudes of Canada's early pioneers. *Older.*

Armstrong, Audrey I.; Sulphur and molasses; home remedies and other echoes of the Canadian past. Smith, J. Merle (illus.). Musson, 1977. 96 pages. $5.95 paper [0-7737-1013-2]

Rural remedies of the pioneers make a useful addition to our folklore. *Older to mature.*

Guillet, Edwin C.; Lives and times of the patriots. U.T.P., 1968. 304 pages. $3.50 paper [0-8020-6088-9]

An account of the Rebellion in Upper Canada, 1837-1838, and the Patriot Agitation in the U.S.A., 1837-1842. *Older to mature.*

Guillet, Edwin C.; Pioneer days in Upper Canada. U.T.P., 1964. 216 pages. $4.50 paper [0-8020-6031-5]

Social life and customs from "sugaring off" to sports and recreation. *Older to mature.*

Guillet, Edwin C.; Pioneer settlements in Upper Canada. U.T.P., 1970. 118 pages. $3.95 paper [0-8020-6110-9]

Recounts the beginnings and development of six early settlements. *Older to mature.*

Jameson, Anna B.; Winter studies and summer rambles in Canada. McClelland, 1965 (1838). 172 pages. $2.25 paper [0-7710-9146-X] (New Canadian Library); Coles, 1972. 1 vol. $19.95 cloth. 3 vols. $13.95 paper (Coles Canadiana Collection)

A gentlewoman's view of York and the countryside of Upper Canada, originally published in 1838. *Older to mature.*

Langdon, Eustella; Pioneer gardens. Holt, 1972. 62 pages. $3.95 paper [0-03-923311-1]

A beautiful book about Canada's earliest gardens includes pioneer recipes, herbal remedies and sketches by pioneers. *Older.*

Minhinnick, Jeanne; At home in Upper Canada. Clarke, Irwin, 1970. 228 pages. $22.50 [0-7720-0106-5]

Profusely illustrated history of domestic life in the pre-confederation home. *Mature.*

Minhinnick, Jeanne; Early furniture in Upper Canada Village. McGraw, 1964. 43 pages. Trade ed. $2.95 [0-7700-0010-X]; educ. $1.50.

About the articles of everyday living, made with personal skill and care and cherished by their owners. *Older.*

Moodie, Susanna; Roughing it in the bush. McClelland, 1962 (c1852). $2.25 paper [0-7710-9131-1] (New Canadian Library); Coles, 1974 (c1852). $13.95 cloth [0-7740-0155-0]; $7.95 paper [0-7740-0156-9] (Coles Canadiana Collection)

By a recent immigrant to Upper Canada who describes pioneer life as she experienced it in the backwoods in the mid 19th century. *Mature.*

Myles, Eugenie Louise; The Emperor of Peace River. Western Producer Prairie, 1977 (1965). 302 pages. $4.95 paper [0-919306-52-7]

Episodes in the life of a pioneer family provide a wealth of information for the history buff. *Older to mature.*

Russell, Loris S.; A Heritage of light: lamps and lighting in the early Canadian home. U.T.P., 1968. $22.50 cloth [0-8020-1530-1]. *Mature.*

Ryder, Huia G.; Antique furniture by New Brunswick craftsmen. McGraw, 1965. 180 pages. $5.95 paper [0-07-092979-3]

Pioneer artifacts show how the colonists furnished their homes. *Mature.*

Stewart, Gordon and **Antonson, Brian;** Canadian frontier annual number three, 1978, illustrated. Antonson, (Douglas & McIntyre), 1978. 128 pages. $4.95 paper [0-919900-30-5]

Articles and stories describing events and individuals before 1900. Bibliographies and sources included. *Older to mature.*

Symons, Harry; Fences. Jefferys, C.W. (illus.); McGraw, (1958) 1974. 155 pages. $4.95 paper [0-07-082203-4]

Fences, gates and stiles used in Ontario from Indian days. Clearly illustrated. *Older.*

Traill, Catherine Parr; Backwoods of Canada. McClelland, 1971 (c1836). $1.95 paper [0-7710-9151-6] (New Canadian Library)

"Being letters from the wife of an emigrant officer illustrative of the domestic economy of British America." This is a slightly edited version. *Mature.*

WORLD HISTORY

Moore, Marion; The United Kingdom: a new Britain. Nelson, 1966. 224 pages. $8.25

A Canadian author outlines the history of Britain, particularly since the beginning of the 20th century. *Mature.*

Ricker, John C. and **Saywell, John T.;** The Story of Western man, Vol I - The Emergence of Europe, Vol II - Europe and the modern world. Clarke, Irwin, 1969. 2 vols. $25.95 (set) [0-7720-0235-5]

Canadian scholars make European history accessible for every man. Well illustrated. *Older to mature.*

Rogers, Edward S.; Forgotten peoples: a reference. Royal Ontario Museum, 1969. 107 pages. $4.00 paper [0-88854-024-8]

The natural, social and supernatural environments of those societies swept aside by Western technology. *Mature.*

Young Delbert A.; According to Hakluyt. Clarke, Irwin, 1973. 197 pages. $6.95 [0-7720-0587-7]

Tales of exploration adapted from Hakluyt's famous *Voyages. Older.*

REFERENCE

Akrigg, G.P.V. and **Akrigg, Helen B.;** 1001 British Columbia place names. Discovery, 1973. 3rd (rev.) ed. 195 pages. $8.95 [0-919624-01-4]

Avis, Walter S. and others; A Concise dictionary of Canadianisms. Gage, 1972. $5.95 paper [0-7715-1968-0] (Dictionary of Canadian English)

Avis, Walter S. and others; The Intermediate dictionary. Gage, 1972. Rev. ed. Grades 6-9 $8.40 [0-7715-1974-5] (Dictionary of Canadian English)

Avis, Walter S. and others; The Senior dictionary. Gage, 1967. Grades 9-13 $10.95 [0-7715-1977-X] (Dictionary of Canadian English)

Banfield, A.F.; The Mammals of Canada. U.T.P., 1974. $25.00 [0-8020-2137-9]

Bourinot, John G.; Bourinot's rules of order. Stanford, Geoffrey H., ed. McClelland, 1977 (c1894) 3rd rev. ed. $4.95 paper [0-7710-8335-1]; $10.00 leatherbound [0-7710-8334-3]

Canada. Department of Agriculture; Frankton, Clarence and **Mulligan, Gerald A.;** Weeds of Canada. Canadian Government, 1977. Rev. ed. 217 pages. $4.50 paper.

Canada. Department of Fisheries and Forestry and **Hosie, R.C.;** Native trees of Canada. Canadian Government 1970. 7th ed. 380 pages. $9.50 cloth [0-660-00279-5]; $6.00 paper.

Canada. Statistics Canada; Canada handbook. Canadian Government, 1979. 376 pages. $3.95 paper [0-660-00870-X]
Well illustrated, useful fact book about Canada's environment, her people and their heritage, the economy, governments and their services.

The Canadian dictionary for children. Collier-Macmillan, 1979. $13.95 [0-02-991210-5]
About 30,000 entries potentially useful through grade 12 with Canadianisms specially noted and a guide to using the dictionary.

Colombo, John Robert (ed.); Colombo's Canadian quotations. Hurtig, 1974. $15.00 [0-88830-079-4]; $35.00 limited edition [0-88830-080-8]

Colombo, John Robert; Colombo's Canadian references. Oxford, 1976. $14.95 [0-19-540253-7]

Dictionary of Canadian biography, Volume I. 1000-1700 Brown, George W. (ed.); and Trudel, Marcel (ed.). U.T.P., 1966. $25.00 [0-8020-3142-0]

Dictionary of Canadian biography, Volume II. 1701-1740 Hayne, David (ed.); and Vachon, André (ed.). U.T.P., 1969. $25.00 [0-8020-3240-0]

Dictionary of Canadian biography, Volume III. 1741-1770 Halpenny, Francess G. (general ed.). U.T.P., 1974. $25.00 [0-8020-3314-8]

Dictionary of Canadian biography, Volume IV. 1771-1800 Halpenny, Francess G. (ed.). U.T.P., 1979. $35.00 [0-8020-3351-2]

Dictionary of Canadian biography, Volume IX. 1861-1870 Halpenny, Francess G. U.T.P., 1976. $25.00 [0-8020-3319-9]

Dictionary of Canadian biography, Volume X. 1871-1880. La Terreur, Marc (ed.). U.T.P., 1972. $25.00 [0-8020-3287-7]
Begun in 1966 with volume one this national biographical dictionary will reach 20 volumes with entries from 1000 A.D. to the mid-20th century. Chronological in arrangement, each volume covers a specific number of years with the entries arranged alphabetically. Also included are related essays such as on the regions and Native peoples of Canada.

A Directory of Canadian plays and playwrights; Playwrights Co-op, 1977. 111 pages. Free.

Duval, Paul; Four decades: the Canadian Group of Painters and their contemporaries. Clarke, Irwin, 1973. 191 pages. $24.95 [0-7720-0553-2]

Encyclopedia Canadiana. Pearson, Kenneth H., ed.; Grolier, 1977. 12th ed. 10 vols. $189.50 [0-7173-1604-9]
The only comprehensive encyclopedia of Canada now in its twelfth revision.

Fergusson, Charles Bruce; Place names and places of Nova Scotia. Mika, 1975. Reprint ed. $30.00 [0-919302-90-4]

Freshwater fishes of Canada; Canadian Government 1979. 996 pages. $12.75.

Guillet, Edwin C.; Early life in Upper Canada. U.T.P., 1963. $25.00 [0-8020-1277-9]

Guillet, Edwin C.; The Pioneer farmer and backwoodsman. U.T.P., 1963. 2 vols. $30.00 boxed [0-8020-1753-3]

Hamilton, Robert M. and **Shields, Dorothy;** The Dictionary of Canadian quotations and phrases. McClelland, 1979. Rev. and enl. ed. 1063 pages. $75.00 [0-7710-3844-5]

From William Aberhart to the Yukon through Coughing and Patent medicines 10,300 entries cross indexed for author, subject and topic.

Hardy, W.G. (ed.); Alberta: a natural history. Hurtig, 1967. 2nd ed. 343 pages. $12.50 [0-88830-004-2]

Holmgren, Eric J. and **Holmgren, P.M.H.;** Over 2000 place names of Alberta. Western Producer, 1977. 3rd ed. $10.95 cloth [0-919306-67-5]; $5.95 paper [0-919306-75-6] 210 pages.

Judd, W.W. (ed.) and **Speirs, J. Murray** (ed.); A Naturalist's guide to Ontario. Hahn, Sylvia (illus.); U.T.P., 1964. $4.00 paper [0-8020-6039-0]

Kalman, Harold; Pioneer churches. de Visser, John (photos); McClelland, 1976. 192 pages $29.50 [0-7710-2700-1]

Kirkpatrick, Daniel (ed.); Twentieth century children's writers. St. Martin's Press (Macmillan of Canada), 1978. 1507 pages. $50.00 [0-312-82413-0]
Bio-bibliographical information on 630 English language authors of fiction, poetry and drama for children is combined with critical essays and some authors' comments. Included are 31 Canadian authors and 12 Canadian contributors.

Klink, Carl F. (ed.); Literary history of Canada: Canadian literature in English. U.T.P., 1976. 2nd ed. 3 Vols.
Vol. 1 $25.00 cloth [0-8020-2211-1];
Vol. 1 $8.95 paper [0-8020-6276-8];
Vol. 2 $25.00 cloth [0-8020-2213-8];
Vol. 2 $8.95 paper [0-8020-6277-6];
Vol. 3 $20.00 cloth [0-8020-2214-6];
Vol. 3 $8.95 paper [0-8020-6278-4];
Boxed set $35.00 [0-8020-6265-2]

Kogon, Marilyn H. (Comp.); Selected free Ontario government publications for children and young adults. Ontario Library Association and Ontario Ministry of Government Services, 1979 3rd. ed. 22 pages. Free. Order from Publications Centre, Ministry of Government Services.

McDonough, Irma (comp.); Profiles C.L.A., 1975. 2nd ed. 159 pages. $6.00 paper [0-88802-110-0]
Interviews with 44 authors and illustrators of Canadian children's books. Portraits and bibliographies included.

MacMillan, Keith and **Beckwith, John;** Contemporary Canadian composers. Oxford, 1975. 248 pages. $14.95 [0-19-540244-8]

MacRae, Marion and **Adamson, Anthony;** Hallowed walls; church architecture in Upper Canada. Clarke, Irwin, 1975. 304 pages. $24.95.
Representative samples of church buildings in the territory of the province of Ontario before 1840.

Manitoba School Library Audio-Visual Association; Connections: writers and the land. M.S.L. A.V.A., 1974. 134 pages. $5.00 paper.
Short biographies of writers connected with Manitoba.

Mellen, Peter; The Group of Seven. McClelland, 1976. new. ed. $29.50 [0-7710-5816-0]; Slipcased $35.00 [0-7710-5815-2]

National Museum of Canada; Birds of Canada. National Museums, 1966. 428 pages. $22.50 [0-660-00126-8] (Biological Series)

National Museum of Canada; The Indians of Canada. National Museums, 1963. 6th ed. 452 pages. $9.75.

Ontario. Ministry of Culture and Recreation; Directory: Native communities and organizations in Ontario. The Ministry, 1980. 105 pages. Free [0-7743-4187-4]
Excellent directory for contact with Native peoples' organizations.

Palardy, Jean; The Early furniture of French Canada. McLean, Eric (tr.); Macmillan, 1978. 412 pages. $14.95 [0-7705-1664-5]
This definitive work on the furniture found in French Canadian homes from the 17th century to the early 19th century is well illustrated with photographs.

Priamo, Carol; Mills. McGraw, 1976. 196 pages. $27.50 [07-082402-9]

Rempel, John I.; Building with wood and other aspects of 19th century building in Ontario. University of Toronto Press, 1967. 287 pages. $19.95 [0-8020-1476-3]

Exceedingly well-illustrated and well-documented account of 19th century wooden buildings in Ontario.

Robinson, Sinclair and **Smith, Donald;** Practical handbook of Canadian French/Manuel pratique du français canadien. Macmillan, 1973. $10.00 cloth [0-7705-1027-2]; $3.95 paper [0-7705-1028-0]

Russell, E.T.; What's in a name? Travelling through Saskatchewan with the story behind 1600 place names. Prentice, 1973. 2nd ed. 364 pages. $5.25 [0-919306-39-X]

Shackleton, Philip; The Furniture of old Ontario. Macmillan, 1978. 399 pages. $14.95 paper [0-7705-1665-3]

Chairs, sofas, beds, tables and other furniture well photographed and catalogued for an authentic view of the work of our early craftsmen.

Story, Norah; The Oxford companion to Canadian history and literature. Oxford, 1967. $24.95 [0-19-540115-8]

Swettenham, John (ed.); Valiant men: Canada's Victoria Cross and George Cross winners. Hakkert, 1973. 234 pages. $14.95 [0-88866-525-3] (Canadian War Museum Historical Publications)

Toye, William (ed.); The Oxford companion to Canadian history and literature: supplement 1967-1972. Oxford, 1973. $12.50 [0-19-540205-7]

Turner, Daisy; Moose Factory Cree. Highway Bookshop, 1975. 49 pages. $2.00 paper [0-88954-026-8]

Tyrchiewicz, Peggy; Ethnic folk costumes in Canada. Hyperion, 1979. 229 pages. $35.00 [0-920534-10-4]

Folk costumes brought to Canada or made here from patterns from various countries are described in detail and illustrated in colour.

Vinay, Jean-Paul; Daviault, Pierre and **Alexander, Henry;** The Canadian dictionary: French/English. McClelland, 1962. 861 pages. $8.95 [0-7710-8715-2] Text ed. $5.95.

Wallace, William Stewart; The Macmillan dictionary of Canadian biography. Macmillan, 1976. 4th ed. $30.00 [0-7705-1462-6]

Walters, Susan (ed.); Canadian almanac and directory. Copp, 1978. $29.50 [0-7730-4019-6]

MAGAZINES FOR YOUNG PEOPLE

The following titles would enhance any children's library although only a few of them have been published specifically for children. Contact the Canadian Periodical Publishers' Association, 54 Wolseley Street, Toronto, Ontario, M5T 1A5 for a checklist of their over 160 member periodicals.

Ahoy; An Atlantic magazine for children. Published by the Junior League of Halifax, P.O. Box 3380, Halifax South P.O., Halifax, N.S. B3J 3J1
Quarterly. $5.00 for one year. Add $1.00 outside Canada. [0317-6126]

General interest magazine has a Down East flavour that non-Atlantic children will want to savour too. Stories, games, puzzles, anecdotes, drawings for 7-13 year olds.

Arctic in Colour; Northern News Services Ltd., Box 2850 Yellowknife, N.W.T. X0E 1H0.
Quarterly. $3.50 for one year.

Each issue has 52 pages of informative articles and beautiful colour photos on the North. The magazine is "published in the North by Northerners."

The Beaver; magazine of the North. Published by Hudson's Bay Company, Hudson's Bay House, 77 Main Street, Winnipeg, Manitoba R3C 2R1.
Quarterly. In Canada; $6.00 for one year; $18.00 for three years (add $1.00 outside Canada) [0005-7517]

"The interests of *The Beaver* cover the territory with which the Company has been or is now associated" - exploration, mining, Native people, geology, animals.

Book Times; Published by The Children's Book Centre, 229 College Street, 5th floor, Toronto, Ontario M5T 1R4.
Four times a year. Available in bulk only. Subscription for four issues: 50 copies $10.00; 100 copies $15.00; 500 copies $50.00.

A four-page news sheet about Canadian books, magazines, authors, and illustrators, written for children. Meant to be distributed in related settings - school and public libraries, bookstores.

Canada and the World; Published by Maclean-Hunter, 481 University Avenue, Toronto, Ontario M5W 1A7.
Monthly, September to May. $6.85 for one year, payment with order. Lower rates for bulk subscriptions. [0043-8170]

Short analytical articles with an historical perspective on current social and political issues, one theme per issue.

Canada Crafts; published by G.P. Page Publications Ltd., 380 Wellington St. W., Toronto, Ontario M5V 1E3.
Bi-monthly. $14.00 for one year. $24.00 two years. $32.00 three years. Outside Canada, add $2.00 postage. [0382-8115]

Well-illustrated in colour, this is of interest to craft professionals, collectors, hobbyists and educators.

Canada Now! Canada Now! Publishers Ltd., P.O. Box 91386, West Vancouver, B.C. V7V 3P1.
36 issues per year $18.00; class sets of ten or more at $15.00 each issue.

"A scholastic magazine of current events and Canadian history keyed to social studies taught in Canadian schools."

Canada West Magazine; Stagecoach Publishing, Box 3399, Langley, B.C. V3A 4R7.
Quarterly. Individuals: $5.00 for one year, $9.00 2 years; $13.00 3 years. Institutions: $6.00 for one year; $11.00 for 2 years; $16.00 3 years [0590-7853]

Articles on people and places that used to be - historic houses, Indian rituals, ghost towns, the pony express and other memorabilia of the West.

Canadian Geographical Journal; Published by The Royal Canadian Geographical Society, 488 Wilbrod Street, Ottawa, Ontario K1N 6M8.
Bi-monthly. $14.00 for one year; outside Canada $16.00 for one year. $2.75 per single copy.

Outstanding coverage of Canadian geography, resources and people.

Chickadee; The Young Naturalist Foundation, 59 Front Street East, Toronto, Ontario M5E 1B3.
Ten issues per year. $8.00 for ten issues, $14.00 for 20 issues, outside Canada add $2.00 per 10 issue subscription. [0707-4611]

A younger version of Owl magazine, this is suitable for children under eight. As well as many colorful illustrations, there are stories, puzzles and games to spark interest in nature.

Conservation Canada; Published by Parks Canada. Order from Information Division, Parks Canada, Ottawa, Ontario. K1A 0H4.
Quarterly. Free.

Colour photographs grace every page of this 28-page bilingual magazine whose articles tell us what is being done to "conserve, preserve and enhance our priceless Canadian heritage."

Cycle Canada; Brave Beaver Pressworks Ltd., 290 Jarvis St., Toronto, Ontario M5B 2C5.
Monthly. $11.95 for one year; $19.95 for two years; $26.95 for three years. (Outside Canada add $4.00) [0319-2822]

For the motorcycle enthusiast.

Flare; Published by Maclean-Hunter, 481 University Avenue, Toronto, Ontario M5W 1A7.
10 issues per year. $7.50 or $10.50 outside Canada. [0708-4927]

Formerly *Miss Chatelaine* this magazine features fashions and fads for teenaged girls and excellent topical articles that echo the feminist slant of *Chatelaine,* its older counterpart.

Harrowsmith; Published by Harrowsmith Magazine, Camden East, Ontario K0K 1J0.
$12.00 for one year; $22.00 for two years. [0381-6885]

Country living, alternative energy, organic gardening, ecology are some of the subjects treated in this comprehensive publication.

Heritage Canada; Published by Heritage Canada, P.O. Box 1358, Station B, Ottawa, Ontario K1P 5R4.
Bi-monthly. Included with membership in Heritage Canada. Family $15.00. Individual $10.00. Senior Citizen $5.00. Life $250.00. Schools and libraries $20.00 [0315-1298]

Concerned with the preservation of Canada's heritage structures and sites.

Magook; Published by Magook Foundation, 254 Bartley Drive, Toronto, Ontario M4A 1G1.
4 issues per year. $7.20 for one year. Back issues are available at $5.00 each [0702-6803]

Magook means *magazine* plus *book*. Every issue of Magook includes a 32-page book and a 16 page magazine bound together. But each 32-page book is also published simultaneously in hard cover and may be ordered from McClelland and Stewart at $4.95 each. The first four books include *The Cottage at Crescent Beach* by Ann Blades; *A Secret in my pocket* by Madeline Kronby; *Snails, slugs, spiders and bugs,* by Trudy L. Rising; *Charlie meets the Goomby* by Paul Bailey. They are all illustrated in full colour and will appeal to children of all ages.

The magazine includes profiles on the authors and illustrators of the books, poems by children, plays and songs and stories by famous Canadians and articles on bookcraft.

Nature Canada; Published by Canadian Nature Federation, 46 Elgin Street, Ottawa, Ontario K1P 5K6. Quarterly. Available with annual membership in Canadian Nature Federation: Regular (individual) $12.00; Regular (family) $15.00; Sustaining $25.00; Active $100.00; Supporting $250.00; Life $500.00. Subscriptions are available to schools and libraries at $15.00 for one year. [0008-2929]

Glossy paper, coloured photographs, well-known writers make Canada's national nature magazine a joy to read.

North/Nord; Published by Department of Indian and Northern Affairs, Ottawa. Bi-monthly. $6.00 for one year; outside Canada $7.50 for one year. [0029-2362]

Excellent source of topical information on all aspects of life in the Canadian North.

Owl; Published by The Young Naturalist Foundation, 59 Front Street East, 3rd floor, Toronto, Ontario. M5E 1B3.
Ten issues per year. $8.00 for 10 issues; $14.00 for 20 issues; outside Canada add $2.00 per 10 issue subscription.

A well-conceived, well-produced magazine intended for children aged 7-13 replaces *The Young Naturalist* and deals with a wide spectrum of outdoor interests - sports, wildlife, ecology, conservation.

Seasons; Published by Federation of Ontario Naturalists, 1262 Don Mills Road, Don Mills, Ontario M3B 2W8. Bi-monthly. Available with annual membership in FON: Individual $17.00; Family $22.00; Supporting $60.00; Life $250.00; Student $12.00; Senior Citizen $10.00; Schools and Libraries $17.00. [0030-3046]

Distinguished Canadian naturalists contribute to a beautifully-produced, colour-illustrated periodical, formerly called *Ontario Naturalist.*

Ski Canada; Published by Terry M. Whelpton, 643 Yonge St., Toronto, Ontario M4Y 2A2.
Bi-monthly. $5.00 one year.

Articles on ski techniques, news of personalities and meets.

Tawow; Published by Department of Indian and Northern Affairs, Ottawa, Ontario K1A 0H4.
Quarterly. $1.50 for each issue; $1.80 outside Canada.

Articles about Indian cultural pursuits, some stories in Cree syllabics, illustrations by Indian artists inform readers about native arts and artists.

PUBLISHERS' SERIES

ADVENTURES IN CANADIAN HISTORY
6 volumes. Macmillan. $1.95 each, paper.

Short accounts of dramatic highlights in Canadian history include Riel's execution of Thomas Scott, the building of the CPR, Elizabeth Simcoe's sojourn in Upper Canada as the wife of Canada's first Lieutenant-Governor. *Older.*

McLaughlin, Florence; First lady of Upper Canada.

Robertson, Robert W.W.; The execution of Thomas Scott. [0-88768-027-5]

Robertson, Robert W.W.; The Law moves west. [0-88768-004-6]

Robertson, Robert W.W.; Sir John A. builds a nation. [0-88768-003-8]

Robertson, Robert W.W.; Sir John A. builds a wall. [0-88768-020-8]

Robertson, Robert W.W.; Stand fast Craigellachie. [0-88768-005-4]

ALL ABOUT SERIES
5 volumes. House of Grant. Prices vary.

Accurate, simple guides to Ontario antique furniture illustrated with clear black-and-white photographs for easy identification. Excellent material for history projects. *Older.*

Ingolfsrud, Elizabeth; All about Ontario chairs. $3.95, paper [0-460-90082-X]

Ingolfsrud, Elizabeth; All about Ontario chests, $3.95, paper [0-460-90083-8]

Ingolfsrud, Elizabeth; All about Ontario cupboards, $4.95, paper [0-460-90084-6]

Ingolsfrud, Elizabeth; All about Ontario desks, $4.95, paper [0-460-90085-4]

Ingolfsrud, Elizabeth; All about Ontario tables, $3.50, paper [0-460-90087-0]

BUCKSKIN BOOKS
12 volumes. Macmillan. Prices vary.

Notable Canadian authors and illustrators combine their efforts to make exciting adventure stories based on incidents in Canadian history. *Middle.*

Ballantyne, Lareine; The Scout who led an army. $2.95, paper [0-7705-1132-5]

Benham, Leslie; The Heroine of Long Point. $4.95, cloth [0-7705-0025-0]

Bramwell, Barbara; Adventure at the mill. $3.95, cloth [0-7705-0026-9]

Clark, Catherine Anthony; The Man with yellow eyes, $4.95, cloth [0-7705-0028-5]; $2.95, paper [0-7705-1131-7]

Leitch, Adelaide; The Great canoe. $3.95, cloth [0-7705-0022-6]

Leitch, Adelaide; Lukey Paul from Labrador. $3.95, cloth [0-7705-0031-5]

McLaughlin, Lorrie; The Trouble with Jamie. $3.95, cloth [0-7705-0033-1]

McLaughlin, Lorrie; West to the Cariboo. $3.95, cloth [0-7705-0023-4]; $1.95, paper [0-7705-1130-9]

Thompson, Frances C.; Escape from Grande Pré. $3.95, cloth [0-7705-0034-X]; $1.95, paper [0-7705-1135-X]

Thompson, Frances G.; Danger in the coves. $3.95, cloth [0-7705-0027-7]

Wood, Kerry; The Boy and the buffalo. $3.95, cloth [0-7705-0030-7]

Wright, Richard; Andrew Tolliver. $3.95, cloth [0-7705-0032-3]

CANADA AT WORK

5 volumes. McGraw. Prices vary.

Well illustrated, comprehensive studies of Canadian industry.
Older to mature.

Dykes, James G.; Canada's automotive industry. $8.82 [0-07-09458-1]

Manchester, Lorne; Canada's aviation industry. $8.82 [0-07-094956-5]

Manchester, Lorne; Canada's fisheries. $7.76 [0-07-09498-8]

Phillips, R.A.J.; Canada's railways. $8.82 [0-07-094957-3]

Walker, Dean; Canada's agriculture. $7.75 [0-07-094979-4]

CANADA: ORIGINS AND OPTIONS

12 volumes projected. Wiley. $4.50 each.

"Designed to encourage the student of social studies to explore our culture and our heritage." Each volume focusses on one specific topic for a succinct but thorough analysis. Six volumes now available. *Older to mature.*

Doughty, Howard A.; British roots. [0-471-99768-4]

Doughty, Howard A.; The First Canadians. [0-471-99770-6]

Doughty, Howard A.; Our legal heritage. [0-471-99765-X]

Munro, Iain R.; Canada and the world wars. [0-471-99773-0]

Munro, Iain R.; Immigration. [0-471-99767-6]

Skidmore, Darrel R.; You and your government. [0-471-99766-8]

THE CANADA SERIES

12 volumes projected. McGraw. $8.95 each.

Profusely illustrated geographies of all the provinces covering industry, government, historical highlights, personalities, environment in a clear concise text. Seven volumes now available. *Older to mature.*

Hocking, Anthony; Manitoba. [0-07-082688-9]

Hocking, Anthony; New Brunswick. [0-07-082686-2]

Hocking, Anthony; Ontario. [0-07-082692-7]

Hocking, Anthony; Prince Edward Island. [0-07-082683-8]

Hocking, Anthony; Quebec. [0-07-082691-9]

Hocking, Anthony; Saskatchewan. [0-07-082689-7]

Hocking, Anthony; The Yukon and the Northwest Territories. [0-07-082694-3]

CANADA'S HERITAGE IN PICTURES

1 volume, more projected. Nelson. $12.95.

Designed to encourage further reading, these pictorial histories carry photographs on every page. *Middle to mature.*

Swainson, Donald; Macdonald of Kingston: first prime minister. [0-17-600739-3]

CANADA'S ILLUSTRATED HERITAGE

16 volume set. McClelland. $99.98 per set.

Canada's social history comes alive in these well illustrated, popular accounts from our beginnings in 1497 to 1970. *Older to mature.*

Atwood, Margaret; Days of the rebels 1815/1840. [0-919644-16-3]

Batten, Jack; Canada moves westward 1880/1890. [0-919644-20-1]

Braithwaite, Max; The Hungry thirties 1930/1940. [0-919644-25-2]

Callwood, June; The Naughty nineties 1890/1900. [0-919644-21-X]

Carroll, Jay; Pioneer days 1840/1860. [0-919644-17-1]

Craig, John; The Years of agony 1910/1920. [0-919644-23-6]

Craig, John; The Crazy twenties 1920/1930. [0-919644-24-4]

Edmonds, Alan; The Years of protest 1960-1970. [0-919644-28-7]

Franklin, Stephen; A Time for heroes. [0-919644-20-1]

Hannon, Leslie; Redcoats and loyalists 1760/1815. [0-919644-15-5]

Horwood, Harold. The Colonial dream 1497/1760. [0-919644-14-7]

Stephenson, William; Dawn of the nation 1860/1870. [0-919644-18-X]

Symington, Fraser; The First Canadians. [0-919644-13-9]

CANADIAN ARTISTS SERIES
(Gage)

3 volumes. Gage. $12.95 each.

Sympathetic biographies of Canadian artists illustrated with representative colour and black and white reproductions of their work, in a well-designed format. *Older to mature.*

Rand, Margaret; Gray, Margaret and **Steen, Lois;** A.J. Casson. [0-7715-9962-5]

Rand, Margaret; Gray, Margaret and **Steen, Lois;** Carl Schaefer. [0-7715-9340-6]

Rand, Margaret; Gray, Margaret and **Steen, Lois;** Charles Comfort. [0-7715-9988-9]

CANADIAN ARTISTS SERIES
(The National Gallery)

7 volumes. The National Gallery. $3.95 each, paper.

Well illustrated, well written monographs that young people can enjoy. *Older to mature.*

Finley, Gerald; George Heriot. [88884-369-0]

Gagnon, François-Marc; Paul-Emile Gagnon [88884-217-6]

Hind, William G.R.; J. Russell Harper. [88884-273-2]

Ostiguy, Jean-René; Charles Huot. [88884-370-4]

Reid, Dennis; Bertram Brooker. [88884-372-0]

Reid, Dennis; Edwin H. Holgate. [88884-314-3]

Varley, Christopher; Frederick H. Varley. [88884-371-2]

CANADIAN BIOGRAPHICAL STUDIES

7 volumes. U.T.P. Prices vary.

Devoted to making little known Canadians and their times better known to the specialist and the general reader, these short readable biographies appear in French and English editions and are designed primarily to assist contributors to the *Dictionary of Canadian Biography/Dictionnaire biographique du Canada. Mature.*

Bumsted, J.M.; Henry Alline. $4.50 paper [0-8020-3247-8]

Gagan, David P.; The Denison family of Toronto. $6.50, cloth [0-8020-3296-6]; $2.95, paper [0-8020-3297-4]

Groulx, Lionel; Roland-Michel Barrin de la Galissonière; $4.50, paper [0-8020-3237-0]

Henderson, J.L.H.; John Strachan. $6.50, cloth. [0-8020-3225-7]

Hodgins, Bruce; John Sandfield MacDonald. $4.50, paper [0-8020-3248-6]

Morton, William L.; Henry Youle Hind. $4.50, paper [0-8020-3278-8]

Wilbur, Richard; H.H. Stevens. $9.50, cloth [0-8020-3339-3]

CANADIAN CRITICAL ISSUES

10 volumes. O.I.S.E. and PaperJacks. Prices vary.

Informative and provocative booklets about controversial issues in present day Canadian society. *Mature.*

From OISE only:

Bourne, Paula; Women in Canadian society. $3.95 paper [0-7744-0123-0]

Eisenberg, John A. and **Bourne, Paula;** The Right to live and die. $2.95 paper [0-7744-0092-7]

Eisenberg, John A. and **Troper, Harold;** Native survival. $3.25 paper [0-7744-0094-3]

Levin, Malcolm and **Sylvester, Christine;** Crisis in Quebec. $2.95 paper [0-7744-0091-9]

Sylvester, Christine and **Harris, Marion;** On strike! $2.95 paper [0-7744-0096-X]

Troper, Harold and **Palmer, Lee;** Issues in cultural diversity. $3.65 paper [0-7744-0124-9]

From PaperJacks only:

Bourne, Paula and **Eisenberg, John A.;** The Law and the police. $1.50 paper [0-7737-7011-9]

Eisenberg, John A. and **MacQueen, Gailand;** Don't teach that! $1.50 paper [0-7737-7012-7]

Levin, Malcolm and **Sylvester, Christine;** Foreign ownership. $1.25 paper [0-7737-7013-5]

CANADIAN FAVOURITES

20 volumes. McClelland. Prices vary.

There are 14 volumes by Lucy M. Montgomery in this series. Please see the annotated entries under her name in the FICTION section under STORIES. Six other popular stories listed below appear in this series. *Older to mature.*

Dunham, Mabel; Kristli's trees. $3.95 paper [0-7710-2920-9]

Faulknor, Cliff; The Smoke horse. $4.50 cloth, $3.95 paper [0-7710-3108-4]

Harris, Christie; Raven's cry. $4.38 cloth, $3.95 paper [0-7710-4033-4]

Hill, Kay; Glooscap and his magic. $5.50 cloth, $4.50 paper [0-7710-4117-9]

McFarlane, Leslie; The Last of the great picnics. $2.75 paper [0-7710-5784-9]

Saunders, Marshall; Beautiful Joe. $3.50 paper [0-7710-7938-7]

CANADIAN HISTORY THROUGH THE PRESS SERIES

7 Volumes. Holt. $4.50 each, paper.

Newspaper articles and editorials reflect contemporary reaction to the issues and events of the 19th and 20th centuries. *Older to mature.*

Bowler, Reginald Arthur; The War of 1812. [0-03-925857-2]

Clark, Lovell C.; The Guibord affair. [0-03-925851-3]

Cross, Michael; Free trade, annexation, and reciprocity. [0-03-925850-5]

Page, Robert, J.D.; Imperialism and Canada, 1895-1903. [0-03-925852-1]

Rasporich, Anthony W.; William Lyon Mackenzie. [0-03-925859-9]

Rea, J.E.; The Winnipeg General Strike. [0-03-925858-0]

Waite, Peter B.; Confederation 1854-1867. [0-03-925854-8]

CANADIAN ILLUSTRATED LIBRARY

4 volumes. McClelland. Prices vary.

Profusely illustrated popular accounts of various Canadian events and personalities. *Older to mature.*

Berton, Pierre; Historic headlines. $6.95 [0-7710-1308-6]

Kilbourn, William; The Making of a nation. $8.95 [0-7710-0035-9]

MacLennan, Hugh; The Colour of Canada. $12.50 [0-7710-0031-6]

Mowat, Farley; Canada north. $5.95 paper [0-7710-0023-5]

CANADIAN JACKDAWS

29 folders. Clarke, Irwin. $4.55 each.

Facsimiles of original resource materials relating to Canadian history and personalities. *Older.*

C2 Riel. [0-7720-0146-4]

C4 Building the C.P.R. [0-7720-0148-0]

C5 The Fur trade. [0-7720-0149-9]

C7 1837: Mackenzie. [0-7720-0151-0]

C8 Dieppe 1942. [0-7720-0152-01]

C9 Bristol & the Cabots. [0-7720-0153-7]

C11 Cartier of St. Malo. [0-7720-0155-3]

C12 The R.C.M.P. [0-7720-0156-1]

C13 The Great Depression. [0-7720-0157-X]

C14 Push to the Pacific. [0-7720-0158-8]

C15 The North-West Passage. [0-7720-0159-6]

C16 Indians of Canada. [0-7720-0160-X]

C17 Canada & the Civil War. [0-7720-0161-8]

C18 Gold in the Cariboo. [0-7720-0162-6]

C19 Laurier. [0-7720-0163-4]

C20 The Maritimes' age of sail. [0-7720-0164-2]

C21 The Fenians. [0-7720-0165-0]

C23 Champlain. [0-7720-0167-7]

C24 Leacock. [0-7720-0168-5]

C25 The War of 1812. [0-7720-0537-0]

C26 Struggle for the 14th colony. [0-7720-0508-7]

C29 The Winnipeg General Strike. [0-7720-053-6]

C33 Stratford. [0-7720-0544-3]

C34 Canadian American Relations. [0-7720-0632-6]

C36 Wings of progress [0-7720-1036-7]

C38 Newfoundland and Confederation. [0-7720-1050-1]

CANADIAN LIVES

5 volumes. Oxford. Prices vary.

Well researched, well written short biographies of famous political figures in Canadian history, suitable for interested young people. *Older to mature.*

Bowsfield, Hartwell; Louis Riel. $5.00 [0-19-540182-4]

Flint, David; William Lyon Mackenzie. $5.00 [0-19-540185-9]

Robertson, Barbara; Wilfrid Laurier. $5.00 [0-19-540185-9]

Swainson, Donald; John A. Macdonald. $5.00 [0-19-540181-6]

Woodcock, George; Amor De Cosmos. $6.25 [0-19-540232-4]

CANADIAN PREHISTORY SERIES

6 volumes. Van Nostrand. $6.95 paper.

Significant archeological findings documented by leading scholars reveal the life of our Native peoples before Jacques Cartier landed in Canada. Colour plates, photographs, diagrams, maps. *Older to mature.*

MacDonald, G.F. and **R.I. Inglis;** The Dig. [0-660-00007-5]

McGhee, Robert; Canadian Arctic prehistory. [0-442-29813-7]

Tuck, James A.; Newfoundland and Labrador prehistory. [0-442-29889-7]

Wright, J.V.; Ontario prehistory. [0-442-29888-9]

Wright, J.V.; Quebec prehistory. [0-442-29831-5]

Wright, J.V.; Six chapters of Canada's prehistory. [0-442-29887-0]

CANADIANA SCRAPBOOK

8 volumes. Prentice-Hall. Order will be processed for 10 copies or multiples of 10 copies, or an individual title only. A package of 10 books is $49.50 list.

Large folio format displays to advantage the numerous photographs and accompanying text that bring significant historical periods of our history into focus. *All ages.*

1. A Nation launched: Macdonald's Dominion 1867-1896 [0-13-6093477]

2. The Great Klondike Gold Rush 1896-1904 [0-13-3639525]

3. A Nation beckons: Canada 1896-1914 [0-13-6092713]

4. Canadians at war 1941-1918 [0-13-1134566]

5. The Confident years: Canada in the 1920's [0-13-1675516]

6. The Depression years: Canada in the 1930's [0-13-1990187]

7. Canadians at war 1939-1945 [0-13-113456-6]

8. Years of promise: Canada 1945-1963 [0-13-971846-X]

THE CANADIANS

54 volumes published, more projected. Fitzhenry and Whiteside. $3.00 each, paper.

Short (about 60 pages each) succinct biographies of Canadian personalities, intended for students. Photos and drawings add to the readers' enjoyment. *Older to mature.*

Barnett, Donald; Poundmaker. [0-88902-221-6]

Bassett, John M. and **A. Roy Petrie;** Allan Napier MacNab. [0-88902-201-1]

Bassett, John M.; Elizabeth Simcoe. [0-88902-204-6]

Bassett, John M.; Henry Larsen. [0-88902-230-5]

Bassett, John M. and **A. Roy Petrie;** Laura Secord. [0-88902-202-X]

Bassett, John M.; Samuel Cunard. [0-88902-206-2]

Bassett, John M.; Timothy Eaton. [0-88902-210-0]

Bassett, John M. and **A. Roy Petrie;** William Hamilton Merritt. [0-88902-200-3]

Benham, Mary Lile; La Vérendrye. [0-88902-676-9]

Benham, Mary Lile; Nellie McClung. [0-88902-219-4]

Benham, Mary Lile; Paul Kane. [0-88902-233-X]

Burns, Florence M.; William Berczy. [0-88902-237-2]

Careless, J.M.S.; George Brown. [0-88902-667-X]

Cochrane, Jean; Kate Aitken. [0-88902-249-6]

Collins, Paul; Hart Massey. [0-88902-241-0]

Cosentino, Frank; Ned Hanlan. [0-88902-248-8]

Damania, Laura; Egerton Ryerson. [0-88902-212-7]

English, John; Arthur Meighen. [0-88902-242-9]

Flint, David; Sir Henry Pellatt. [0-88902-659-9]

Gardner, Alison; James Douglas. [0-88902-222-4]

Gillen, Molly; Lucy Maud Montgomery. [0-88902-244-5]

Granatstein, J.L.; Mackenzie King. [0-88902-228-3]

Green, Lorne; Sandford Fleming [0-88902-671-8]

Hacker, Carlotta; Crowfoot. [0-88902-238-0]

Hacker, Carlotta; E. Cora Hind. [0-88902-666-1]

Hall, D.J.; Clifford Sifton. [0-88902-223-2]

Hayes, W.S.; Beaverbrook. [0-88902-500-2]

James, Donna; Emily Murphy. [0-88902-234-8]

McDougall, Bruce; Charles Mair. [0-88902-240-2]

McDougall, Bruce; John Wilson Murray. [0-88902-672-6]

McNaught, Kenneth; J.S. Woodsworth [0-88902-663-7]

Mayles, Stephen; William Van Horne. [0-88902-216-X]

Metcalf, Vicky; Catherine Schubert. [0-88902-243-7]

Murphy, Larry; Thomas Keefer. [0-88902-227-5]

Neering, Rosemary; Emily Carr. [0-88902-207-0]

Neering, Rosemary; Louis Riel. [0-88902-214-3]

Percy, H.R.; Joseph Howe. [0-88902-220-8]

Petrie, A. Roy; Alexander Graham Bell. [0-88902-209-7]

Petrie, A. Roy; Joseph Brant. [0-88902-217-8]

Petrie, A. Roy; Sam McLaughlin. [0-88902-205-4]

Ray, Janet; Emily Stowe. [0-88902-236-4]

Redekop, Magdalene; Ernest Thompson Seton. [0-88902-661-0]

Saunders, Robert; R.B. Bennett. [0-88902-653-X]

Sealey, D. Bruce; Jerry Potts [0-88902-678-5]

Shaw, Margaret M.; Frederick Banting. [0-88902-229-1]

Sheffe, Norman; Casimir Gzowski. [0-88902-211-9]

Sheffe, Norman; Goldwin Smith. [0-88902-224-0]

Smith, James K.; Alexander Mackenzie. [0-88902-225-9]

Smith, James K.; David Thompson. [0-88902-213-5]

Spiegel, Martin; Wilfrid Laurier. [0-88902-245-3]

Stewart, Roderick; Norman Bethune. [0-88902-203-8]

Sturgis, James; Adam Beck. [0-88902-246-1]

Waite, Peter; John A. Macdonald. [0-88902-231-3]

Wilson, Mary C.; Marion Hilliard. [0-88902-215-1]

Woodcock, George; Gabriel Dumont. [0-88902-239-9]

CANADIANS ALL SERIES

3 volumes. Methuen. $4.95 each, paper.

Well and not so well known Canadians whose lives will inspire young people. *Older to mature.*

Angus, Terry and **White, Shirley;** Canadians all. [0-458-91270-0]

Angus, Terry and **White, Shirley;** Canadians all 2. [0-458-93860-2]

Kahn, Charles and **Kahn, Maureen;** Canadians all 3. [0-458-94250-2]

CAREERS CANADA

26 volumes. Supply and Services Canada. $1.00 paper, each.

Reliable information collected 1975-1978, about various types of Canadian occupations will assist readers to choose suitable vocations. *Older to mature.*

1. Careers in construction.
2. Clerical occupations.
3. Mechanical repair occupations.
4. Electronic data processing occupations.
5. Careers in recreation and sports.
6. Careers in social sciences.
7. Careers in protective services.
8. Careers in personal services.
9. Careers in the hospitality industry.
10. Careers in sales
11. Careers in drafting.
12. Careers in social work and social welfare.
13. Vocations in religion.
14. Careers in natural sciences.
15. Careers in health services.
16. Careers in banking and finance.
17. Careers in insurance and real estate.
18. Careers in agriculture.
19. Careers in transportation.
20. Technicians in applied arts.
21. Careers in mining and mineral processing.
22. Technicians in science and engineering.
23. Careers in fishing and fish processing.
24. Careers in forestry and logging.
25. Careers in petroleum and natural gas.
26. Careers in printing.

CHARLIE CHOPPERS SERIES

9 volumes projected. Wholesome Press. $6.95 each, paper.

Charlie Choppers is a "brightly illustrated little boy who smiles his way through the food rules" and learns about nutrition and health. One volume available. *Middle.*

Goresht, Anne; Charlie Choppers grows and grows.

THE CREDIT VALLEY SERIES

17 volumes. Boston Mills Press. From $3.00 to $5.95 paper.

THE HALTON COUNTY SERIES

4 volumes. Boston Mills Press. From $4.00 to $5.95, paper.

THE WELLINGTON COUNTY SERIES

3 volumes. Boston Mills Press. From $3.00 to $5.95, paper.

This press, located in Cheltenham, Ontario, is representative of regional publishing at its best. Although the materials are not primarily for children, they do add another dimension to the study of local history. The *Great horseshoe wreck, Milton, Steam trains through Orangeville* are representative titles. *Older to mature.*

DOCUMENTS IN CANADIAN HISTORY

4 volumes. Ontario Institute for Studies in Education. Prices vary.

The Canadian Studies Foundation encouraged the preparation of primary resource materials to be used in the teaching of Canadian history. These were developed by French- and English-Canadian teachers for supplementary reference use in elementary and secondary schools. Useful for all libraries. *Mature.*

1. Debates about Canada's future 1868-1896. $6.75 [0-7744-0148-6]
2. Lower Canada in the 1830's. $6.75 [0-7744-0149-4]
3. New France 1713-1760. $6.55 [7744-0144-3]
4. Upper Canada in the 1830's. $7.20 [0-7744-0143-5]

EDIBLE WILD PLANTS OF CANADA SERIES

4 volumes. National Museum of Natural Sciences. Prices vary.

Szczawinski, Adam F. and **Nancy J. Turner;** Edible garden weeds of Canada. $8.95 [660-00026-1]

Szczawinski, Adam F. and **Nancy J. Turner;** Wild green vegetables of Canada. $9.95 [660-10342-7]

Turner, Nancy J. and **Adam F. Szczawinski;** Edible wild fruits and nuts of Canada. $9.95 [660-00128-4]

Turner, Nancy J. and **Adam F. Szczawinski;** Wild coffee and tea substitutes of Canada. $6.95 [660-00090-3]

ELEMENTS SERIES

4 volumes. PMA Books. $4.95 each, paper.

Inspired anthologies of Canadian writing focused on subjects related to the elements, well illustrated, well designed, and well edited by Peter Carver. *Mature.*

Air. [0-88778-163-2]
Earth. [0-88778-162-4]
Fire. [0-88778-164-0]
Water. [0-88778-165-9]

FACE-OFF SERIES

3 volumes. EMC Corporation, St. Paul, Minnesota (Dent), 1973. $6.55 each.

Short novels about boys and hockey illustrated by Kenneth M. Shields and written by Scott Young. *Middle.*

Learning to be captain. [0-912022-58-2]

The Moscow challengers. [0-912022-57-4]

The Silent one speaks up. [0-912022-59-0]

THE 5W SERIES

11 volumes. Royal Ontario Museum. $1.25 each, paper

This series of illustrated booklets has been written by members of the Royal Ontario Museum staff, designed as introductions to diverse subjects.

Brett, K.B.; Women's costume in early Ontario. [0-88854-050-7]

Brett, K.B.; Women's costume in Ontario 1867-1907. [0-88854-063-9]

Needler, W.; Jewellery of the ancient Near East. [0-88854-057-4]

Rogers, E.S.; False face society of the Iroquois. [0-88854-059-0]

Russell, L.S.; Lighting the pioneer Ontario home. [0-88854-061-2]

Russell, L.S.; The Mastodon. [0-88854-055-8]

Stevens, G.; Early Ontario furniture. [0-88854-062-0]

Stevens, G.; Early Ontario glass. [0-88854-051-5]

Swinton, W.E.; Dinosaurs of Canada. [0-88854-054-X]

Swinton, W.E.; Evolution. [0-88854-056-6]

Tovell, W.M.; The Niagara Escarpment. [0-88854-052-3]

FOLKTALE SERIES

8 volumes. Kids Can. $2.95 each, paper.

Meaningfully illustrated bilingual retellings of folk tales originating in the countries that people multicultural Canada. *Middle to older.*

Bannerji, Himani; The Two sisters. [0-919964-15-X]

Bertelli, Mariella; The Shirt of the happy man. [0-919964-17-6]

Chandon, Odarka; Kyrylo, the tanner. [0-919964-16-8]

Cox, Rita; How trouble made the monkey eat pepper. [0-919964-14-1]

Johnston, Basil; How the birds got their colours. [0-919964-19-2]

Ling, Frieda; The Maiden of Wu Long and Lau, Mee-Shan; The Axe and the sword. [0-919964-18-4]

McDougall, M.M.; The Little rooster's diamond penny. [0-919964-21-4]

Mascayano, Ismael; The Daughter of the sun. [0-919964-20-6]

FOOTPRINTS IN TIME

4 volumes. Dent. Prices vary.

Documentary sourcebooks of Canadian, Ontario and British history and early exploration. Illustrations include contemporary newspaper items, diary entries, photographs and maps. *Older to mature.*

Reid, Raymond A.; Footprints in time: Ontario. Dent, 1967. $4.50 paper [0-460-91743-9]

Richardson, Edwin A. (ed.) and **Thexton, James D.** (ed.); Footprints in time: a sourcebook in British history. Dent, 1963. $4.50 cloth [0-460-91735-8]

Smith, H. Murray (ed.); Footprints in time: a sourcebook in Canadian history for young people. Dent, 1962. $4.00 cloth [0-460-91737-4]

Trant, Ross; Footprints in time: a sourcebook in the history of discovery. Dent, 1970. $3.95 cloth [0-460-91739-0]

THE GAGE CANADIAN STUDIES SERIES

4 volumes. Gage. $9.95 each.

Useful for general reference in any library these textbooks deal with Canadian socio-economic developments. *Mature.*

Mitchner, E.A. and others; Forging a destiny: Canada since 1945. [0-7715-8529-2]

Stewart, Roderick and **McLean, Neil;** Forming a nation: the story of Canada and Canadians. Book 1[0-7715-8519-5]

Stewart, Roderick and McLean, Neil; Forming a nation: The story of Canada and Canadians. Book 2 [0-7715-8521-7]

Wood, Dean and **Remnant, Robert;** The People we are: Canada's multicultural society.

GEOLOGICAL GUIDE BOOKS

5 volumes. Ontario. Ministry of Natural Resources. $2.00 each, paper.

Straightforward resumés of the general geology of four areas in Ontario and descriptions of various points of geological interest near access routes in these areas. Written for the novice the guide books include colour and black and white photographs of the geology and scenery of the areas, a glossary of technical terms, and an appendix of localities where specimens may be obtained. The fifth guide book gives an account of Ontario's official mineral - the amethyst. *Mature.*

Hewitt, D.T.; Geology and scenery, Peterborough, Bancroft and Madoc area.

Ontario. Ministry of Natural Resources; Geology and scenery, north shore of Lake Superior.

Pye, E.G.; Geology and scenery, Rainy Lake and east to Lake Superior.

Robertson, J.A. and **Card, K.D.;** Geology and scenery, north shore of Lake Huron Region.

Vos, M.A.; Amethyst deposits of Ontario.

GINN STUDIES IN CANADIAN HISTORY

19 volumes, and teacher's manual. Ginn. $43.56 per set (one of each title) $9.00 packet of five (same title)

Short, profusely illustrated accounts of historical events, written especially for students. *Middle.*

Allaby, Eric; Shipbuilding in the Maritimes. [7702-0131-8]

Andrews, Elizabeth; Ellen Elliott: a pioneer. [7702-0135-0]

Andrews, R.J.; Battle at Quebec 1759. [0-7702-0111-3]

Andrews, R.J.; The fur fort. [7702-0107-5]

Andrews, R.J.; Soldier at Quebec: 1759. [7702-0121-0]

Andrews, R.J.; Spy at Quebec: 1759. [7702-0127-X]

Andrews, R.J.; The Voyageurs. [7702-0101-6]

Brennan, Terence J.; The timber trade in the Ottawa Valley. [7702-0129-6]

Coatsworth, David; Farmers of the east: Huron Indians. [7702-0141-5]

Coatsworth, Emerson, S.; Nomads of the Shield: Ojibway Indians. [7702-0105-9]

Coatsworth, Emerson S.; Treaties and promises: Saulteaux Indians. [7702-0133-4]

Feather, Donald and **Waters, George;** Fort York. [7702-0125-3]

Harper, Peter; Gold Rush in the Cariboo. [7702-0137-7]

Hawkes, Christopher; Sainte-Marie among the Hurons. [7702-0123-7]

Smith, D.C.; Colonists at Port Royal. [7702-0103-2]

Smith, D.C.; The Seigneury of Longueuil. [7702-0117-2]

Symington, D.F.; Hunters of the Plains: Assiniboine Indians. [7702-0119-9]

Symington, D.F.; Seafaring warriors of the west: Nootka Indians. [7702-0109-1]

Wilson, K.; Life at Red River: 1830-1860. [7702-0115-6]

GREAT STORIES OF CANADA

21 volumes. Macmillan of Canada. Prices vary.

Competent writers have contributed to this series "to recount history in story form, in a manner appealing to the young reader," Josephine Phelan's *The Ballad of D'Arcy McGee,* Pierre Berton's *The Golden Trail,* Joseph Schull's *The Salt-Water Men* represent the best of the series and some of the best Canadian historical writing for children. *Older.*

Berton, Pierre; The Golden trail. $4.95, cloth [0-7705-1052-3]; $2.95, paper [0-7705-1053-1]

Campbell, Marjorie Wilkins; The Nor'westers. $4.95, cloth [0-7705-1054-X]; $2.95, paper [0-7705-1055-8]

Campbell, Marjorie Wilkins; Savage river. $1.95, paper [0-7705-0097-5]

Chalmers, J.W.; Red River adventure. $5.95, cloth [0-7705-0137-0]

Fairley, T.C.; The True north. $2.95 paper [0-7705-0989-4]

Farrar, F.S.; Arctic assignment. $4.95, cloth [0-7705-1056-6]; $2.95, paper [0-7705-1057-4]

Ferguson, Robert D.; Man from St. Malo. $4.95, cloth [0-7705-1058-2]; $2.95, paper [0-7705-1059-0]

Goodspeed, D.J.; The Good soldier. $2.95 paper [0-7705-0994-0]

Haig-Brown, Roderick; Captain of the Discovery. $4.95, cloth [0-7705-1060-4]; $2.95, paper [0-7705-1061-2]

Lambert, Richard S.; Mutiny in the Bay. $1.95, paper [0-7705-0988-6]

Lambert, Richard S.; Redcoat sailor. $4.95, cloth [0-7705-0136-2]; $1.95, paper [0-7705-0988-6]

Longstreth, T. Morris; The Scarlet force. $4.95, cloth [0-7705-1062-0]; $2.95, paper [0-7705-1063-9]

McCourt, Edward; Buckskin brigadier. $4.95, cloth [0-7705-0131-1].

Miller, Orlo; Raiders of the Mohawk. $4.95, cloth [0-7705-0128-1]

Phelan, Josephine; The Ballad of D'Arcy McGee. $4.95, cloth [0-7705-0158-3]; $1.95, paper [0-7705-0996-7]

Phelan, Josephine; The Bold heart. $4.95, cloth [0-7705-0135-4]

Ritchie, C,T.; The First Canadian. $4.95, cloth [0-7705-0149-4]

Schull, Joseph; The Salt-water men. $1.00, paper [0-7705-0991-6]

Wilson, Clifford; Adventures from the Bay. $4.95 [0-7705-0150-8]

Wood, Kerry; The Great chief. $1.95, paper [0-7705-0990-8]

Wood, Kerry; The Queen's cowboy. $1.95, paper [0-7705-0992-4]

GROWTH OF A NATION SERIES

9 volumes. Fitzhenry. $2.95 each, paper.

Intended for school use, these brief illustrated social histories illuminate specific periods in Canadian life. *Middle.*

Neering, Rosemary and **Garrod, Stan;** Building a new life. [0-88902-072-3]

Neering, Rosemary and **Gregory, Richard;** Building of the railway. [0-88902-177-5]

Neering, Rosemary; Fur trade. Gregory, Richard (illus.) [0-88902-179-1]

Neering, Rosemary; Gold rush; Gregory, Richard (illus.) [0-88902-175-9]

Neering, Rosemary and **Garrod, Stan;** In the pioneer home. [0-88902-187-2]

Neering, Rosemary and **Garrod, Stan;** Life in New France. Smith, Merle (illus.) [0-88902-181-3]

Neering, Rosemary and **Garrod, Stan;** Life of the Loyalists. Smith, Merle (illus.) [0-88902-182-1]

Neering, Rosemary; Northwest Mounted Police. Gregory, Richard (illus.) [0-88902-176-7]

Neering, Rosemary; Settlement of the West. Gregory, Richard (illus.) [0-88902-178-3]

THE HISTORY OF CANADIAN CITIES

2 volumes. Lorimer. Prices vary.

Developed by the National Museum of Man each book is illustrated with photographs that record all aspects of each city's life story. *Mature.*

Artibise, Alan; Winnipeg: an illustrated history. $19.95, cloth [0-88862-150-7]; $11.95, paper [0-88862-151-5]

Foran, Max; Calgary: an illustrated history. $19.95, cloth [0-88862-224-4]

HIYOU SERIES

4 volumes. Commcept. $7.65 each.

Four weighty volumes in a "Canadian Language Arts Programme" for grades four through seven which can nevertheless serve as excellent anthologies of Canadian writing for young people. *Middle to mature.*

Book 1. Hiyou tillicum. [0-88829-030-6]
Book 2. Hiyou tumtum. [0-88829-032-2]

Book 3. Hiyou waw-waw [0-88829-034-9]
Book 4. Hiyou muckamuck. [0-88829-036-5]

HOW THEY LIVED IN CANADA

5 volumes. Douglas & McIntyre. $6.95 each.

These well illustrated, simply written social histories of our Native peoples' life before the white man came will inform any reader. *Middle to older.*

Campbell, Maria; People of the buffalo. [0-88894-089-0]

Campbell, Maria; Riel's people. [0-88894-222-2]

McConkey, Lois; Sea and cedar. [0-88894-042-4]

Marshall, Ingeborg; The Red ochre people. [0-88894-157-9]

Ridington, Robin and **Ridington, Jill;** People of the trail. [0-88894-221-4]

THE ILLUSTRATED NATURAL HISTORY OF CANADA SERIES

12 volumes. Natural Science (McClelland) $10.95 each.

Beautifully illustrated, well-researched and readable books on the natural history and indigenous fauna of Canadian geographical regions. *Mature.*

Allen, Robert Thomas; The Great Lakes. [0-919644-01-5]

Bodsworth, Fred; The Pacific coast. [0-919644-03-1]

Braithwaite, Max; The Western plains. [0-919644-07-4]

Drew, Wayland, et al; The Nature of fish. [0-919644-12-0]

Drew, Wayland, et al; The Nature of mammals. [0-919644-11-2]

Edwards, Yorke; The Mountain barrier. [0-919644-05-8]

Knight, James A., et al; The Nature of birds. [0-919644-10-4]

Lefolii, Ken; The St. Lawrence Valley. [0-919644-04-X]

Livingston, John; Canada: the subcontinent. [0-919644-09-0]

Moon, Barbara; The Canadian shield. [0-919644-08-2]

Russell, Franklin; The Atlantic coast. [0-919644-06-6]

Wilkinson, Douglas; The Arctic coast. [0-919644-02-3]

IN THE PUBLIC INTEREST LAW SERIES

10 volumes, more projected. I.P.I. (libraries); Gage (schools); French editions from Editions Champlain. $5.00 each, paper.

These pamphlets attempt to rationalize Canadian law for the layman giving everyday examples and court decisions; each one has a glossary, bibliography and index. Teachers' manuals are available. *Mature.*

Cohl, K.A.; I.P.I. update 1979. [0-920702-18-X]

Cohl, K.A.; Sexuality and the law. [0-920702-10-4]

Cohl, K.A.; Tort law. [0-920702-14-7]. Also available in French as: La Loi sur les torts. [0-920936-02-4]

Deibert, Karl; Criminal law. [0-920702-02-3]. Also available in French as: Le droit criminel. [0-920936-04-0]

Deibert, Karl; Law and the labour force. [0-920702-08-2]

Merker, M.; Consumer law. [0-920702-00-7]

Merker, M.; Family law. [0-920702-04-X]. Also available in French as: Le droit familial. [0-920936-06-7]

Ungar, Susan; An Introduction to law. [0-920702-06-6]. Also available in French as: Introduction au droit. [0-920936-00-8]

Ungar, Susan; Student rights and responsibilities. [0-920702-12-0]

Worldmann, Peter I. and **McMurray, Hilarie;** Human rights and the law. $6.95 [0-920702-16-3]

IN YOUR COMMUNITY

3 volumes. Dent. $2.95 each, paper.

How the community is served by its social service workers. *Younger.*

Dobson, Murray; Dobson, Vera and **Peters, James;** The Letter carrier. [0-460-92925-9]

Peters, James and **Dobson, Murray;** The Policeman. [0-460-94138-0]

Peters, James; Peters, Julie and **Dobson, Murray;** The Firefighter. [0-460-91669-6]

INDIANS OF CANADA SERIES

6 volumes. Royal Ontario Museum, 1970. $1.00 each.

Short, general histories of the Indians of Canada by E.S. Rogers conclude with brief notes on present day trends. *Older.*

The Indians of Canada: A Survey. [88854-037-X]

Iroquoians of the Eastern Woodlands. [88854-038-8]

Algonkians of the Eastern Woodlands. [88854-039-6]

Indians of the Plains. [88854-040-X]

Indians of the North Pacific Coast. [88854-041-8]

Indians of the Subarctic. [88854-042-6]

KIDS LIKE US

12 volumes. Methuen. Prices below.

These multicultural readers by Beverley Allinson and Barbara O'Kelly feature four youngsters of different ethnic backgrounds - Chinese, Chilean, Trinidadian and Jamaican - who are friendly neighbours in Toronto. *Middle to older.*

$8.95 per set, paper (use ISBN 0-458-92130]; $3.95 each title.

Click. [0-458-92150-5]

Flashback. [0-458-92110-6]

Trips. [0-458-92170-0]

Wallpaper. [0-458-92130-0]

$8.95 per set, paper (use ISBN 0-458-92850]; $3.95 each title.

Groaning ups. [0-458-924-90-3]

Short stop. [0-458-925-10-1]

Small talk. [0-458-925-00-4]

Turkey pops. [0-458-924-80-6]

$8.95 per set, paper (use ISBN 0-458-93460]; $3.95 each title.

The Hardcastle legacy. [0-458-93140]

The Phantom sailors. [0-458-93150]

The Secret formula. [0-458-93120]

The Westwoods monster. [0-458-93130]

KIDS OF CANADA SERIES

9 volumes. Lorimer. $6.95 each.

Meant for beginning readers these short simple stories deal with everyday problems faced by ordinary kids. Realistic full colour illustrations. *Younger.*

Allison, Rosemary; The Pillow. [0-88862-245-7]

Atwood, Margaret and **Barkhouse, Joyce;** Anna's pet. [0-88862-249-X]

Dewdney, Selwyn; The Hungry time. [0-88862-261-9]

Dickson, Barry; Afraid of the dark. [0-88862-255-4]

Kidd, Bruce; Hockey showdown. [0-88862-251-1]

Kidd, Bruce; Who's a soccer player. [0-88862-253-8]

Laurence, Margaret; Six darn cows. [0-88862-247-3]

O'Young, Leoung; Mike and the bike. [0-88862-257-0]

We make Canada shine: poems by children. $3.95 paper [0-88862-288-0]

MAKWA BOOKS

6 volumes. Peguis. $1.50 each, paper.

Primarily used with the 4 to 7 age group among Native children learning to read these simple books appeal to beginning readers anywhere. *Younger.*

Dalby, Lois and **McCrie, Jeanette;** The Bang book. [0-919566-15-4]

Dalby, Lois and **McCrie, Jeanette;** Grandma knows. [0-919566-12-X]

Dalby, Lois and **McCrie, Jeanette;** Here I go. [0-919566-14-6]

Dalby, Lois and **McCrie, Jeanette;** Jack and Jet. [0-919566-13-8]

Dalby, Lois and **McCrie, Jeanette;** A Little mouse. [0-919566-16-2]

Dalby, Lois and **McCrie, Jeanette;** The New baby. [0-919566-17-0]

MINI BOOKS FOR MINI HANDS

4 volumes. Tundra (Collins) $0.69 each, paper.
Whimsical and appealing small books for very small people. *Younger.*

Andrews, Jan.; An elephant/Un éléphant Ella. [0-88776-063-5]

Andrews, Jan.; A moth/Une mite Pouf. [0-88776-065-1]

Stevenson, Marla; A toad/Un crapaud Bufo. [0-88776-064-3]

Stratford, Philip; A dog/Un chien Olive. [0-88776-062-7]

MULTICULTURAL CANADA SERIES

4 volumes. Van Nostrand. $4.95 each, paper.

Historical profiles of single families through several generations that explore the contributions to Canadian society made by particular ethnic, racial and religious groups. *Older.*

Burke, Marguerite V.; The Ukrainian Canadians. [0-442-29863-3]

Flint, Joanne; The Mennonite Canadians. [0-442-29747-5]

Ito, Roy; The Japanese Canadians. [0-442-29891-9]

Mastrangelo, Rocco; The Italian Canadians. [0-442-29775-0]

NATURAL HISTORY NOTEBOOK SERIES

3 volumes. The National Museum of Natural Sciences. $2.00 each.

Illustrated by Charles Douglas these one page "fillers" include a line drawing and a succinct description of animals, birds, reptiles, amphibians and insects found in Canada. *Middle.*

Natural History Notebook No. 1 [0-660-00092-X]

Natural History Notebook No. 2 [0-660-00094-6]

Natural History Notebook No. 3. [0-660-10341-9]

NORTHERN LIGHTS

6 volumes. PMA Books. $6.95 each.

Well edited by Mary Alice Downie these personal adventures woven around a fragment of Canadian life will involve beginning readers in memorable experiences. *Younger to middle.*

Downie, Mary Alice; The Last ship. Calvert, Lissa (illus.) [0-88778-201-9]

Hamilton, Mary; The Sky caribou. Perna, Debi (illus.) [0-887778-203-5]

McSweeney, Susanne; The Yellow flag. Clark, Brenda (illus.) [0-88778-204-3]

Rawlyk, George; Streets of gold. O'Young, Leoung (illus.) [0-88778-202-7]

Swainson, Donald and **Eleanor;** The Buffalo hunt. Smith, Mark (illus.) [0-88778-206-X]

Tanaka, Shelley; Michi's doll. Berg, Ron (illus.) [0-88778-205-1]

THE OLYMPIC LIBRARY OF CANADA

6 volumes. Colban of Canada, 400 Dundas St. W., Suite 201, Whitby, Ontario L1N 2M7. Set of 6 $15.00 or $2.95 each, paper.

Covering all amateur sports represented at the modern Olympic games, each volume describes the history and development, rules and regulations and training and coaching methods for a particular sport. *Older.*

Beddoes, Dick; Skating. [0-88966-052-2]

Mellor, Bob; Skiing. [0-88966-050-6]

O'Brien, Andy; Bobsled and luge. [0-88966-056-5]

Pennington, Bob; All about Olympians. [0-88966-235-5]

Roxborough, Henry H.; The Olympic story. [0-88966-048-4]

Smith, Maurice; Ice hockey. [0-88966-054-9]

ORACLES

15 pamphlets. Order from Loans Officer, National Loans Programme, Communications Division, National Museum of Man, 921 St. Laurent Blvd., Ottawa K1A 0M8. Free.

Short, popular, illustrated pamphlets also available in French. *Older.*

The Beothuks

The Borden system of site identification

The Confederation café

Eskimo history

Indian rattles

The Iroquois

Kung Fu

Land of the maple leaf

Making do: The depression years in Alberta

On Canadian identity

Ontario prehistory

Skin, snow, stone and bone

The Story of Nuliajuk

Traditional Canadian folk music

OXFORD CANADIAN PICTORIAL SERIES

14 volumes, more projected. Oxford. $12.95 each.

Outstanding colour photographs with captions and short introductions give us a pictorial representation of specific places and regions, some recreating the past, e.g. *Fortress of Louisburg. Middle to older.*

Barrett, Wayne; Kings Landing. [0-19-540301-0]

Barrett, Wayne; Prince Edward Island. [0-19-540276-6]

Cormier, Romeo; Image of Acadia. [0-19-540330-14]

de Visser, John; Newfoundland and Labrador. [0-19-540336-3]

Drummond, Michael; Montreal and its countryside. [0-19-540308-8]

Fitzgerald, Owen; Cape Breton. [0-19-540295-2]

Fitzgerald, Owen; Fortress of Louisburg. [0-19-540302-9]

Fowler, Peter; Bruce Trail country. [0-19-540299-5]

Fowler, Peter; Cottage country. [0-19-540300-2]

Haas, Rudi; Ottawa, our nation's capital. [0-19-540340-1]

Hines, Sherman; Nova Scotia, lighthouse route and the Annapolis Valley. [0-19-540319-3]

Redivo, Hugo; The Skanagan. [0-19-540286-3]

Simpkins, Bill; Chinook county; Alberta south. [0-19-540307-X]

von Baich, Paul; The Yukon. [0-19-540303-7]

PAPER SCULPTURES

3 volumes. National Museums of Canada, Marketing Services Division, Ottawa K1A 0M8. 8 pages each. $1.75 each, paper.

Bilingual informational booklets are intended for children aged twelve and up. The centre pages of the booklet can be pulled out, cut up, shaped, assembled, and glued to make a life-like three-dimensional coloured paper sculpture. *Older.*

Old Fourlegs: a "living fossil"/Le vieux quadrupède, "fossile vivant". [0-660-00010-5]

Triceratops, a Dinosaur/Le triceratops, un dinosaure. [0-660-00020-2]

The Polar Bear/L'ours blanc. [0-660-00021-0]

PONA SERIES

8 volumes projected. Fitzhenry. $3.95 each, paper.

A realistic picture of the lives of modern Canadian Native people developed by the Canadian Association in Support of the Native Peoples in cooperation with the Ontario Ministry of Education. *Older.*

Beaudry, Lindsay; Kawin. [0-88902-143-0]

Benedict, Rebecca and **Wahl, Chris;** St. Regis Reserve. [0-88902-137-6]

Cockburn, Bruce; Native country record (recording). $3.95 [88902-1449]

Monture, Sharon and **McSweeney, John;** Fort Albany Reserve. [0-88902-138-4]

PRIME MINISTERS OF CANADA

5 volumes. McGraw. $14.95 each.
Profusely illustrated full length biographies of the prime ministers, setting them in the social and political milieu of their times. *Mature.*

Bothwell, Robert; Pearson, his life and world. [0-07-082305-7]

Clippingdale, Richard; Laurier, his life and world. [0-07-082302-0]

English, John; Borden, his life and world. [0-07-082303-0]

Granatstein, J.L.; Mackenzie King, his life and world. [0-07-082304-9]

Waite, P.B.; Macdonald, his life and world. [0-07-082301-4]

ROM NORTH AMERICAN INDIAN CHARTS

6 charts. Royal Ontario Museum. $4.25 each.
Full colour wall posters illustrating various aspects of the culture of our Native people as well as specific artifacts of three principal tribes. *All ages.*

Assiniboine Indians. [0-88855-014-5]
Musical instruments. [0-88855-015-4]
Naskapi Indians. [0-88855-018-9]
Quillwork. [0-88855-016-2]
Toys and games. [0-88855-017-0]
Woodland Cree Indians. [0-88855-019-7]

SPORTS AND RECREATION SERIES

36 volumes. Colban of Canada, 400 Dundas St. W., Suite 201, Whitby, Ontario L1N 2M7. 32 pages each. $2.50 paper. $2.00 to schools.

Short, clear, illustrated books explain the basic elements of sports and games to 6-16 year olds. *Middle to mature.*

Banitz, K.E.; Basic skating is fun. Sinclair, D.R. (illus.) [0-88966-156-1]

Banitz, K.E.; Cross country skiing. Ford, Eric (illus.) [0-88966-011-5]

Banitz, K.E.; Five-pin bowling is fun. Ford, Eric (illus.) [0-88966-098-0]

Banitz, K.E.; The game of soccer. Ford, Eric (illus.) [0-88966-004-2]

Banitz, K.E.; Hooray for hockey. Raynor, Gordon (illus.) [0-88966-002-6]

Banitz, K.E.; Softball is fun, McRae, Jock (illus.) [0-88966-003-4]

Banitz, K.E.; T-Softball is fun. Dermaut, Beatrice (illus.) [0-88966-035-2]

Banitz, K.E.; Table tennis. Ford, Eric (illus.) [0-88966-009-3]

Banitz, K.E.; T-Ball is fun, Raynor. Gordon (illus.) [0-88966-001-8]

Craig, John; Archery is fun. Ford, Eric (illus.) [0-88966-024-5]

Craig, John; Baseball is fun, Raynor. Gordon (illus.) [0-88966-033-6]

Craig, John; Basketball is fun. Ford, Eric (illus.) [0-88966-015-8]

Craig, John; Boxing is fun, Raynor. Gordon (illus.) [0-88966-041-7]

Craig, John; Boys' gymnastics are fun! Ford, Eric (illus.) [0-88966-106-5]

Craig, John; Field hockey is fun! Jacob, Hersh (illus.) [0-88966-037-9]

Craig, John; Floor hockey is fun! Moir, Bill (illus.) [0-88966-100-6]

Craig, John; Football is fun! Raynor, Gordon (illus.) [0-88966-017-4]

Craig, John; Free-style wrestling. Manley, Stanley (illus.) [0-88966-021-2]

Craig, John; Girls' gymnastics are fun! Dermaut, Beatrice (illus.) [0-88966-108-1]

Craig, John; Greco-Roman wrestling. Ford, Eric (illus.) [0-88966-023-9]

Craig, John; Lacrosse is fun! Ford. Eric (illus.) [0-88966-027-1]

Craig, John; Running is fun; Sinclair. D.V. (illus.) [0-88966-062-X]

Craig, John; Team handball. Jacob, Hersh (illus.) [0-88966-019-0]

Craig, John; Volleyball is fun. Ford, Eric (illus.) [0-88966-013-1]

Craig, John; Waterpolo is fun. Jacob, Hersh (illus.) [0-88966-031-X]

Griffin, Rowlan; Epis is fun; Ford, Eric (illus.) [0-88966-092-1]

Haunsberger, Leo; Judo is fun. Ford, Eric (illus.) [0-88966-122-7]

Milburn, G.N. Squash is fun! Moir, Bill (illus.) [0-88966-252-5]

Muir, Randy; Tobogganing is fun! Illus. by the author. [0-88966-243-6]

O'Bryan, Maureen; Netball is fun! Ford, Eric (illus.) [0-88966-130-8]

O'Bryan, Maureen; Synchronized swimming is fun! Dermaut, Beatrice (illus.) [0-88966-172-3]

O'Bryan, Maureen; Tennis is fun! Dermaut, Beatrice (illus.) [0-88966-029-8]

O'Bryan, Maureen; Tin can curling. Muir, Randy (illus.) [0-88966-177-4]

Terhune, Dave; Enjoy the guitar. Moir, Bill (illus.) [0-88966-262-2]

Towson, R.T.; Snorkeling is fun! Jacob, Hersh (illus.) [0-88966-256-8]

Wipper, Kirk; Snowshoeing is fun! Ford, Eric (illus.) [0-88966-254-1]

STUDIES IN CANADIAN GEOGRAPHY

6 volumes. U.T.P. Prices vary.

Interpret the main characteristics and unique attributes of the geographic regions of Canada–environment, settlement, economy, political-territorial structure and main cities–using graphs and maps. Reliable readable studies for mature readers and for reference purposes. *Mature*.

Gentilcore, R. Loma; Ontario. $10.00 cloth [0-8020-1919-6]; $5.50 paper [0-8020-6160-5]

Grenier, Fernand; Quebec. $12.50 cloth [0-8020-1918-8]; $5.50 paper [0-8020-1918-8]

MacPherson, A.G.; The Atlantic provinces. $12.50 cloth [0-8020-1916-1]; $5.50 paper [0-8020-6158-3]

Robinson, J.L.; British Columbia/Colombie britannique. $5.50 paper [0-8020-6162-1]

Smith, P.J.; The Prairie provinces/Les provinces de la prairie. $5.50 paper [0-8020-6161-3]

Wonders, W. C.; The North/Le nord. $12.50 cloth [0-8020-1923-4]; $5.50 paper [0-8020-6164-8]

SUPERPEOPLE SERIES

3 volumes. Fitzhenry. $6.95 each, cloth; $3.95 each, paper.

Short (48 pages) readable biographies of well-known Canadians in sports, illustrated with action photographs, written by Fred McFadden. *Middle*.

Abby Hoffman. [0-88903-050-2]

Bobby Clarke. [0-88903-045-6]

Ken Dryden. [0-88903-048-0]

TEACHERS AND WRITERS EDUCATION PROJECT RESOURCE GUIDES

10 volumes and introductory handbook. The Writers' Development Trust, 86 Bloor St. W., Toronto. $2.00 each, or set of 10 for $15.00, paper.

Developed by teams of teachers across Canada these resource guides will assist high school teachers to develop dynamic courses in Canadian literature. They are also excellent guides to individual study for mature readers. *Mature*.

1. The North/Native peoples.
2. Coming of age in Canada.
3. The Immigrant experience.
4. New Land/New language.
5. Family relationships.
6. Action/Adventure.
7. Quebec literature in translation.
8. Images of biculturalism.
9. Social realism.
10. Women in Canadian literature.

THEMES IN CANADIAN LITERATURE

17 volumes. Macmillan. Prices vary.

A short introduction prefaces poems, plays, stories, articles and excerpts from Canadian writing on specific themes, one per volume. Readers experience the authors' writing, not writing about their writing. Meant for courses in Canadian studies, the anthologies are excellent introductions to themes in Canadian literature. *Older to mature.*

Angus, Terry (ed); The Prairie experience. $2.80 [0-7705-1260-7]

Arnason, David (ed.); Isolation in Canadian literature. $2.80 [0-7705-1270-4]

Bailey, Leuba (ed.); The Immigrant experience. $2.95 [0-7705-1261-5]

Foley, James (ed.); The Search for identity. $2.95 [0-7705-1262-3]

Ford, Theresa (ed.); Canadian humour & satire. $2.95 [0-7705-1263-1]

Hale, Alice (ed.); and **Sheila Brooks** (ed.); The Depression in Canadian literature. $2.80 [0-7705-1365-4]

Hesse, M.G. (ed.); Childhood and Youth in Canadian literature. $3.00 [0-7705-1598-3]

Hodgins, Jack (ed.); The Frontier Experience. $2.80 [0-7705-1264-X]

Hodgins, Jack (ed.); The West Coast experience. $2.80 [0-7705-1366-2]

McCullough, Elizabeth (ed.); The Role of women in Canadian literature. $2.80 [0-7705-1265-8]

Mowat, William and **Christine** (ed.); Native peoples in Canadian literature. $2.80 [0-7705-1268-2]

Nowlan, Michael O. (ed.); Canadian myths & legends. $2.95 [0-7705-1364-6]

Nowlan, Michael O. (ed.); The Maritime experience. $2.80 [0-7705-1266-6]

Saint-Pierre, Gaston (ed.); The French-Canadian experience. $3.40 [0-7705-1363-0]

Stevens, John (ed.); The Ontario experience. $2.80 [0-7705-1362-X]

Stevens, John (ed.); The Urban experience. $2.80 [0-7705-1267-4]

Wilson, Lionel (ed.); The Artist in Canadian literature. $2.95 [0-7705-1269-0]

TORONTO PUBLIC LIBRARY BOARD LOCAL HISTORY HANDBOOKS

2 volumes. Toronto Public Library. $2.00 each, paper.

Well-designed, well-illustrated and well-written local histories. *Older to mature.*

1. Myrvold, Barbara; North Toronto in pictures, 1889-1912.

2. Hutcheson, Stephanie; Yorkville in pictures, 1853-1883. [0-919486-69-X]

WE BUILT CANADA

8 volumes published, more projected. Book Society. $2.95 each, paper.

Short, illustrated social histories on Canadian pioneers for students. *Middle to older.*

Davies, Colin; Louis Riel and the new nation. [0-7725-5293-2]

Gregor, Alexander D.; Vilhjalmur Stefansson and the Arctic. [0-7725-5257-8]

Osborne, K.W.; R.B. Russell and the labor movement. [0-7725-5255-6]

Sealey, D. Bruce; Cuthbert Grant and the Métis. [0-7725-5285-1]

Sealey, D. Bruce; The Mounties and law enforcement. [0-7725-5292-4]

Wilson, Case; Donald Smith and the Canadian Pacific Railway. [0-7725-5289-4]

Wilson, Keith; George Simpson and the Hudson's Bay Company. [0-7725-5286-X]

Wright, Helen K.; Nellie McClung and women's rights. [0-7725-5290-8]

WILD RIVERS

7 volumes. Parks Canada.
$1.50 each, paper.

Clear and informative booklets on the topography of the areas in which the rivers flow; useful for experienced canoeists planning white-water trips. *Mature.*

Alberta

Central British Columbia

James Bay and Hudson Bay

Newfoundland and Labrador

Quebec North Shore

Saskatchewan

Yukon Territory

WOMEN AT WORK

12 volumes. Heath. $9.50 for set of 5. $9.50 for series of 4, paper.

Three series of four books each meant as readers for grades 2, 3 and 4, but entirely suitable as library resource material on working women. Based on the careers of real women, the books are well-written and illustrated with meaningful photographs. *Younger to older.*

Series for Grade 2

Allinson, Beverley and **Lawrence, Judith;**

Behind the scenes. [0-669-00536-3]

Clowning around. [0-669-00534-7]

Hammer and tongs. [0-669-00535-5]

Hand and glove. [0-669-00537-1]

Series for Grade 3

Allinson, Beverley and **Lawrence, Judith;**

Doctor Mary's animals. [0-669-95216-8]

Ellie sells fish. [0-669-95208-7]

Maryon makes shapes. [0-669-05190-0]

Myra builds a house. [0-669-95224-9]

Series for Grade 4

Allinson, Beverley and **Lawrence, Judith;**

Let's take a vote. [0-669-95331-8]

Open wide. [0-669-95349-0]

Ready for take-off. [0-669-95323-7]

Take one. [0-699-96315-6]

WOMEN IN CANADIAN LIFE

4 volumes. Fitzhenry. $4.95 each, paper.

Planned as historical studies on the role of women in specific areas of Canadian society. These short, illustrated books aptly introduce their subjects. *Older.*

Cochrane, Jean; Women in Canadian politics. [0-88903-053-7]

Cochrane, Jean; Hoffman, Abby and **Kincaid, Pat;** Women in Canadian sports. [0-88903-052-9]

Dranoff, Linda Silver; Women in Canadian law. [0-88903-051-0]

McClung, M.G.; Women in Canadian literature. [0-88903-054-5]

ZAP SERIES

9 volumes. Fitzhenry. $3.95 each, paper.

"A compelling conglomeration of fact, story, poetry, history, legend and folklore, games and interviews with a sprinkling of things to do." *Middle to older.*

Zap eating. [0-88902-205-X]

Zap fire. [0-88902-251-8]

Zap flying. [0-88902-257-7]

Zap hockey. [0-88902-256-9]

Zap magic. [0-88902-252-6]

Zap monsters. [0-88902-081-2]

Zap music. [0-88902-253-4]

Zap underground. [0-88902-255-7]

Zap water. [0-88902-254-2]

ZOO BOOK SERIES

8 volumes published, more projected. Heath. $1.35 each, paper.

Sixteen page booklets written by Judy Ross and designed to appeal to animal lovers and zoo visitors include well-chosen colour photos and enough pertinent facts to satisfy young students. *Younger to older.*

Brum the Siberian tiger. [0-669-00822-2]

Dassen the penguin. [0-669-00845-1]

Falstaff the hippopotamus. [0-669-00848-6]

Khan the camel. [0-669-00847-8]

Lobo the timber wolf. [0-669-00823-0]

Mias the orangutan. [0-669-00846-X]

Snowflake the polar bear. [0-669-00820-6]

Tequila the African elephant. [0-669-00821-4]

AWARD WINNING BOOKS

THE AMELIA FRANCES HOWARD-GIBBON AWARD

This award for the best illustrated children's book of the year has been presented since 1971 by the Canadian Association of Children's Librarians. A committee of CACL members chooses the winning book and the award is presented at the annual CLA conference in June of the year following the award year. The illustrator must be a Canadian citizen, and the book must be published in Canada. The prize is a sterling gilt medal suitably engraved.

1971 *The Wind Has Wings:* poems from Canada, compiled by Mary Alice Downie and Barbara Robertson. Illustrated by Elizabeth Cleaver. Toronto, Oxford, 1968.

1972 *A Child in Prison Camp,* by Shizuye Takashima. Illustrated by the author. Montreal, Tundra, 1971.

1973 *Au-delà du soleil/Beyond the Sun,* by Jacques de Roussan. Illustrated by the author. Montreal, Tundra, 1972.

1974 *A Prairie Boy's Winter,* by William Kurelek. Illustrated by the author. Montreal, Tundra, 1973.

1975 *The Sleighs of My Childhood/Les traineaux de mon enfance,* by Carlo Italiano. Illustrated by the author. Montreal, Tundra, 1974.

1976 *The Prairie Boy's Summer,* by William Kurelek. Illustrated by the author. Montreal, Tundra, 1975.
Runner up: *The Witch of the North,* by Mary Alice Downie. Illustrated by Elizabeth Cleaver. Ottawa, Oberon, 1975.

1977 *Down by Jim Long's Stage,* by Al Pittman. Illustrated by Pam Hall. St. Johns, Breakwater, 1976.
Runner up: *Québec je t'aime/Quebèc I Love You,* by Miyuki Tanobe. Illustrated by the author. Montreal, Tundra, 1976.

1978 *The Loon's Necklace,* by William Toye. Illustrated by Elizabeth Cleaver. Toronto, Oxford, 1977.
Runner up: *Garbage Delight,* by Dennis Lee. Illustrated by Frank Newfeld. Toronto, Macmillan, 1977.

1979 *A Salmon for Simon,* by Betty Waterton. Illustrated by Ann Blades. Vancouver, Douglas & McIntyre, 1978.
Runner up: *Great Canadian Animal Stories,* ed. Muriel Whitaker. Illustrated by Vlasta van Campen. Edmonton, Hurtig, 1978.

1980 *The Twelve Dancing Princesses,* by Janet Lunn. Illustrated by Laszlo Gal. Toronto, Methuen, 1979.
Runners up: *Great Canadian Adventure Stories,* edited by Muriel Whitaker. Illustrated by Vlasta van Campen. Edmonton, Hurtig, 1979; and *The Olden Days Coat,* by Margaret Laurence. Illustrated by Muriel Wood. Toronto, McClelland, 1979.

BEAVER TROPHY

The Hudson's Bay Company Retail Store in Edmonton, Alberta has presented the Beaver Trophy annually since 1965 for the best unpublished manuscripts in four categories: non-fiction, fiction, adult and juvenile. To qualify the author must have been a resident of Edmonton or its immediate environs, within a radius of 100 miles, for six months preceding January first of the award year. The $500 prize is presented in November. Judges are named by the Edmonton Branch of the Canadian Authors' Association. The winners in the juvenile category follow.

1967 *Last Voyage of the Unicorn,* by Delbert Young. Toronto, Clarke, Irwin, 1979.

1975 *The Quest of the Golden Gannet,* by Dorothy Barnhouse. St. John's, Breakwater, 1979.

THE CANADA COUNCIL AWARD FOR CHILDREN'S LITERATURE/ LE PRIX LITTERAIRE DU CONSEIL DES ARTS POUR LA JEUNESSE

This award was established in 1975 and included two annual prizes of $5,000 in recognition of outstanding contributions to Canadian literature for children in the English and French languages. There are now four annual prizes of $5,000 each to accommodate outstanding contributions to the illustration of children's books in both languages as well. All books for children written or illustrated by Canadian citizens in the year preceding the award presentation are eligible, whether published in Canada or abroad. (See PRIX DE LITTERATURE DE JEUNESSE for the French language awards.)

1976 *Shantymen of Cache Lake,* by Bill Freeman. Toronto, Lorimer, 1975.

1977 *The Wooden People,* by Myra Paperny. Toronto, Little Brown, 1976.

1978 *Listen for the Singing,* by Jean Little. Toronto, Clarke, Irwin, 1977.

1979 *Hold Fast,* by Kevin Major. Toronto, Clarke, Irwin, 1978. (Literature) *A Salmon for Simon,* by Betty Waterton. Illustrated by Ann Blades. Vancouver, Douglas & McIntyre, 1978. (Illustration)

1980 *Days of Terror,* by Barbara Claassen Smucker. Toronto, Clarke, Irwin, 1979. (Literature) *The Twelve Dancing Princesses,* by Janet Lunn. Illustrated by Laszlo Gal. Toronto, Methuen, 1979. (Illustration)

CANADIAN CHILDREN'S BOOK AWARD

Little, Brown and Company established the Canadian Children's Book Award in 1956. The award of $1,000 is given occasionally, and no oftener than every two years, to encourage the writing of original children's books by Canadian authors. Any unpublished manuscript by a resident of Canada is eligible.

1958 *Nkwala,* by Edith L. Sharp. Toronto, Little, Brown, 1958.

1961 *Mine for Keeps,* by Jean Little. Toronto, Little Brown, 1962.

1965 *The White Calf,* by Cliff Faulknor. Toronto, Little, Brown, 1965.

1967 *Strange Summer in Stratford,* by Norah A. Perez. Toronto, Little, Brown, 1968.

1976 *The Wooden People,* by Myra Paperny. Toronto, Little, Brown, 1976.

1977 *The Snailman,* by Brenda Sivers. Toronto, Little, Brown, 1978.

THE CANADIAN LIBRARY ASSOCIATION BOOK-OF-THE-YEAR FOR CHILDREN AWARD

This is the longest-standing Canadian award given annually for the best children's book, chosen by a committee of members of the Canadian Association of Children's Librarians, a section of the Canadian Library Association. The award is presented at the annual CLA conference in June of the year following the award year. To merit consideration a book must have been published in Canada, written by a Canadian citizen, or written on a Canadian subject. Regulations governing the award have been changed a number of times; therefore two awards were given in 1966. The prize is a sterling gilt medal suitably engraved. (See CACL children's book awards, 1947-1978 in *Canadian Library Journal,* August 1978, pp. 259-268)

1947 *Starbuck Valley Winter,* by Roderick Haig-Brown. New York, Morrow, 1943.
1948 No award.
1949 *Kristli's Trees,* by Mabel Dunham. Toronto, McClelland, 1948.
1950 *Franklin of the Arctic,* by Richard S. Lambert. Toronto, McClelland, 1949.
1951 No award.
1952 *The Sun Horse,* by Catherine Anthony Clark, Toronto, Macmillan, 1951.
1953 No award.
1954 No award.
1956 *Train for Tiger Lily,* by Louise Riley, Toronto, Macmillan, 1954.
1957 *Glooskap's Country and other Indian tales,* by Cyrus Macmillan. Toronto, Oxford, 1955.
1958 *Lost in the Barrens,* by Farley Mowat. Toronto, Little, Brown, 1956.
1959 *The Dangerous Cove,* by John F. Hayes. Toronto, Copp Clark, 1957.
1960 *The Golden Phoenix and other French-Canadian fairy tales,* by Marius Barbeau. Retold by Michael Hornyansky. Toronto, Oxford, 1958.
1961 *The St. Lawrence,* by William Toye. Toronto, Oxford, 1959.
1962 No award.
1963 *The Incredible Journey: a tale of three animals,* by Sheila Burnford. Toronto, Little, Brown, 1961.
1964 *The Whale People,* by Roderick Haig-Brown. London, Collins, 1962.
1965 *Tales of Nanabozho,* by Dorothy M. Reid. Toronto, Oxford, 1963.
1966 *The Double Knights: more tales from round the world,* by James McNeill. Toronto, Oxford, 1964.
1966 *Tikta'liktak: an Eskimo legend,* by James Houston. Toronto, Longman, 1965
1967 *Raven's cry,* by Christie Harris. Toronto, McClelland, 1966.
1968 *The White Archer: an Eskimo legend,* by James Houston. Toronto, Longman, 1967.
1969 *And To-morrow the Stars: the story of John Cabot,* by Kay Hill. New York, Dodd, Mead, 1968.
1970 *Sally Go Round the Sun: 300 songs, rhymes and games of Canadian children,* by Edith Fowke. Toronto, McClelland, 1969.
1971 *Cartier Discovers the St. Lawrence,* by William Toye. Toronto, Oxford, 1970.
1972 *Mary of Mile 18,* by Ann Blades. Montreal, Tundra, 1971.
1973 *The Marrow of the World,* by Ruth Nichols. Toronto, Macmillan, 1972.
1974 *The Miraculous Hind,* by Elizabeth Cleaver. Toronto, Holt, 1973.
1975 *Alligator Pie,* by Dennis Lee. Toronto, Macmillan, 1974. Runner up: *Slave of the Haida,* by Doris Andersen. Toronto, Macmillan, 1974.
1976 *Jacob Two Two Meets the Hooded Fang,* by Mordecai Richler. Toronto, Little, Brown, 1975. Runner up: *The Prairie Boy's Summer* by William Kurelek. Montreal, Tundra, 1975.
1977 *Mouse Woman and the Vanished Princesses,* by Christie Harris. Toronto, McClelland, 1976. Runner up: *Simon and the Golden Sword,* by Frank Newfeld. Toronto, Oxford, 1976.
1978 *Garbage Delight,* by Dennis Lee. Toronto, Macmillan, 1977. Runner up: *Underground to Canada,* by Barbara Smucker. Toronto, Clarke, Irwin, 1977.
1979 *Hold Fast,* by Kevin Major. Toronto, Clarke, Irwin, 1978. Runner up: *A Salmon for Simon,* by Betty Waterton. Vancouver, Douglas and McIntyre, 1978.
1980 *River Runners,* by James Houston. Toronto, McClelland, 1979.
Runners up: *The Olden Days Coat,* by Margaret Laurence. Toronto, McClelland, 1979; and *Days of Terror,* by Barbara Claassen Smucker. Toronto, Clarke, Irwin, 1979.

COLLIER-MACMILLAN AWARD

This $500 award was first presented in 1974 for the best Canadian juvenile manuscript submitted to the Collier-Macmillan advertised competition. It is awarded sporadically.

1974 *Star Maiden: an Ojibwa legend of the first water lily,* by Patricia Robins and illustrated by Shirley Day. Toronto, Collier-Macmillan, 1975.

1976 *Alphavegetabet,* by Louise Ellis. Toronto, Collier-Macmillan, 1976.

GOVERNOR-GENERAL'S LITERARY AWARD

The Governor-General's Literary Awards were established in 1936 by the Canadian Authors Association and were so called with the agreement of John Buchan, Lord Tweedsmuir, then Governor-General of Canada, as a permanent recognition of literary merit. The awards took the form of a bronze medal and were presented to the authors of the best books of poetry, fiction, non-fiction and juvenile literature. In 1959 The Canada Council undertook the administration of the awards and the winning authors now win a prize of $5000 and a specially-bound copy of their books. The juvenile award was discontinued in 1959.

1950 *Franklin of the Arctic,* by Richard S. Lambert. Toronto, McClelland, 1949.

1951 *The Great Adventure,* by Donalda Dickie. Toronto, Dent, 1950.

1952 *A Land Divided,* by John F. Hayes. Toronto, Copp Clark, 1951.

1953 *Cargoes on the Great Lakes,* by Marie McPhedran. Toronto, Macmillan, 1952.

1954 *Rebels Ride at Night,* by John F. Hayes. Toronto, Copp, Clark, 1953.

1955 *The Nor'Westers,* by Marjorie W. Campbell. Toronto, Macmillan, 1954.

1958 *The Great Chief,* by Kerry Wood, Toronto, Macmillan, 1957.

1959 *Nkwala,* by Edith L. Sharp. Toronto, Little, Brown, 1958.

MACMILLAN OF CANADA CONTEST

The Macmillan of Canada Contest was held in 1962. The award of $5,000 was given for the best story written for young readers aged eight to ten, based on incidents in Canadian history.

1962 *The Great Canoe,* by Adelaide Leitch. Toronto, Macmillan, 1962.

THE RUTH SCHWARTZ FOUNDATION AWARD

This award of $2,000 was established in 1975 in memory of Toronto bookseller, Ruth Schwartz. The prize is given for the best children's book written in English and published in Canada, chosen annually by the Canadian Booksellers' Association or other jury designated by the Ontario Arts Council.

1976 *Jacob Two-Two Meets the Hooded Fang,* by Mordecai Richler. Toronto, McClelland & Stewart, 1975.

1977 *The Violin,* by Robert Thomas Allen. Toronto, McGraw, 1976.

1978 *Garbage Delight,* by Dennis Lee. Toronto, Macmillan, 1977.

1979 *Hold Fast,* by Kevin Major. Toronto, Clarke, Irwin, 1978.

1980 *Days of Terror,* by Barbara Claassen Smucker. Toronto, Clarke, Irwin, 1979.

TORONTO IODE AWARD

An award established by the Municipal Chapter of Toronto Independent Order of the Daughters of the Empire in cooperation with the Toronto Public Library Board is made annually to an author or illustrator of a children's book written or illustrated by a Canadian citizen residing in Toronto or surrounding area. The award carries a prize of $500 presented in March following the award year.

1974 *A Prairie Boy's Winter,* by William Kurelek. Montreal, Tundra, 1973.
1975 *Alligator Pie,* by Dennis Lee. Toronto, Macmillan, 1974.
1976 *How the Kookaburra Got His Laugh,* by Aviva Layton, Toronto, McClelland, 1975.
1977 *The Loon's Necklace,* by William Toye. Toronto, Oxford, 1977.
1978 Laszlo Gal for his illustrations in: *My Name is Not Odessa Yarker,* by Marion Engel. Toronto, Kids Can Press, 1977. *The Shirt of the Happy Man,* by Mariella Bertelli. Toronto, Kids Can Press, 1977. *Why the Man in the Moon is Happy,* by Ronald Melzack. Toronto, McClelland, 1977.
1979 *The Twelve Dancing Princesses,* by Janet Lunn. Toronto, Methuen, 1978.

THE VICKY METCALF AWARD

This $1,000 Award is donated by Mrs. Vicky Metcalf and administered by the Canadian Authors' Association. The prize is given solely to stimulate writing for children and awarded annually to an author for his/her body of work of interest to young people.

1963 Kerry Wood
1964 John F. Hayes
1965 Roderick Haig-Brown
1966 Fred Swayze
1967 John Patrick Gillese
1968 Lorrie McLaughlin
1969 Audrey McKim
1970 Farley Mowat
1971 Kay Hill
1972 William E. Toye
1973 Christie Harris
1974 Jean Little
1975 Lyn Harrington
1976 Suzanne Martel
1977 James Houston
1978 Lyn Cook
1979 Cliff Faulknor

VICKY METCALF SHORT STORY AWARD

Presented annually by the Canadian Authors' Association to a Canadian citizen or landed immigrant for the best children's short story published in Canada in the year prior to the award year. The selection is made by an independent panel of judges, and the award carries a prize of $500. The winner is announced as soon as the selection is final. Presentations are made at the annual awards dinner of the Canadian Authors' Association.

1978 McDougall, Marina. "The Kingdom of the Riddles" in *Ready or Not,* edited by Jack Booth. (Language Patterns Impressions, Reading Series) Toronto. Holt, 1978.

PROFESSIONAL MEDIA

PROFESSIONAL TOOLS

Admittance restricted: the child as citizen in Canada. The Canadian Council on Children and Youth; CCCY, 1978. $8.95 paper [0-920786-00-6]

This report of the Canadian Council on Children and Youth focuses on the crucial needs of children: economic support, health care, protection and education, the special needs of Native children, and ends with a perspective on children's rights.

Amey, L.J.; The Canadian school-housed public library, illustrated with photographs and charts. Dalhousie University Libraries and School of Library Service, 1979 (Occasional Paper Number 24). 488 pages. $7.50 + $.50 postage. [0-7703-0159-2]

This large volume brings together all essential information on the school-housed public library, stressing the Canadian experience.

Andersen, Lorri; Aubrey, Irene; and **McDiarmid, Louise;** Storytellers' rendezvous: Canadian stories to tell to children. Louie, BoKim (illus.). Canadian Library Association, 1979. $15.00 paper [0-88802-132-1]

Especially chosen for storytellers by storytellers these Canadian stories, folk tales, legends and poems offer excellent fare for story hours. Telling time and age suitability are included.

Blostein, Fay; New paperbacks for young adults. Ontario Library Association, 1979. 127 pages. $1.95 [0-88968-022-7]

Thematic guide with brief annotations arranged by age groups (12-15 years, 12-18 years and 16-18 years). Some Canadian titles included.

Branscombe, Frederic (ed.); and **Newsom, Harry** (ed.); Resource services for Canadian schools. McGraw, 1977. $4.95 paper [0-07-082619-6]

Principles and guidelines that affect school library services reflecting an integrated approach to print and non-print materials and the influence of larger units of service on the individual school resources.

Brotin, Delores and **Donald Gail;** Contentions: an analysis of Canadian literature curricula. CANLIT, 1976. 73 pages. $4.00 paper [0-9690564-3-5]

A research report of Canadian literature used in 54 curricula in Canadian schools.

Burdenuk, Gene (ed.); An Annotated guide to selection sources for secondary school resource centres. OLA, 1977. $3.00 paper [0-88969-005-7]

Canada. Department of Indian Affairs and Northern Development; About Indians: a listing of books, 3rd ed. Information Kiosk, Department of Indian Affairs and Northern Development, Ottawa K1A 0H4, 1975. Free.

An excellent bibliography, arranged by grade levels from kindergarten to grade six and up, includes Canadian and other titles. A new edition is expected in 1981. Order from regional offices of the Department of Indian Affairs or from the Information Kiosk in Ottawa.

Canadian books in Canadian schools: a case study; report of the Work Group on Educational and Library Materials of the Toronto Board of Education, October, 1976. Association of Canadian Publishers, 70 The Esplanade, 3rd floor, Toronto, M5E 1R2, 1977. 41 pages. $2.50 paper.

The Toronto Board of Education commissioned a work group on educational and library materials to discover Canadian inclusions in the schools. Recommendations include a three-year catch-up to expand Canadian collections.

Cuddy, Mary Lou and **Scott, James I.;** British Columbia in books; an annotated bibliography. Douglas & McIntyre, 1974. 144 pages. $6.95 paper [0-88894-066-1]

Although dated this bibliography indicates the diversity of regional publishing.

Fasick, Adele M. and **England, Claire;** Children using media; reading and viewing preferences among the users and non-users of the Regina Public Library. Research report. Centre for Research in Librarianship, Faculty of Library Science, University of Toronto, January 1977. 79 pages. $10.00 paper. Order from: R. Yeo, Regina Public Library, Regina, Saskatchewan.

This first Canadian research report on children's library services surveys "reading and viewing preferences among the users and non-users of the Regina Public Library."

Fasick, Adele M.; What should libraries do for children? Parents, Librarians and Teachers view materials and services in South Central Regional System (Ontario). South Central Regional Library Board, 220 Dundurn Street South, Hamilton L8P 4K7, 1978. 156 pages. $10.00 paper.

Research study into the services offered to children in the South Central Library Region of Ontario whose findings emphasize the wider promotion of services and materials among the potential users.

Hale, Alice K.; An Introduction to teaching Canadian literature. Atlantic Education, 1975. 53 pages. $3.00 paper.

A teacher's resource booklet developed by the Lighthouse Learning Program "to promote educational excellence through the use of local resources."

Hauck, Philomena; Sourcebook on Canadian women. Canadian Library Association, 1979. $10.00 paper [0-88802-126-7]

Annotated bibliography on books, periodicals, pamphlets audiovisual materials and general information sources related to women and their concerns. "Books for liberated children" lists about 20 items.

Henderson, Diane (ed.); Guide to basic reference materials for Canadian libraries. UTP, 1977. 5th ed. $15.00 looseleaf [0-8020-2224-3]

Hodgetts, A.B.; Teaching Canada for the 80's: a guide for Canadian studies. OISE, 1978. 136 pages. $6.25 paper [0-7744-0167-2]

A four part curriculum plan highlights this proposal for teaching Canadian studies.

Jarvi, Edith T. (ed.); **McLean, Isabel** (ed.) and **MacKenzie, Catherine** (ed.); Canadian selection: books and periodicals for libraries. UTP, 1978. 1060 pages. $35.00 [0-8020-4554-5]

Annotated, selective listing of Canadian books for a well-stocked library. No children's books are listed but it is valuable as a reference resource for librarians working in public libraries.

Kogan, Marilyn H. and **Whalen, George;** Handbook for school library organization. McGraw, 1980. 224 pages. $14.95 [0-07-077833-7]

This complete guide combines detailed, thorough cataloguing procedures with up to date information on computerization, commercial cataloguing and networking.

Kogan, Marilyn, comp.; Selected Ontario government publications for schools and libraries. Ontario Library Association and Ontario Ministry of Government Services, 1979. 22 pages. Free (limited)

About 150 free and inexpensive government publications useful for Canadian studies.

Let's tell a story; kit of 3/4" U-matic video-cassette and bibliographies. Midwestern Regional, 1979. $45.00 per kit.

An excellent videotape on the various techniques and forms of storytelling with lists of stories, tips and books on storytelling.

Levetzow, Joanna von; Toy libraries; how to start a toy library in your community, illustrated with drawings. Canadian Association of Toy Libraries, 50 Quebec Avenue, Suite 1207, Toronto, M6P 4B4, 1978. 24 pages. $3.00 paper, plus 26¢ postage.

This basic guide to help organizations establish a toy lending service includes a brief history of toy lending, the aims of the Canadian Association of Toy Libraries and a chapter on safety.

Library programming handbook 1979. Lethbridge Public Library, Lethbridge, Alberta T1J 4C4, 1979. $6.00 paper.

Seventy-one successful library programs used in libraries across Canada.

Light, Beth and **Strong-Boag, Veronica;** True daughters of the north: Canadian women's history. OISE, 1980. 210 pages. $11.95 [0-7744-0185-0]

An introductory essay and an annotated bibliography of materials on Canadian women's history from the 17th century on.

McClear, Mary-Eileen; You can come too. Powell, Ann (illus.). Midwestern Regional, 1978. 13 pages. $0.50/ paper.

A colouring book serves as a simple introduction to the public library and its services.

Manitoba School Library Audio-Visual Association; Looking for Manitoba government publications: an annotated bibliography of books and pamphlets. MSLAVA, 1978. $5.00 paper.

Manitoba school librarians have assumed a provincial responsibility in producing this list of government publications of use for Canadian studies courses.

Matheson, Edward C. (ed.); and **Thorne, Eunice A.** (ed.); The Book trade in Canada 1980/L'Industrie du livre au Canada. Ampersand, 1980. Annual. $18.00 paper [0-920262-08-2]

Includes pertinent information on publishers and distributors, sales agents and wholesalers, industry-related organizations, booksellers, and literary awards and prizes.

Ontario. Ministry of Education; People of Native ancestry: a resource guide for the intermediate division. 2nd ed. Ontario Ministry of Government Services, 1977. 62 pages. Free.

The 26-page bibliography lists books, periodicals, films, newspapers, videotapes and other media, resource centres, Native organizations, friendship centres and publishers.

Ontario. Ministry of Education. Ministry of Culture and Recreation; Resource list for a multicultural society. Maxwell, Janet; Rubess, Banuta; Sabanski, Indra; Dodd, Dorothy-Jean (comp.). Ministry of Government Services, Publications Service, 1977. 626 pages. $3.00 paper.

Lists resources from 185 national and cultural groups as well as some under general subject areas such as multi-culturalism and prejudice.

Page, James E. (ed.); Seeing ourselves; films for Canadian studies. NFB, 1979. 210 pages. $3.95 paper [0-7722-0001-7]

Excellent guide to films of potential value to teaching Canadian studies includes grade levels and critical questions.

Pilkey, Doris; A Library pocketful: self serve ideas. The Author, 40 Windridge Drive, Markham, L3P 1V1, 1979. 7th ed. 150 pages. $5.00 paper.

A host of ideas and activities to keep children reading highlight this school library handbook.

Pluscauskas, Martha; and **Butler, Marian** (eds.); Canadian books in print: author and title index, 1979. $75.00 [0068-8398]; [0-8020-4577-4]

This invaluable index to Canadian publications is now further enhanced by three updates per year on microfiche, hence the higher price.

Pluscauskas, Martha and **Butler, Marian** (eds.); Canadian books in print: subject guide. U.T.P., 1979. $35.00 [0-315-1999]; [0-8020-4578-2]

Subject access to Canadian titles makes collection building easier for libraries.

Robinson, Paul; After survival: a teacher's guide to Canadian resources. PMA Books, 1976. 329 pages. $15.00 cloth [0-88778-147-0]; $8.95 paper [0-88778-150-0]

Deals with Canadian resource materials suitable for the subjects taught in Canadian schools. A polemic and a grand apologia for a nationalistic bias in education. No index.

Robinson, Paul; Where our survival lies; students and textbooks in Atlantic Canada. Atlantic Institute of Education, 5244 South Street, Halifax, N.S. B3J 1A4, 1979. 107 pages. $4.00 [0-7703-0155-X]

Examines seriously and thoroughly the textbook situation in the four Atlantic provinces regarding Atlantic and Canadian content.

Ryder, Dorothy E. (ed.); Canadian reference sources: a selective guide. CLA, 1973. $10.00 [0-88802-093-7] Supplement (1975) $7.00 [0-88802-106-2]

Invaluable guide to Canadian reference books for library collection building.

Schlukbier, George; Children's Services Survey 1979, conducted by Info Bank. Southwestern Regional Library System, 1979. 252 pages. $15.00 paper.

In celebration of International Year of the Child the Southwestern Regional Library System in Windsor sponsored a survey of children's library services supported by the Ministry of Culture and Recreation. This is the final report.

Snow, Kathleen M. and **Hauck, Philomena;** Canadian materials for schools. McClelland, 1970. Trade $6.50 [0-7710-8285-1]; text $5.25 [0-7710-8198-7]

Although somewhat dated this outline encourages the use of Canadian materials in Canadian school curricula.

Sources and resources; a handbook for teacher-librarians in British Columbia. B.C. Ministry of Education, 1978. 80 pages. Inquire from Publication Services Branch, Ministry of Education, 878 Viewfield Rd., Victoria V9A 4V1.

Concise, readable and to the point information on official B.C. school library policy, efficient acquisition, organization and circulation of library resource materials.

Taylor, Donna (ed.); The Great Lakes region in children's books. Green Oak Press, 9339 Spicer Road, Brighton, Michigan 48116, 1980. $16.95 [0-931600-01-4]

Selective, annotated list of books about the Great Lakes States and Ontario. The Canadian section was compiled by Pat Tomey.

Tudor, Dean (ed.); **Tudor, Nancy** (ed.); and **Biesenthal, Linda** (ed.); Canadian book review annual. PMA Books 1975-1977, 1975 ed.; $27.50 net. [0-88778-133-0]; 1976 ed. $27.50 net; [0-88778-161-6]; 1977 ed. $29.50 net [0-88778-179-9]

"Evaluative guide to Canadian English-language trade books and a selection of important college and educational titles" and significant children's books.

University of British Columbia; Women's Resources Centre; Annotated bibliography for women's studies for high school students. UBC, 1976. 126 pages. $5.00 paper.

Covers 11 subject areas including politics, the law, education and history of women in Canada.

Weihs, Jean; Lewis, Shirley and **Macdonald, Janet;** Non book materials; the organization of integrated collections. Canadian Library Association, 1979. 2nd ed. $8.00 paper.

Comprehensive manual for all aspects of a media centre's collection. Interprets AACR2 and is a companion volume to that code.

Wilkinson, J.P.; Canadian juvenile fiction and the library market. Canadian Library Association, 1976. $5.00 paper [0-88802-112-7]

A research study into the publisher-librarian connection regarding the availability of Canadian children's books from the publisher and in the library.

Wood, Dean D.; Multicultural Canada: a teacher's guide to ethnic studies. O.I.S.E., 1978. 138 pages. $10.50 paper [0-7744-0175-3] (Curriculum Series 36]

The bibliography/resource list of 566 items is a bonus in this trans-disciplinary approach to planning courses in ethnic studies.

You asked for it: a guide for preschool storyhours, presented by Walden Public Library. North Central Regional Library System, 334 Regent St. South, Sudbury, P3C 4E2, 1977. 81 pages. $6.00 paper, outside the North Central Region.

This guide to 32 successful preschool storyhours is a handy reference for busy librarians who need a repertory fast.

LITERARY HISTORY AND CRITICISM

Amtmann, Bernard; A Bibliography of Canadian children's books and books for young people 1841-1867/Livres de l'enfance et livres de la jeunesse au Canada 1841-1867. Bernard Amtmann, 1529 Sherbrooke Street West, Montreal H3G 1L7, 1977. VII, 124 pages. $25.00 paper.

Amtmann, Bernard; Early Canadian children's books 1763-1840; a bibliographical investigation into the nature of early Canadian children's books and books for young people/Livres de l'enfance et livres de la jeunesse au Canada 1763-1840; étude bibliographique. Bernard Amtmann, Bibliographic investigations of works "suitable for and available to juvenile readers, even if not always intended for them" published and printed in Canada up to 1867. Sources and locations are cited.

Atwood, Margaret; Survival: a thematic guide to Canadian literature. Anansi, 1972. $4.95 paper [0-88784-613-0]

"A criticism, a manifesto, and a collection of personal and subversive remarks" about Canadian fictional writing on nature, animals, the Native people, explorers and settlers, among other subjects illuminating the theme of survival.

Birdsall, Peter, and **Broten, Delores;** Mind war: book censorship in English Canada. Canlit, 1978. 66 pages. $5.00 paper [0-920566-01-4]

A collection of newspaper articles on book censorship chronologically arranged from 1935 to 1978. Index to censored books included.

Colombo, John Robert (comp.) and others; CDN SF & F: a bibliography of Canadian science fiction and fantasy. Hounslow Press, 128 pages. 1979. $4.95 paper [0-88882-036-4]

Out-of print titles are included in this annotated bibliography.

Cutt, Margaret Nancy; Ministering angels. Five Owls Press, 1979. 226 pages. [0-903838-01-X]

This study of 19th century evangelical writing for children is available only through membership ($15.00) in The Friends of the Osborne and Lillian H. Smith Collections, Boys and Girls House, Toronto Public Library, 40 St. George Street, Toronto M5S 2E4.

Desbarats, Peter; What they used to tell about: Indian legends from Labrador. McClelland, 1969. $10.95 [0-7710-2689-7]

Collected by the department of anthropology in the University of Montreal these legends of the Montagnais-Naskapi Indians of Northern Quebec and Labrador reflect a mythological antiquity that conveys a primitive, natural regard for all living things, quite different from the usual European approach to folklore.

deVries, Leonard; Flowers of delight. Toronto Public Libraries, 1965. $15.00 [0-919486-21-5]

"Culled from the Osborne Collection of early children's books, an agreeable garland of prose and poetry for the instruction and amusement of little masters and misses and their distinguished parents, embellished with some 750 elegant woodcuts and engravings on wood and copper of which upwards of 125 are neatly coloured, selected with the greatest care from books for juvenile minds 1765-1830."

Egoff, Sheila (ed.); **Stubbs, Gordon T.** (ed.) and **Ashley, L.F.** (ed.); Only connect; readings on children's literature. Oxford, 1980 (1969). $8.95 paper [0-19-540309-6]

A well-chosen collection of essays on children's literature includes two by Sheila Egoff.

Egoff, Sheila; The Republic of childhood: a critical guide to Canadian children's literature in English. Oxford, 1975. 2nd ed. $12.50 cloth [0-19-540231-6]; $7.95 paper [0-19-540233-2]

An historical survey of Canadian children's books published after 1950, dealing with legends, fantasy, folk and fairytales, historical fiction, animal biography, history, biography and five other categories, among them illustration and design.

Fee, Margery and **Cawker, Ruth** (comps.); Canadian fiction, an annotated bibliography. PMA, 1976. 170 pages. $15.00 cloth [0-88778-134-9]; $8.95 paper [0-88778-140-3]

Intended to assist teachers to develop Canlit courses, this bibliography includes works of more than 100 writers classified under 32 broad subject headings.

Fowke, Edith; Henderson, Carole and **Brooks, Judith** (comps.); A bibliography of Canadian folklore in English. York University, 1976. Prelim. ed. 146 pages. $2.75 paper.

Listings of folklore items defined as "the material handed on by tradition whether by word of mouth or by custom and practice."

Fowke, Edith (comp.); Folklore of Canada. McClelland, 1976. 349 pages. $10.00 [0-7710-3202-1]

Presents a "representative cross-section of the various kinds of folklore found in Canada . . . not reshaped by writers seeking to popularize it" - from the Native peoples, Canadiens, Anglo-Canadians and the "Canadian Mosaic."

Granatstein, J.L. (ed.) and **Stevens, Paul** (ed.); Canada since 1867: a bibliographical guide. Samuel-Stevens, 1977. 2nd ed. 204 pages. $9.95 cloth [0-88866-583-0]; $4.95 paper [0-88866-584-9]

The editors select the best books and "focus on the most recent research and writing in the major areas of Canadian historical writing."

Is anybody out there listening? A study of sexism in high schools. Videotape, 1/2" reel to reel, 30 minutes, $50.00; video cassette, 3/4" tape, 30 minutes, $75.00. E and A Productions, 396 Davisville Ave., Toronto M5S 1A5, 1978.

Young people frankly delve into the incidence of sexism in their teachers, courses, textbooks and outside reading.

Meet the Author Kits. The Children's Book Centre, 229 College Street, Toronto, M5T 1R4. $12.00 each kit; $20.00 for first two kits.

The kits include poster-photographs and bio-bibliographies on Canadian authors and illustrators. Kit No. 1 includes Ann Blades, Elizabeth Cleaver, James Houston, Dennis Lee, Farley Mowat, Patti Stren. Kit No. 2 includes Laszlo Gal, Christie Harris, Monica Hughes, Jean Little, Frank Newfeld, Barbara Smucker.

Midwestern Regional Library System; Jean Little. Midwestern Regional Library System, 637 Victoria St. N., Kitchener N2H 5G4, 1979. Videotape, 24 minutes. $25.00.

Interview format captures the author's vitality and personality.

Midwestern Regional Library System; Sue Ann Alderson. Midwestern Regional Library System, 637 Victoria St. N., Kitchener N2H 5G4, 1979. Videotape, 28 minutes. $25.00.

The author discusses the influences on her career, her successes and failures, and personal anecdotes.

Ontario. Royal Commission on Book Publishing; Background papers. Ontario Queen's Printer and Publisher, 1972. 395 pages. $5.00 cloth [0-7743-0000-0]; $3.75 paper [0-7743-0001-9]

Excellent comprehensive analysis of Canadian publishing through 19 research papers that explore relevant concerns: copyright, bookstores, marketing of educational books, public and school libraries, and children's books among them.

Ontario. Royal Commission on Book Publishing; Canadian publishers and Canadian publishing. Ontario Queen's Printer and Publisher, 1972. 371 pages. $5.00 cloth [0-7743-0002-7]; $3.75 paper [0-7743-0003-5]

The final report of the Royal Commission appointed by the Ontario government in December 1970 includes 70 recommendations which were the outgrowth of 185 briefs presented mainly in public hearings and 19 specially commissioned research papers.

Pacific Rim Conference on Children's Literature, U.B.C., 1976. One ocean touching. Scarecrow, 1979. 252 pages. $12.00 [0-8108-1199-5]

Papers given at the first Pacific Rim Conference include contributions by Ivan Southall, Leon Garfield, Suzanne Martel and Claude Aubry.

Robeson, Virginia and **Sylvester, Christine;** Teaching Canadian studies: an evaluation of print materials. O.I.S.E., 1980. 340 pages. $18.95. [0-7744-0184-2]

Evaluations of nearly 500 publications in Canadian history, geography, social issues and other studies reviewed by over 300 specialists.

Schwarz, Herbert T; Tales from the smokehouse. Odjig, Daphne (illus.). Hurtig, 1976. $8.95 cloth; $4.95 paper [0-88830-122-7]

Thirteen stories drawn from the Ojibway, Mohawk, Naskapi and other Indian tribal lore reveal the dynamic sexuality inherent in Indian life and legend.

Sorfleet, John Robert (ed.); L. M. Montgomery: an assessment. Canadian Children's Press, 1976. $3.95 paper [0-920512-00-3]

Eight critical articles on the work of one of Canada's best-known writers in celebration of the 100th anniversary of her birth in 1874. First appeared in *Canadian Children's Literature*, No. 3, 1975.

Stevens, James; Sacred legends of the Sandy Lake Cree. Ray, Carl (illus.). McClelland, 1977. $5.95 paper [0-7710-8342-4]

Carl Ray, grandson of one of the most revered medicine men in the Sandy Lake district, shares these legends through the telling and his drawings in the first printed record ever made of them.

Symons, Tom; The Symons report. McClelland, 1977. 205 pages. $1.95 paper [0-7710-8380-7] Out of print; see below.

An abridged version of volumes 1 and 2 of ***To know ourselves***, the Report of the Commission on Canadian Studies, is now available only from the Book and Periodical Development Council, 86 Bloor St. West, Toronto, M5S 1M5. It is free but send 50 cents to cover mailing costs.

Thomas, Clara; Our nature, our voices. Porcépic, 1973. 175 pages. $3.75 paper [0-88770-618-5]

A chronological guide to Canadian literature with short biobibliographical essays on 47 authors.

A Token for friends. The Friends of the Osborne and Lillian H. Smith Collection, 40 St. George St., Toronto M5S 2E4. 1979. 48 pages. $5.00.

This small memento contains a tribute to Edgar Osborne, a description of the Osborne Collection and Osborne's first catalogue, partially annotated.

Toronto public libraries; The Osborne collection of early children's books, 1476-1910: a catalogue, St. John, Judith (ed.); Toronto Public Libraries, 1966. Vol. 1 $25.00 [0-919486-25-8]; Vol 2 $30.00 [0-919486-55-X]

Two comprehensive annotated catalogues of early children's books housed in Boys and Girls House, originally donated by Edgar G. Osborne and enlarged by donations and acquisitions.

Waterston, Elizabeth; Survey: a short history of Canadian literature. Methuen, 1973. $4.65 paper [0-458-90930-0] (Methuen Canadian Literature Series)

Very brief general history of Canadian literature.

PERIODICALS

BCSLA reviews. School Librarians' Association. British Columbia Teachers' Federation, 105-2235 Burrard Street, Vancouver, V6J 3H9. 5 issues in the school year. $15.00 subscription for BCTF members, $20.00 subscription for non-BCTF members, $7.00 subscription for students.

Books in Canada. Canadian Review of Books Ltd., 366 Adelaide Street East, Suite 432, Toronto, Ontario M5A 1N4. Monthly. $9.95 per year [0045-2564]

Canadian children's literature. a journal of criticism and review; Canadian Children's Literature Association, Box 335, Guelph, Ontario N1H 6K5; Quarterly. $11.00 per year for institutions; $9.00 per year for individuals. Single issues $3.25.

Canadian government publications catalogue. 171 Slater Street, Ottawa, Ontario, K1A 0S9. Quarterly plus yearly index. $20.00. $4.00 per copy.

Canadian materials for schools and libraries. Canadian Library Association, 151 Sparks Street, Ottawa, Ontario, K1P 5E3; Four times a year. $15.00 per year. $4.00 per copy [0317-4654]

Canadian periodical index. Canadian Library Association, 151 Sparks Street, Ottawa, Ontario, K1P 5E3; Monthly. Subscription on a service entry basis.

The Canadian reader. Reader's Club of Canada Ltd., 35 Britain Street, Toronto, Ontario M5A 1R7. Free to members of Reader's Club; $8.00 a year for non-members. [0008-4891]

Children's book news. Published by The Children's Book Centre, 229 College Street, 5th Floor, Toronto, Ontario M5T 1R4. Four times per year. Free [0705-0038]
Available free of charge to those who request inclusion on the mailing list, this four-page broadside features news from bookstores, schools and libraries, reviews of current Canadian books for children and articles on authors, illustrators, publishers, for adults.

Emergency librarian; Dyad Services, P. O. Box 4696, Station D, London, Ontario N5W 5L7. Bimonthly. $12 per year for individuals, $15 per year for institutions. [0315-8888].
Devoted to children's library issues and literature in the school and public library fields. Reviews and bibliographies included.

Free! the newsletter of free materials and services. Dyad Services, P.O. Box 4696 Station C, London, Ontario N5W 5L7. Bimonthly. $10 per year. [0708-4625]

In review. Canadian books for young people. Libraries and Community Information, 77 Bloor Street West, 7th Floor, Toronto, Ontario M7A 2R9. Quarterly. Free in Ontario; $14.00 for three years elsewhere. [0019-3259]

Ontario government publications monthly checklist. Publications Centre, Printing Services Branch, Ministry of Government Services, 3B7 Macdonald Block, Queen's Park, Toronto, Ontario M7A 1N8. Free.

Quill & Quire. 59 Front Street East, Toronto, Ontario M5E 1B3; Monthly with supplements. $16.00 per year [0033-6491]

The World of children's books, a review of children's literature in English. Jon C. Scott, English Department University of Alberta, Edmonton, T6G 2E5. Bi-annual. $4.50 in Canada; $5.00 in the USA and Great Britain. Cheques payable to Jon C. Stott.

Y-A hotline. Professor L. J. Amey, School of Library Service, Dalhousie University, Halifax, Nova Scotia B3H 4H8. Six issues, irregularly, for $3.50 [0701-8894].

Library science students share their research and critical appraisals with the field in this periodical devoted to subjects of interest to young people and their librarians.

CONTACTS

Associations concerned with children's literature

Canadian Association of
Children's Librarians
Canadian Library Association
151 Sparks Street
Ottawa, Ontario K1P 5E3

Canadian School Library Association
Canadian Library Association
151 Sparks Street
Ottawa, Ontario K1P 5E3

The Children's Book Centre
229 College Street
Toronto, Ontario M5T 1R4

Children's Services Guild
Ontario Library Association
73 Richmond Street West
Toronto, Ontario M5H 1Z4

IBBY - Canadian Section
Membership Secretary
Box 501
Etobicoke, Ontario M9C 4V5

International Liaison Officer IBBY
Chief, Children's Literature Section
The National Library
Ottawa, Ontario K1A 0N4

Associations intéressées aux livres pour les jeunes

Association canadienne pour
l'avancement de la littérature de
jeunesse, (A.C.A.L.J.),
C.P. 2152,
Succursale Jacques-Cartier,
Sherbrooke, J1J 3Y2.
(819) 565-5660

Communication-Jeunesse,
445, St-François-Xavier,
Bureau 21,
Montréal, H2Y 2T1.
(514) 844-5939

IBBY-Canadian Section/UILJ-Section
canadienne
Chef de la section de littérature de
jeunesse,
Bibliothèque nationale du Canada,
Ottawa, Ontario K1A 0N4

Bookstores

The Children's Book Centre publishes a list of bookstores carrying Canadian children's books in ***The Children's Book News***. The following are a few representative stores:

Longhouse Bookshop
630 Yonge Street
Toronto, Ontario M4Y 1Z8
416-921-9995

The Children's Book Store
604 Markham Street
Toronto, Ontario M6G 2L8
416-535-7011

The Bookery of Ottawa
463 Sussex Drive
Ottawa, Ontario K1N 6Z4
613-238-1428

A Pair of Trindles Bookshoppe
Old Red Store
Historic Properties
Halifax, Nova Scotia B3J 1W5
902-423-7528

The Bookworm's Den
Grosvenor Park Shopping Centre
Saskatoon, Saskatchewan S7H 0T8
306-373-3411

The Village Bookshop
10212 - 140 Street
Edmonton, Alberta T5N 2L4
403-452-3791

Duthie's Books for Children
915 Robson Street
Vancouver, B.C. V6Z 1A5
604-684-4496

Distributeurs de livres français

Editions Champlain Ltd.,
107 Church Street,
Toronto, M5C 2G5.
(416) 364-4345

Librairie Caron,
251 est, Ste-Catherine,
Montréal, H2X 1L5.
(514) 845-5698

Librairie de La Capitale,
75, rue Elgin,
Ottawa, K1P 5B8.
(613) 236-7287

Librairie Coin du Livre (Central) Ltée.,
263, rue Dalhousie,
Ottawa, K1N 7E3.
(613) 235-7886

Librairie La Courte Echelle,
4627, St-Denis,
Montréal, H2J 2L4.
(514) 288-8522

Librairie Dussault Ltée,
8955 boul. St-Laurent,
Montréal, H2M 1M6.
(514) 384-8760

Librairie Garneau,
47-49 Buade,
Québec, G1R 4A2.
(418) 692-4282

Librairie Leméac,
371 ouest, boul. Laurier,
Montréal, H2V 2K6.
(514) 273-2841

Lidec Inc.,
1083, rue Van Horne,
Montréal, H2V 1J6.
(514) 274-6521

Librairie Renaud-Bray,
5219, Côte-des-Neiges,
Montréal, H3T 1Y1.
(514) 342-1515

Librairie Scholaire Canadienne
2244, rue Rouen,
Montréal, H2K 1L5.
(514) 527-3425

Librairie Servidec,
202-A, rue Main,
Ottawa, K1S 1C6.
(613) 237-5576

Livres canadiens pour la jeunesse

LIVRES D'IMAGES

Anfousse, Ginette; La cachette. La Courte échelle, 1976. 20 pages. $3.95 [0-88570-004-X]

L'histoire d'une petite fille, possédant un tamanoir, et qui n'ayant personne avec qui jouer, invite le lecteur à jouer avec elle à cache-cache. Illustrations vivantes et colorées. Cassette et disque disponibles. *Tout-petits.*

Anfousse, Ginette; La chicane. La Courte échelle, 1978. 24 pages. $3.95 [0-88570-015-5] (Etoile filante)

Une chicane est survenue entre Ji et Cloclo. Un autre album de qualité d'un auteur qui sait parler à l'enfant. Cassette et disque disponibles. *Tout-petits.*

Anfousse, Ginette; Mon ami Pichou. La Courte échelle, 1976. 20 pages. $3.95 [0-8870-005-8]

C'est l'automne. Pichou, un tamanoir, est de mauvaise humeur parce qu'il ne peut plus manger des fourmis. Sa propriétaire, une petite fille, tente de le consoler en lui disant que l'été reviendra. Les illustrations ont la simplicité du dessin d'enfant. Cassette et disque disponibles. *Tout-petits.*

Anfousse, Ginette; La varicelle. La Courte échelle, 1978. 24 pages. $3.95 [0-88570-014-7] (Etoile filante)

Ji et Pichou, son bébé - tamanoir - mangeur de fourmis - pour-vrai, sont séparés à cause de cette maladie embêtante. Un texte court accompagne les illustrations pleines d'humour, de gaiété. Cassette et disque disponibles. *Tout-petits.*

Asselin, Claude; Un petit nuage. Héritage, 1977. 28 pages. $1.95 [0-7773-2513-6]

Des illustrations nettes suivent un texte simple pour raconter l'histoire d'un petit nuage esseulé. *Tout-petits.*

Beaudet, Sarah; Kingsley, Nina et **Leblanc, Michou;** C'est quoi la garderie? Lesco, Robert (illus.). Editions l'Etincelle, 1974. 16 pages. $1.75 broché.

Le livre illustre plusieurs concepts important qu'un enfant devrait apprendre dans une garderie. Les activités dans ce livre représentent la situation actuelle dans la garderie populaire. *Tout-petits.*

Bussières, Simone; Le petit sapin qui a poussé sur une étoile. Chabot, Cécile (illus.). Les Presses Laurentiennes, 1972. 21 pages. $4.00 (Perce-Neige)

Légende du premier arbre de Noël laissé tout près de la crèche par l'étoile des Mages. Tout-petits, débutants.

Choquette, Pauline; La souris bleue et les papillons cosmonautes. Marie-Anastasie (illus.). Lidec, 1969. 26 pages. $0.50¢

Plus aventureuse que ses soeurs, Farfelette, la petite souris bleue décide d'accompagner les trois papillons cosmonautes dans leur voyage sur la lune. *Tout-petits.*

Corriveau, Monique; Cécile. Corriveau, Marie-Noël (illus.). Editions Jeunesse, 1968. 34 pages. $2.50

Cécile reçut le premier prix du concours littéraire de la Commission du Centenaire, dans la catégorie des Livres pour enfants. Le livre contient trois histoires ravissantes. *Tout-petits.*

Desparois, Lucille; Pirouette cacahuète; conte de Tante Lucille. Gagnon, Cécile (illus.). Editions Héritage, s.d. 16 pages. $1.59 (Albums Héritage)

Marcel, un petit garçon très gourmand, fait un rêve qui lui permettra de corriger son vilain défaut. *Tout-petits.*

Duchesne, Christiane; Lazaros Olibrius. Editions Héritage, 1975. 13 pages. $2.75

L'entente cordiale réalisée par le rire. *Tout-petits.*

Duchesne, Christiane; Le loup, l'oiseau et le violoncelle. La Courte échelle, 1978. 24 pages. $3.95 [0-88570-012-0] (Etoile filante)

Une histoire originale mettant en scène un loup "gentil" qui se lie d'amitié avec un oiseau. Facile à lire. Illustrations de grande qualité. *Tout-petits.*

Duchesne, Christiane; Le serpent vert. Editions Héritage, 1978. 16 pages. $2.50 [0-7773-2514-4] (Les enfants du roi Cléobule)

Histoire d'un serpent et d'un oeuf racontée en quelques mots et magnifiquement illustrée. *Tout-petits.*

Duchesne, Christiane; Le triste dragon. Editions Héritage, 1975. 13 pages. $2.75 [0-7773-2512-8]

Cette fantaisie est pleine de joie de vivre. *Tout-petits.*

Gagnon, Cécile; Les boutons perdus. Héritage, 1979. 16 pages. $0.99¢ [0-7773-4315-0] (Brindille)

Emmanuelle qui perd les boutons verts de son manteau part à leur recherche. *Tout-petits.*

Gagnon, Cécile; Plumeneige. Dansereau, Suzanne (illus.). Héritage, 1980. s.p. $2.50 [0-7773-2534-9]

Un bonhomme de neige prend vie et s'anime. Album attrayant. *Tout-petits.*

Gauthier, Bertrand; Dou Ilvien. Gay, Marie-Louise (illus.). La Courte échelle, 1978. 32 pages. $4.95 broché. [0-88570-016-3] (Etoile filante)

C'est une histoire policière, mais avec la différence qu'elle est humoristique et fantastique. *Moyens.*

Gauthier, Bertrand; Hou Ilva. Gay, Marie-Louise (illus.). La Courte échelle, 1976. 31 pages. $4.95 [0-88570-008-2] (Etoile filante)

Un conte fantaisiste et humoristique composé d'une série d'épisodes bizarres. Une lecture un peu spéciale. *Moyens.*

Gouin, Suzanne; Le ciel amoureux. La Courte échelle, 1979. 24 pages. $5.95 broché [2-89201-010-3]

Une langue poétique embellit le texte de ce livre bien illustré. *Débutants.*

Hébert, Marie-Francine; Abécédaire. Tibo, Gilles (illus.). La Courte échelle, 1979. 32 pages. $5.95 [2-89021-009-X]

Un abécédaire surprenant, fantaisiste et comique qui prétend donner le goût de la lecture et de l'écriture et où on repasse majuscules et minuscules, les écritures en script et cursives. Difficile à lire et à utiliser. Disque ou cassette, et guide d'activités d'animation et d'utilisation pédagogique sont disponibles chez l'éditeur. Certaines pages sont agaçantes à lire. *Débutants.*

Julandré; Une puce dans l'espace. Loranger, Francine (illus.). Héritage, 1976. 32 pages. $2.50 [0-7773-2502-0] (Albums Héritage)

Le grand désir de Pucette, la petite puce est d'aller dans le ciel bleu. Un jour, elle apprend qu'une immense fusée ira bientôt sur la lune. Pucette décide d'y aller et, grâce à son ingéniosité, elle sera la première puce à marcher sur la lune. *Tout-petits.*

Lapointe, Jocelyne; La maison aux couleurs. Les Presses Laurentiennes, 1970. 23 pages. $3.00 (Perce-Neige)

Cet album merveilleux, rempli d'illustrations, déborde de gaieté, de couleurs et de soleil. Raconté dans un style clair et précis. *Tout-petits.*

Larose, Céline; Petit soulier. Larose, Pierre (illus.). Leméac, 1979. s.p. $8.95 [2-7609-9830-4]

Un soulier perdu à la recherche de son compagnon. *Tout-petits.*

Larose, Céline; Une tomate inquiète. Larose, Pierre (illus.). Leméac, 1979. s.p. $8.95 [2-7609-9829-0]

Une tomate s'interroge sur son identité. Ouvrage imprimé en gros caractères avec illustrations simples et originales. *Tout-petits.*

Ledoux, Lucie; La 8e merveille. Lidec, 1979. 22 pages. $6.75 [2-7608-1502-1] (Albums Lidec)

Quand une petite fille ferme les yeux, elle voyage très loin - et "sans un sou en poche." *Débutants.*

Lefrançois, Alexis; Eglantine et Mélancolie. Bassery, Christine (illus.). Grasset, 1979. s.p.

Histoire d'amour entre une vieille maison, Eglantine, et une chèvre, Mélancolie. Ecriture précise, illustrations luxuriantes. *Tout-petits.*

Major, Henriette; Les 5 frères. Gagnon, Cécile (illus.). Héritage, 1979. 16 pages. $0.99¢ [0-7773-4314-2] (Brindille)

Major, Henriette; Doudou les assiettes. Major, Henriette (illus.). Héritage, 1979. 16 pages. $0.99¢ [0-7773-4316-9] (Brindille)

Major, Henriette; Kapuk. Gagnon, Cécile (illus.). Héritage, 1979. 16 pages. $0.99¢ [0-7773-4318-5] (Brindille)

Trois petits albums qui amuseront les petits. *Tout-petits.*

Major, Henriette; Un drôle de petit cheval bleu. Gaucher, Guy (illus.). C.P.P./Leméac, 1967. 58 pages. $4.95 (Coccinelle)

Un petit cheval bleu pas comme les autres. Illustrations humoristiques et caricaturales. *Tout-petits.*

Major, Henriette; La surprise de dame Chenille. C.P.P./Leméac, 1970. 48 pages. $4.95 (Premiers Pas)

L'histoire de dame Chenille qui, le temps venu, trouve un endroit confortable pour se reposer et se transforme en un très beau papillon. *Tout-petits.*

Mérinat, Eric; Les perles de pluie. Fontannaz, Lucienne (illus.). La Courte échelle, 1975, 1979. 27 pages. $4.95 broché. [2-89021-004-9]

Conte dans lequel un chat est intrigué par les perles que trois lézards portent entre leurs pattes. Lorsqu'il apprend que les perles ont un pouvoir magique, le chat décide de partir à la recherche de l'une de ces perles. *Débutants.*

Plante, Raymond; Une fenêtre dans ma tête. Paré, Roger (illus.). La Courte échelle, 1979. 2 vols. $2.95 [2-89021-000-6] $3.95. [2-89021-011-1]

Oeuvre un peu spéciale où l'imagination de l'enfant est sans cesse sollicitée. Illustrations gaies et amusantes. Prix Conseil des arts du Canada, 1980 pour les illustrations. *Tous-petits, débutants.*

Pomminville, Louise; L'Abécédaire de Pitatou. Leméac, 1979. 54 pages. $9.95 [2-7609-9831-2]

Présentation agréable, cependant l'auteur a choisi de ne représenter dans l'illustration que quelques mots de chaque liste. *Tout-petits.*

Pomminville, Louise; Pitatou et la Gaspésie. Leméac, 1973. 23 pages. $5.95

Les oiseaux de la forêt de Nulle-Part visitent la Gaspésie et s'émerveillent devant la mer, le rocher percé, les fous de bassan et les macareux. *Tout-petits.*

Pomminville, Louise; Pitatou et le printemps. Leméac, 1972. 25 pages. $5.95

Au pays des merveilleux oiseaux de la forêt de Nulle-Part, c'est le printemps et on s'apprête à fêter le retour de Pitapatte l'oiseau migrateur, le grand voyageur. *Tout-petits.*

Pomminville, Louise; Pitatou et le sport amateur. Leméac, 1976. 38 pages. $5.95 [0-7761-9824-6]

Les oiseaux de la forêt de Nulle-Part organisent et participent à une olympiade. *Tout-petits.*

Pomminville, Louise; Pitatou et les pommiers. Leméac, 1972. 25 pages. $5.95

Petit conte sur les oiseaux de la forêt de Nulle-Part qui découvrent les pommiers et écoutent Pitaguitare le troubadour des bois. *Tout-petits.*

Pomminville, Louise et **Deprez, Marie Rose;** Pitatou et la neige. Pomminville, Louise (illus.). Leméac, 1978. 28 pages. $7.95 [0-7761-9827-0]

Les merveilleux oiseaux de la forêt de Nulle-Part transmettent encore une fois, leur message d'amour et d'amitié. *Tout-petits.*

Rioux, René; Cléo. Lapointe, Michèle (illus.). Héritage, 1975. 35 pages. $0.99¢ [0-7773-2501-2]

Ayant échappé de justesse au grand oiseau jaune, Cléo, la petite chenille rouge, décide d'abandonner ses amies les chenilles vertes. Le lendemain, ces dernières décident de partir à la retrouvaille de leur amie et secourent Cléo qui allait être mangé par Monsieur Croque. *Tout-petits.*

Sarrasin, Francin; Pétale. Deschamps, Yves (illus.). Paulines, 1975. 14 pages. $0.95¢

Un petit garçon apprend les joies et les peines de l'amitié en se liant d'amitié avec un oiseau. *Tout-petits.*

Scalabrini, Rita; La famille Citrouillard. Leméac, 1974. 23 pages. $4.95

Généalogie de la famille Citrouillard souche de Melon-Doux du côté du père et de Poirot du côté de la mère. *Tout-petits.*

Scalabrini, Rita; La famille Citrouillard au temps des sucres. Leméac, 1976. 32 pages. $4.95 [0-7761-9825-4]

Un texte très didactique et des dessins vivants et poétiques apprennent aux enfants la fabrication du sirop d'érable. *Tout-petits, débutants.*

Scalabrini, Rita; La famille Citrouillard aux poissons des chenaux. Leméac, 1979. s.p. $8.95 [2-7609-9828-2]

Un album tout-à-fait réussi sur un événement annuel à Trois-Rivières. *Tout-petits, débutants.*

Scalabrini, Rita; Le petit Chocola Cho. Leméac, 1972. 25 pages. $4.95

Histoire d'un petit train Chocola Cho qui se promène à travers champs et salue ses amis, les bouleaux, les pins et les vaches. *Tout-petits.*

Soulières, Robert; Le bal des chenilles. Lemieux, Michèle (illus.). Pierre Tisseyre, 1979. 22 pages. $1.95 [2-89051-016-6]

Une chenille, seule pour le bal, fait passer une annonce et trouve ainsi un papillon pour l'accompagner . . . Illustrations en noir et blanc. *Tout-petits.*

Soulières, Robert; Max le magicien. Valcourt, Christiane (illus.). La Courte échelle, 1979. 24 pages. $3.95 [2-89021-008-1]

Les gants magiques de Max lui procurent tout ce qu'il désire . . . jusqu'au jour où Max ne désire plus rien et découvre la vraie vie. *Moyens.*

Suzie; Les amis de Pierrot. Paulines, 1974. 14 pages. $0.95¢

Un petit garçon découvre l'amitié. *Tout-petits.*

Suzie; La bottine vagabonde. Paulines, 1975. 14 pages. $0.95¢

Une bottine difforme trouve le bonheur en s'installant dans la forêt. *Tout-petits.*

Suzie; Les trois petits sapins. Paulines, 1974. 14 pages. $0.95¢

La réalisation des rêves de trois sapins. *Tout-petits.*

Thériault, Yves; Cajetan et la taupe. Poirier, Michel (illus.). Paulines, 1979. 15 pages. $2.75 broché. [2-89039-016-0] (Contes du pays)

Cajetan, un petit garçon, est bon pour une taupe qui en retour le sauve du froid. *Tout-petits.*

Vaillancourt, Lise; Les Greseaux. Lidec, 1969. 31 pages. $5.70 [2-7608-1501-3] (Albums Lidec)

Les Greseaux sont des personnages imaginaires qui ont "les yeux ronds, les pieds longs, un nombril comme de raison." *Tout-petits.*

Valiquette, Yolande; Le temps du plastique. Lidec, 1979. s.p. $7.95 [2-7608-1504-8]

Conte écologique conçu et imagé par l'auteur. Vocabulaire riche. Illustrations avant-gardistes. *Moyens.*

Vallières, Anne; Ouram. Leméac, 1973. 16 pages. $4.50 (Littérature de Jeunesse)

Histoire d'un animal bizarre, moitié ours, moitié hippopotame. *Tout-petits.*

BANDES DESSINEES

Bastien, Gabriel; Monsieur Petit pois au soleil. Héritage, 1974. $0.99¢ [0-7773-2031-2]

Bastien, Gabriel; Monsieur Petit pois: Dialoguer. Héritage, 1975. $0.99¢ [0-7773-2032-0]

Bastien, Gabriel; Monsieur Petit pois: Ombre et lumière. Héritage, 1975. $0.99¢ [0-7773-2033-9]

Des illustrations charmantes aux couleurs agréables, peu de texte. Humour tranquille. ***Grands, aînés.***

Brault, André et **Henri Desclez;** Nic et Pic. Héritage/Société Radio-Canada, 1978. s.p. [0-7773-0807-X]

Les marionnettes Nic et Pic créées pour la télévision racontent quelques-unes de leurs aventures. Illustrations en noir et blanc. ***Tout-petits, débutants.***

Cailloux, Michel; Nic et Pic: Complot en Amérique du Sud. Poirier, Claude et Serge Wilson (illus.). Héritage/Société Radio-Canada, 1977. $1.29 [0-7773-2015-0]

Cailloux, Michel; Nic et Pic: Le dangereux inventeur. Poirier, Claude et Serge Wilson (illus.). Héritage/Société Radio-Canada, 1974. $1.29 [0-7773-2012-6]

Cailloux, Michel; Nic et Pic: La Fée draglonne. Poirier, Claude et Serge Wilson (illus.). Héritage/Société Radio-Canada, 1975. $1.29 [0-7773-2010-X]

Cailloux, Michel; Nic et Pic: Le génie de l'érablière. Poirier, Claude et Serge Wilson (illus.). Héritage/Société Radio-Canada, 1975. $1.29 [0-7773-2013-4]

Cailloux, Michel; Nic et Pic et le pirate. Poirier, Claude et Serge Wilson (illus.). Héritage/Société Radio-Canada, 1977. $1.29 [0-7773-2016-9]

Nic et Pic sont des souris marionnettes réalisées par Pierre Régimbald et Nicole Lapointe pour une série télévisée. Divertissant. ***Débutants.***

Munson, Harold; Koli. Orion, 1979. 23 pages. [2-89124-004-9]

Personnifiant la vie d'un manchot. Illustrations en noir et blanc. ***Débutants.***

LECTURE FACILE

Allen, Robert Thomas; Le violon. Martin, Claire (trad.). Pierre Tisseyre, Cercle du livre de France, 1976. 79 pages. $6.95 [0-7753-0092-6]

Né du film *Le violon*, c'est une histoire d'amour entre un enfant, un vieillard et un violon. Les photographies sont de George Pastic. *Débutants.*

Bussières, Simone; Les fables des trois commères. Bédard, Laurent (illus.). Les Presses Laurentiennes, 1962. 32 pages. $1.75

Trois contes amusants et humoristiques: l'aventure de monsieur et madame Bobby (l'histoire de deux chiens), Ratapon le chat et Tigris le rat, et l'histoire du petit canard qui voulait se faire paon. *Débutants.*

Carbet, Marie-Madeleine; Contes de Tantana. Léveillé, Jacques (illus.). Leméac, 1980. 187 pages. $8.95 [2-7609-9833-9]

Dans une langue imagée, l'auteur raconte les expériences d'enfants antillais et québécois. Plus une étude de moeurs qu'un livre de contes. *Moyens.*

Champagne, Edith; Le vieil homme aux bulles. de Beney, Gabriel (illus.). Paulines, 1979. 15 pages. $2.75 broché. [2-89039-021-7] (Contes du pays)

Des cheveux d'un gentil vieil homme que personne ne connaît et n'a jamais vu sortent des bulles qui inondent de joie ceux pour qui elles sont créées. *Débutants.*

Côté, Louis-Philippe; La fée d'Azur. Pelletier, Marie Gravel (illus.). Les Contes du Bocage. s.d. 30 pages. $2.70

Belle légende québécoise où la fée d'azur est enfin délivrée par Pierre-Pierre le frère de Jean-Jean. *Débutants.*

Côté, Louis-Philippe; Les huîtres magiques. Méthé, Louise (illus.). La Courte échelle, 1975. 29 pages. $4.95 broché.

Un conte de fée où un prince recherche son épouse qui a disparu le jour du mariage. Il traverse pays et océans pour la retrouver dans les forêts du Saguenay. Illustrations charmantes. Cassette et disque disponibles. *Débutants.*

Côté, Louis-Philippe; Le prince Sourire et le lys bleu. Tibo, Gilles (illus.). La Courte échelle, 1975, 1979. 32 pages. $4.95 broché. [2-89021-005-7]

Un conte de fée, du genre traditionnel, où le prince Sourire est protégé par sa marraine (une fée) et le lys bleu, sa fleur protectrice. *Débutants.*

Coulombe, Pauline; Mon ami parmi les oiseaux. Dunnigan, Huguette (illus.). Paulines, 1979. 15 pages. $2.75 [2-89039-018-7] (Contes du pays)

Un récit lent et tendre qui raconte l'amitié entre un vieillard et un petit garçon. *Débutants.*

Gagnon, Cécile; L'Epouvantail et le champignon. Héritage, 1978. 126 pages. $2.50 broché. [0-7773-4411-4] (Pour lire avec toi)

Un petit recueil de contes très frais dans lequel les enfants retrouveront les mêmes personnages que dans le précédent livre de l'auteur-illustrateur, *Plume-neige,* dans la même collection. *Débutants, moyens.*

Gagnon, Cécile; Plumeneige. Héritage, 1976. 126 pages. $2.50 [0-7773-4405-X] (Pour lire avec toi)

Une série de charmantes histoires se déroulant au village de Plumetis, ayant pour thèmes principaux l'hiver et la neige. *Débutants.*

Gauthier, Bertrand; Etoifilan. Pednault, Gilles (illus.). La Courte échelle, 1975. 29 pages. $4.95 [0-88570-003-1] (Etoile filante)

Protégé par l'étoile et ses deux amis, la mouche à feu et le papillon, Etoifilan ne manquera plus jamais de travail et pourra ainsi continuer à danser et à chanter. Disque et cassette disponibles. *Débutants.*

Lachance, Jeanne; Le voyage de Lapin Noir. Bédard, France (illus.). Héritage, 1977. 125 pages. $1.95 [0-7773-4406-8] (Pour lire avec toi)

Roman de science fiction facile. Lapin Noir et ses amis visiteront une planète bien étrange après un voyage à bord d'une sphère qu'ils ont trouvée en forêt. Les illustrations constituent un support intéressant au texte. *Débutants.*

LeBel, Louise; Histoires à réinventer. Gage, 1980. 96 pages. $5.50 [0-7715-2502-8]

Un texte qui présente quelques contes d'enfants des quatre coins du pays. Questions à la fin de chaque histoire et lexique. Aquarelles de l'auteur. *Moyens.*

Loranger, Francine; Tourbillon, le lutin de la Côte-Nord. Shelton, Danielle (illus.). Héritage, 1977. 121 pages. $2.50 broché [0-7773-4407-6] (Pour lire avec toi)

L'auteur sait parler de réalités d'aujourd'hui sans quitter le terrain onirique propre au conte. *Débutants.*

Major, Henriette; Les contes de l'arc-en-ciel. Shelton, Danielle (illus.). Héritage, 1976. 124 pages. $2.50 [0-7773-4401-7] (Pour lire avec toi)

Dix contes très courts pour ceux qui aiment le rêve et la fantaisie. *Débutants, moyens.*

Major, Henriette; Un jour, une rivière. Cornuel, Pierre (illus.). La Farandole, 1978. 29 pages. $6.25 [2-7047-0088-5]

Un petit Algonquin, qui croyait posséder une rivière, accepte de partager sa rivière avec les animaux, les poissons et les humains. *Débutants.*

Renaud, Bernadette; Emilie, la baignoire à pattes. Bédard, France (illus.). Héritage, 1976. 126 pages. $2.50 [0-7773-4400-9] (Pour lire avec toi)

Les aventures cocasses d'Emilie, la baignoire à pattes qui n'accepte pas facilement d'être rejetée au hangar par ses maîtres après les avoir servis si longtemps. *Débutants.*

Renaud, Bernadette; La maison tête de pioche. Ledoux, Lucie (illus.). Héritage, 1979. 124 pages. $2.50 [0-7773-4415-7] (Pour lire avec toi)

Une vieille maison vient d'être achetée par un jeune couple qui commence aussitôt à la restaurer. Interprétant mal ces bonnes intentions, elle leur en fait voir de toutes les couleurs. De l'humour, un texte vivant grâce aux nombreux dialogues. *Débutants.*

Renaud, Bernadette; La révolte de la courtepointe. Ledoux, Lucie (illus.). Fides, 1979. 95 pages. $5.95 [2-7621-0961-2]

Julie reçoit une courtepointe à Noël. Très déçue de ces vieilles guenilles qu'elle juge inutiles, elle s'endort ce soir-là en pleurant . . . Une histoire amusante et une héroïne bien sympathique. *Débutants, moyens.*

Roy, Gabrielle; Courte-Queue. Olivier, François (illus.). Editions internationales Alain Stanké, 1979. s.p. $6.95 broché. [2-7604-0053-0]

Le conte de la chatte Courte-Queue qui réussit à sauver ses petits en les escamotant. Prix Conseil des arts du Canada, 1980. *Moyens.*

Roy, Gabrielle; Ma vache Bossie. Pomminville, Louise (illus.). Leméac, 1976. 46 pages. $5.95 [0-7761-9823-8]

Une petite fille reçoit comme cadeau de fête une vache que l'on nomme Bossie. *Moyens.*

Thériault, Yves; Nakika, le petit algonquin. Lapointe, Nicole (illus.). Leméac, 1962. 23 pages. $4.95 (Collection Castor)

Nakika est sûrement le plus malheureux des algonquins, car tous se moquent de son nom. Tout va en s'aggravant jusqu'au jour où, grâce à un pouvoir magique, il devient l'algonquin le plus respecté du village. *Débutants.*

Thériault, Yves; Nauya le petit esquimau. Brosseau, Claude (illus.). Beauchemin, 1963. 62 pages. $4.95 [0-7750-0180-5]

Petit esquimau du Grand Nord canadien, Nauya est un petit garçon déterminé qui n'a qu'un seul défaut. Il aime bien jouer des tours. *Débutants.*

Thériault, Yves; Zibou et Coucou. Leméac, 1964. 23 pages. $3.95 (Collection Castor)

Zibou et Coucou sauvent Oiseauville d'une grande catastrophe et sont, par la suite, honorés pour leur dévouement. *Débutants.*

Vigneault, Gilles; Les quatre saisons de Piquot. Barrett, Hugh John (illus.). Nouvelles éditions de l'Arc, 1979. 36 pages et disque. $12.95 [2-89016-000-9]

Un petit chef-d'oeuvre littéraire déclamé sur disque. Merveilleux, attrayant. *Débutants.*

Villeneuve, Jocelyne; Contes des quatre saisons. Bédard, France (illus.). Héritage, 1978. 125 pages. $2.50 [0-7773-4412-2] (Pour lire avec toi)

Sept courtes histoires, variées et joliment illustrées, cependant d'inégal intérêt. *Débutants, moyens.*

Warnant-Coté, Marie-Andrée; L'enchanteur du pays d'Oz. Devlin, Michèle (illus.). Héritage, 1977. 125 pages. $2.50 [0-7773-4410-6] (Pour lire avec toi)

Une adaptation intéressante d'un classique. La présentation est soignée et attrayante. *Débutants.*

Wilscam, Lynda; Les mots ... de Picotine - L'homme aux ballons. Gagnon, Cécile (illus.). Héritage, 1977. 108 pages. $2.50 [0-7773-4406-8] (Pour lire avec toi)

Picotine et ses amis ont de la difficulté à comprendre un vendeur de ballon. Plaira tout particulièrement à ceux qui connaissent Picotine. *Débutants, moyens.*

Wilson, Serge; Marie-Mardi. Le secret d'Anthime. Devlin, Michèle (illus.). Héritage, 1978. 123 pages. $2.50 [0-7773-4414-9] (Pour lire avec toi)

Marie-Mardi, fée apprentie, doit accomplir une mission au pays des humains. C'est le début d'une aventure mouvementée. *Débutants, moyens.*

Zola, Mélanie; Le loup blanc. Holt, 1973. 28 pages. $1.95 [0-03-929462-5]

Un loup montre sa reconnaissance à deux enfants qui ont demandé à leur père de l'épargner, lorsque ces derniers s'égarent dans la forêt. *Débutants.*

ROMANS

Aubert de Gaspé, Phillipe; Les anciens canadiens. Fides, 1970. 360 pages. $5.95 [0-7755-0201-4] (Bibliothèque canadienne-française)

Deux amis, l'un Ecossais, l'autre Français, deviennent ennemis par la guerre de la conquête (1760). *Grands, aînés.*

Aylwin, Louise; Raminagradu: histoires ordinaires pour enfants extraordinaires. Editions du Jour, 1975. 96 pages. $4.50

Un recueil de contes merveilleux, fantastiques et philosophiques. Les illustrations sont linéaires et le texte manuscrit. *Moyens, grands.*

Benoît, Jean; Le tournoi. Paulines, 1976. 157 pages. $4.50 relié [0-88840-576-6] $2.75 broché [0-88840-581-2]

Voici la suite de *Une . . . Deux . . . Trois prises. T'es mort,* bien que ces deux romans peuvent être lus séparément avec intérêt. Roman sportif très vivant. *Moyens.*

Benoît, Jean; Une . . . deux . . . trois prises. T'es mort. Paulines, 1976. 149 pages. $4.50 relié. [0-88840-576-6]; $2.75 broché. [0-88840-581-2] (Jeunesse-pop)

Une équipe de baseball, Le Pee-Wee du Saint-Mathias, grâce à un nouvel instructeur dynamique et compétent, réussit à se classer pour le tournoi du parc Lafontaine. *Moyens.*

Bernard, Maria; Les morceaux de soleil de Memnoukia. Jeunesse, 1969. 138 pages. $2.50 [0-7752-4071-8] (Karim)

A l'époque de la Nouvelle-France, deux fillettes découvrent le monde gaspésien quand elles sont en quête du mystérieux secret des Abénaquis. *Moyens.*

Boulizon, Guy; Alexandre et les prisonniers des cavernes. Knaff, Jean Christian (illus.). Fides, 1979. 169 pages. $7.95 broché. [0-7621-0732-6] (Goéland)

Sept jeunes scouts français et un jeune Québécois se trouvent soudain engagés dans une aventure dans le monde souterrain des cavernes, plein d'enchantements et de pièges. *Grands.*

Bourque, Sophie; Le paradis terrestre. Editions Le livre du pays, 1979. 59 pages. $3.00 [2-920095-00-5] (Clauchar)

Le récit écrit et illustré par un enfant raconte une étonnante aventure qui a mené jusqu'au paradis terrestre. Imprimé en caractères de manuscrit. Illustrations primitives. *Moyens.*

Burnford, Sheila; L'incroyable randonnée. G.P., 1965. 185 pages. $4.20 [103-239-0A] (Rouge et or Souveraine)

Deux chiens et un chat mis en pension dans le Nord de l'Ontario, parcourent plusieurs milles afin de retrouver leur foyer. Traduction de *The Incredible journey. Moyens, grands.*

Chabot, Cécile; Et le cheval vert. Fides, 1980. 144 pages. $8.50 [2-7621-1008-4] (Goéland)

Trois petites filles vivent à la campagne, à l'ombre d'un merveilleux et tendre quotidien. Elles grandissent et c'est la fin des rires et des jeux. Contes qui permettront de cavaler sur les plages de l'enfance. *Grands.*

Charland, Jean-Pierre; Le naufrage. Editions du Jour, 1975. 110 pages. $3.50 [0-7760-0649-5]

Une histoire palpitante, inquiétante qui apprend agréablement comment est fait un sous-marin et comment on y vit. Prix Marie-Claire Daveluy. *Grands, aînés.*

Choquette, Adrienne; Je m'appelle Pax: histoire d'un chien heureux qui médite sur son bonheur. Les Presses Laurentiennes, c1974. 56 pages. $4.95 [2-89015-008-9]

Histoire d'un chien boxer choyé de tous et très heureux de son sort. Abondamment illustré de photographies. *Moyens.*

Clément, Béatrice; Malmenoir le mauvais. Editions Jeunesse, 1964. 144 pages. $2.50 (Brin d'herbe)

Trois contes de jadis et de naguère. Le premier date du temps des Croisades. Les deux autres racontent des incidents de la vie d'enfants de la Nouvelle-France, menacés par les Iroquois ou par la guerre de 1760. *Moyens.*

Clermont, Marie-Andrée; Alerte au lac des loups. Bergeron, André (illus.). Fides, 1980. 138 pages. $8.50 [2-7621-1000-9] (Goéland)

Au coeur des Laurentides, une dizaine d'adolescents campent insouciants jusqu'à ce qu'ils flairent le mystère. *Grands, aînés.*

Corriveau, Monique; Les compagnons du soleil. Fides, 1976. 3 vols. $9.95 chacun. [0-7755-0592-7] [0-7755-0593-5] [0-7755-0594-3]

Voici une trilogie passionnante de science-fiction où deux mondes s'affrontent. *Grands, aînés.*

Corriveau, Monique; Le garçon au cerf-volant. Méthé, Louise (illus.). Fides, 1974. 137 pages. $7.95 [0-7755-0515-3]

Un livre de qualité rempli d'aventures, plein de beauté et de poésie. Le roman de l'amitié entre un père et son fils. *Moyens.*

Corriveau, Monique; La petite fille du printemps. Pomminville, Louise (illus.). Fides, 1978. 124 pages. $7.95 [0-7755-0705-9] (Goéland)

Publiée il y a 12 ans pour la première fois, cette histoire d'orpheline malheureuse sera populaire auprès de nombreux lecteurs. *Moyens.*

Corriveau, Monique; Patrick et Sophie en fusée. Héritage, 1975, 1979. 265 pages. $3.50 [7773-3400-3] (Galaxie)

Durant leurs vacances, les jumeaux, Vincent et Sophie, montent à bord d'une fusée et voyagent à travers le temps. Sophie en profite pour écrire un livre racontant l'extraordinaire aventure qu'ils vivent dans une tribu Micmac. *Moyens.*

Corriveau, Monique; Les saisons de la mer. Méthé, Louise (illus.). Fides, 1975. 154 pages. $7.95 (Goéland)

Histoire de Marie-Lou et de son frère David, vivant dans le décor d'une petite île au large de Terre-Neuve. *Grands.*

Corriveau, Monique; Le secret de Vanille. Crespo, Colette (illus.). Jeunesse, 1972. (c1962). 131 pages. $2.50 (Brin d'herbe)

Un captivant roman mystère. Une histoire riche de couleur locale et de vie enfantine. *Moyens.*

Corriveau, Monique; Le Wapiti. Wilson, Mélinda (illus.). Fides, 1978. 177 pages. $7.95 [0-7755-0685-0] (Goéland)

C'est un roman historique, nous sommes en Nouvelle-France au XVIIème siècle. Egalement un roman d'aventures avec l'histoire de Mathieu, un Wapiti chez les indiens Seskanous. *Grands, aînés.*

Côté, Maryse; Les chandeliers d'argent. Héritage, 1975. 125 pages. $2.95 broché [0-7773-3007-5]

Vers 1689, une flotte anglaise attaque la ville de Québec. François, fait prisonnier, accompagne un officier anglais qui convoite les chandeliers d'argent de la chapelle des Jésuites et réussit à déjouer ses plans. Un roman historique. *Grands.*

Darios, Louise; Chat Alexandre au Brésil. Shaker, Ihab (illus.). Héritage, 1976. 220 pages. $2.95 [0-7773-3009-1] (Katimavik)

Le chat Alexandre, journaliste québécois, est chargé de faire une série de reportages au Brésil pour Radio-Chachacha de Montréal. *Grands.*

Darios, Louise; Le chat Alexandre d'un Canada à l'autre. Shaker, Ihab (illus.). Héritage, 1980. 266 pages. $3.50 [0-7773-3014-8] (Katimavik)

Une investigation des décors et de la population canadienne. Croquis amusants. Humour tranquille. *Grands.*

Daveluy, Paule; Une année du tonnerre 1: La maison des vacances. Thérien, Lise (illus.). Fides, 1977. 137 pages. $4.95 [0-7755-0662-1] (Goéland)

Daveluy, Paule; Une année du tonnerre 2: Rosanne et la vie. Thérien, Lise (illus.). Fides, 1977. 137 pages. $4.95 [0-7755-0663-X] (Goéland)

Condensé, retravaillé et mise au présent de *L'été enchanté. Drôle d'automne, Cet hiver là,* du genre d'intrigue sentimentale. *Grands, aînés.*

De Roquebrune, Robert; Les habits rouges. Guberek, Josée (illus.). Fides, 1978. 135 pages. $7.95 [0-7755-0684-2] (Goéland)

Roman d'amour et de moeurs ainsi que roman historique situé aux temps de la rebellion des "Fils de la Liberté." Un classique réédité pour les jeunes d'aujourd'hui. *Aînés.*

De Roquebrune, Robert; La Seigneuresse. Fides, 1977. 270 pages. $8.95

Une intrigue amoureuse avec une dimension historique raconte la vie dans la Nouvelle Colonie, les moeurs indiennes, les guerres, mais surtout l'histoire vraie de Louise de Normandville, belle, fortuné, et prise entre deux amours. *Aînés.*

Des Rivières, Madeleine-M.; Ronde autour de mon pays. Bouchard, Jacqueline (illus.). Editions Jeunesse, 1968. 126 pages. $2.50 (Brin d'herbe)

Contes typiques des différentes provinces du Canada. *Moyens.*

Deslongchamps, Roxanne; Les Ozerov - v.l. - L'héritier. Girard, Paule (illus.). Fides, 1978. 273 pages. $5.95 [0-7755-0686-9] (Espace-temps)

Très bon roman d'aventures. Le lecteur suivra avec intérêt Karel, héritier du trône à 14 ans, et l'histoire de la famille Ozerov. *Grands, aînés.*

Elmont, Fred; Les petits chaperons de toutes les couleurs. Boisvert, Irène (illus.). Stanké-Quinze, 1976. 192 pages. $6.50 [0-88566-009-9]

Des contes amusants, bien écrits, aux illustrations intéressantes, qui nous font rencontrer cinq nouveaux chaperons: le Jaune, le Blanc, le Rose, le Bleu et le Vert. *Moyens.*

Gagnon, Geneviève; 22,222 milles à l'heure. Editions de l'Actuelle, 1972. 75 pages. $1.00

Récits très simple de science-fiction. *Moyens.*

Gagnon, Maurice; Le fils du grand Jim. Héritage, 1974. 250 pages. $2.95 [0-7773-3002-4] (Katimavik)

L'histoire du petit Jim, plutôt chétif mais déterminé, qui atteindra le sommet d'une prestigieuse carrière dans la ligue nationale comme gardien de but. *Moyens.*

Gagnon, Maurice; Simon. Héritage, 1975, 1979. 222 pages. $2.95 [0-7773-3006-7]

Le portrait intime d'un de ces joueurs professionels qui jouent au hockey dans une grande équipe. *Moyens.*

Gaudreault-Labrecque, Madeleine; Alerte ce soir à 22 heures. Editions Hurtubise HMH, 1979. $5.95 broché. [2-89045-209-3] (Hurtubise HMH Jeunesse)

Une aventure de Michel Labre dans un monde de grandes découvertes scientifiques. *Grands, aînés.*

Gaudreault-Labrecque, Madeleine; Vol à bord du Concordia. Editions Hurtubise HMH, 1979. $4.95 broché [2-89045-210-7] (Hurtubise HMH Jeunesse)

La disparition du livre de bord contenant les renseignements techniques de haute importance précipite un grand émoi. *Grands, aînés.*

Grandbois-Paquin, Gabrielle; La petite fille aux yeux rouge. Bergeron, André (illus.). Fides, 1978. 169 pages. $7.95 [0-7755-0672-9] (Goéland)

La petite Bernadette Rousseau a perdu sa mère et ce drame vivra en elle toute sa jeunesse. Cette histoire de la mère d'Alain Grandbois nous plonge dans l'atmosphère du début du siècle. Prix Alvine Bélisle 1978. *Grands, aînés.*

Guèvremont, Germaine; En pleine terre. Bergeron, André (illus.). Fides, 1976. 140 pages. $7.95 [0-7755-0598-6] (Goéland)

Réédition du premier ouvrage de l'auteur paru en 1942. Un recueil de quatorze tableaux paysans et de quatre contes de la région soreloise transmettant l'héritage des ancêtres et leur parlure savoureuse. *Aînés.*

Guèvremont, Germaine; Le Survenant. Fides, 1974. 224 pages. $4.50 [0-7755-0197-2] (Bibliothèque canadienne-française)

Le drame de l'extinction de la dynastie paysanne des Beauchemin. *Aînés.*

Hays, Wilma Pitchford; Le tambour de Montcalm. Côté, Maryse (trad.). Héritage, 1974. 202 pages. $2.95 broché. [0-7773-3003-2]

Les aventures de Pierre de Mont tantôt espion du gouverneur Vaudreuil, tantôt tambour du général Montcalm. Traduction de *Drummer boy for Montcalm. Grands.*

Hémon, Louis; Maria Chapdelaine. Fides, 1970. 216 pages. $3.95 [0-7755-0355-X] (Bibliothèque canadienne-française)

Un tableau de la vie des colons du Lac Saint-Jean. *Aînés.*

Jacob, Michèle; Feuilles de thym et fleurs d'amour. Actuelle. s.d. 78 pages. $1.00

La vie dans le sous-bois est dépeinte dans les mots réalistes et imaginatifs d'un jeune auteur de quatorze ans. *Débutants, moyens.*

Leclerc, Félix; Le fou de l'île. Fides, 1970. 216 pages. $4.50 [0-7755-0265-0] (Bibliothèque canadienne-française)

Un fou et son cerf-volant viennent déranger des gens tranquilles. *Aînés.*

Lefebvre, Reynald; Les voyageurs du temps. Guberek, Josée (illus.). Fides, 1978. $2.95 (Espace-Temps)

Deuxième prix Marie-Claire Daveluy 1973. Roman de science-fiction où l'objet de l'intrigue est la machine à voyager dans le temps. Long et inégal. *Grands, aînés.*

Loranger, Francine; Chansons pour un ordinateur. Bouchard, Laurent (illus.). Fides, 1980. 101 pages. $8.50 [2-7621-1001-7] (Goéland)

Un vaisseau spacial change de trajectoir. Perdus dans le cosmos, ses occupants tentent de reprendre leur route. *Grands.*

Loranger, Francine; Le renard rose. Bédard, Frances (illus.). Héritage, 1976. 121 pages. $2.50 [0-7773-4404-1] (Pour lire avec toi)

Monsieur La Belette est chargé de retrouver le Renard Rose qui a disparu très mystérieusement lors de la présentation de la pièce de théâtre qu'il avait lui-même composée pour fêter le Carnaval d'hiver. *Moyens.*

Major, Henriette; A la conquête du temps. Jeunesse, 1970. 126 pages. $2.50 [0-7772-4077-7] (Karim)

Une invention permit à un frère et une soeur de retourner aux temps d'Etienne Brûlé et de revivre à Ville-Marie de 1689. *Moyens.*

Major, Henriette; Le club des curieux. Fides, 1967. 122 pages. $4.95 (Collection les quatre vents)

Les aventures d'une bande de jeune curieux qui arrivent à percer le mystère de la disparition de l'oncle Horace. *Moyens.*

Major, Henriette; Elise et l'oncle riche. Devlin, Michèle (illus.). Fides, 1979. 110 pages. $7.95 [2-7621-0731-8]

A treize ans, âge du premier amour, des joies et des peines, de l'adolescence, une jeune montréalaise rêve d'un oncle riche et d'une vie meilleure. *Grands.*

Markoosie; Le harpon du chasseur. Martin, Claire (trans.). Arnaktauyok, Germaine (illus.). Cercle du Livre de France, 1971. 95 pages. $3.95

Un roman esquimau traduit de l'anglais, *Harpoon of the hunter.* C'est une histoire de survie dans le nord canadien. *Grands.*

Martel, Suzanne; Jeanne, fille du roy. Poirier, Michelle (illus.). Fides, 1974. 254 pages. $7.95 (Goéland)

Le roman de Jeanne, courageuse "fille du roi," qui débarque en Nouvelle France, un pays où la vie est dure et isolée, les Iroquois menacent et l'hiver est rigoureux. *Grands.*

Martel, Suzanne; Les Montcorbier. v.1. - L'apprentissage d'Arahé. Fides, 1979. 368 pages, $13.95 [2-7621-0781-4] v.2 - Première armes - *1918*. Fides, 1979. 432 pages. $13.95 [2-7621-0782-2]

Récit dramatique, coupé d'incidents humoristiques ou tragiques, raconte les aventures d'Arnaud de Montcorbier, garçon attachant et casse-cou, à la fois musicien et bagarreur, l'épreuve et la fierté de son frère aîné, le duc Paul de Montcorbier. Sur un fond historique, celui de la guerre de 1914-1918, l'action se dessine dans une atmosphère mi-orientale, mi-européenne. *Aînés.*

Martel, Suzanne; Pi-oui. Héritage, 1974, 1979. 186 pages. $3.50 [0-7773-3004-0] (Katimavik)

L'histoire de la vie quotidienne de Pi-oui, un jeune joueur de hockey. *Moyens.*

Martel, Suzanne; Titralak, cadet de l'espace. Héritage, 1974, 1979. 282 pages. $3.50 [0-7773-3401-7] (Galaxie)

Un roman de science-fiction, très animant, dans lequel les héros voyagent à travers le temps et l'espace. *Moyens.*

Maxine; Le petit page de Frontenac. Lemieux, André (illus.). Pedagogia, 1963. 160 pages. $2.00

Le petit Jean est recueilli par les Iroquois après le massacre de Lachine. Revenu à Québec, il devient le page du gouverneur. *Moyens.*

Miville-Deschenes, Jean; La mafia du pensionnat. Fides, 1964. 106 pages. $4.95 (Collection les quatre vents)

Dans un carnet, Jacques relate les activités et les ruses employées par la mafia en vue de combattre les injustices infligées aux pensionnaires. *Moyens.*

Mitchell, W.O.; Qui a vu le vent? Cercle du Livre de France, 1974. 294 pages. $5.50 [0-7753-0038-1]

Une enfance en Saskatchewan au cours des années 1920-1930. Traduction de *Who Has Seen The Wind. Aînés.*

Montpetit, Charles; Moi ou la planète. Actuelle, 1973. 101 pages. $1.00

Un premier roman. Un roman science-fiction vif et imaginatif. *Grands.*

Mowat, Farley; Perdus dans le Grand Nord. Laffont, 1974. 242 pages. $6.55 [413-089-41B] (Plein Vent)

Aventures de deux jeunes, un Canadien et un Indien, dans une nature superbe mais hostile. Traduction de *Lost in the Barrens. Grands, aînés.*

Munsterhjelm, Eric; Canilou. Côté, Maryse (trad.). Héritage, 1979. 142 pages. $4.95 [0-7773-3011-3]

Né d'un père loup et d'une mère chienne esquimaude, Canilou apprend à évoluer parmi humains et animaux. Roman inoubliable pour les amis des animaux et de la nature. Traduction de *A Dog named Wolf. Grands.*

Perol, Huguette; Le grand exode de François d'Acadie. Amitié - G.T. Rageot, 1974. 155 pages. $6.55 [2-7002-0048-9]

Un roman historique dans le cadre de la déportation des Acadiens. *Grands.*

Pilon, Daniel; Les silences de la croix-du-sud. Actuelle, 1972. 77 pages. $1.00

Ce livre d'aventure raconte l'expédition lancée en quête d'un temple mystérieux caché dans la brousse du Brésil. Une histoire parfaite pour la jeunesse canadienne. *Grands.*

Proulx, Jean-Baptiste; L'enfant perdu et retrouvé ou Pierre Cholet. Cholette-Longtin, Suzanne (illus.). Fides, 1978. 124 pages. $7.95 [0-7755-0706-7] (Goéland)

Ouvrage fictif ou réel, nul le sait. C'est une nouvelle édition dont la première datant de 1887 fut l'un des récits les plus populaires du Canada français. Il raconte les pérégrinations d'un homme, kidnappé alors qu'il était enfant, maintenant à la recherche de ses parents. *Grands.*

Raillet, René; Le sergent Trois-Rivières: aventures du temps où le Canada était français. Philippon, Patrick (illus.). Magnard, 1971. 90 pages. $7.05 (Fantasia)

Un roman d'aventures romanesques et historiques se déroulant aux derniers temps de la Nouvelle France. *Grands.*

Renaud, Bernadette; Le chat de l'oratoire. Michaud, Josette (illus.). Fides, 1978. 90 pages. $7.95 [0-7755-0697-4] (Goéland)

Une émouvante histoire d'amitié entre un chat et le jeune organiste de l'Oratoire St. Joseph. Ceux qui aiment les chats sauront apprécier ce roman un peu spécial. *Grands, moyens.*

Richler, Mordecai; Jacob Deux-Deux et le vampire masqué. Simard, Jean (trad.). Wegner, Fritz (illus.). Pierre Tisseyre, 1977. 93 pages. $3.95 [7753-0098-5] (Deux solitudes - juvénile)

Le héros de ce roman - conte est Jacob, que sa manie de répéter deux fois les choses pour que les adultes l'écoute, mènera bien loin . . . Traduction de *Jacob Two-Two and the Hooded Fang. Moyens.*

Rocher, Suzanne; Les Cailloux voient du pays. Girard, Paule (illus.). Fides, 1980. 157 pages. $8.50 [2-7621-0974-4] (Goéland)

Anne raconte les aventures cocasses et émouvantes vécues par sa famille lors d'un voyage en roulotte à travers le Canada et les Etats-Unis. *Grands.*

Rocher, Suzanne; Le dernier-né des Cailloux. Faucher, Guy (illus.). Fides, 1975. 95 pages. $7.95 (Goéland)

Anne a gagné, à l'occasion d'un concours, un jeune épagneul qu'elle amène à la maison et qui bientôt est adopté par toute la famille. *Moyens.*

Roy, Gabrielle; Ces enfants de ma vie. Stanké, 1977. 212 pages. $7.95 [0-88566-065-X]

Récits évoquant la vie de l'auteur comme jeune institutrice au Manitoba, les années trente et les enfants issus de cultures différentes aux besoins de leur âge, de sécurité et d'amour. *Aînés.*

Roy, Gabrielle; La petite poule d'eau. Beauchemin, 1970. 272 pages. $9.80

Deux nouvelles racontant les efforts des Tousignant installés à la Petite Poule d'Eau dans le nord du Manitoba, pour faire instruire les enfants, et, les pérégrinations d'un capucin original. *Aînés.*

Sabella, Monique; L'inconnue des Laurentides. Paulines, 1972. 124 pages. $1.00 broché. (Jeunesse-pop)

Prix Marie-Claire Daveluy 1971. Un gentil livre simple, facile à lire. Aventure de vacances. *Moyens.*

Savard, Félix-Antonine; Menaud maître draveur. Fides, 1970. 214 pages. $4.50 [0-7755-0162-X] (Bibliothèque canadienne-française)

Roman-poème. Un plaidoyer vibrant pour la sauvegarde du patrimoine national et un hymne à la liberté. *Aînés.*

Sernine, Daniel; Organisation Argus. de Beney, Gabriel (illus.). Paulines, 1979. 113 pages. $4.50 [2-89039-014-4]

Le jeune Marc Alix et son oncle le docteur Guillon sont mêlés à une affaire d'espionnage scientifique. Face à des adversaires impitoyables, Marc recevra une révélation stupéfiante sur l'identité d'êtres extra-terrestres. *Grands.*

Smucker, Barbara; Les chemins secrets de la liberté. Daveluy, Paule (trad.). Pierre Tisseyre, 1978. 161 pages. $6.95 broché. [0-7753-0114-0]

Julilly et Lisa, jeunes esclaves noires, tentent de s'enfuir vers le Canada où elles trouveront la liberté. Cette histoire excellente est bien traduite. Traduction de *Underground to Canada. Grands.*

Sutal, Louis; Le piège à bateaux. de Beney, Gabriel (illus.). Paulines, 1973. 123 pages. $2.75 [0-88840-400-X]

Un roman policier et d'anticipation. Trois personnages extra-terrestres visitent la Terre et enquêtent sur la disparition de bateaux dans le Golfe Saint-Laurent. *Grands.*

Thériault, Yves; Agaguk. Editions de l'Actuelle, 1963. 320 pages. $6.00 [0-7752-0001-8]

Sorte de long reportage documentaire sur les contrées, les gens, les moeurs du Grand Nord canadien. *Aînés.*

Thériault, Yves; Ashini. Fides, 1961. 145 pages. $3.50 0-7755-0283-9 (Bibliothèque canadienne-française)

"Epopée de la liberté et de la grandeur, ce roman chante, dans une langue majestueuse et d'une grande richesse de sonorités, l'âme de la race montagnaise." *Aînés.*

Thériault, Yves; Le ru d'Ikoué. Poirier, Michelle (illus.). Fides, 1977. 123 pages. $7.95 [0-7755-0631-1] (Goéland)

Ikoué, un jeune Algonquin, découvre un ruisselet qui lui apprend à devenir un homme. Ce roman empreint de nature et de poésie a d'abord paru chez le même éditeur en 1963. *Grands, aînés.*

Voidy, Jeanne; Les contes de la source perdue. Hurtubise, 1978. 117 pages. $5.95 [0-7758-0130-5]

Un recueil de contes qui louent la vie à la campagne, le retour à la terre. *Aînés.*

Yates, Elizabeth; En avant, voyageurs! Daveluy, Paule (trad.). Héritage, 1977. 223 pages. $4.95 [0-7773-3008-3]

Une histoire sur les voyageurs du Canada français. Traduction de *With Pipe, paddle and song. Grands.*

LEGENDES

Aladdin et la lampe merveilleuse. Fière, Martine (illus.). Fides, 1976. s.p. $3.95 [0-7755-0614-1]

Un des contes des mille et une nuits raconté par Schéhérazade. Illustrations colorées et attrayantes. *Moyens.*

Aubry, Claude; Légendes du Canada français. Editions de l'Espoir, 1977. 191 pages. $8.45 (Large vision)

Dans un texte imprimé en gros caractères, l'auteur reprend les dix légendes parues dans l'album *Le violon magique* et y ajoute *Le loup de Noël* et *Le roi des Mille-Isles. Moyens et plus.*

Aubry, Claude; Le loup de Noël. Demionenko, Alex (illus.). L'Espoir, 1978. 48 pages. $9.95

Maître Griboux, loup des Laurentides, est trop vieux pour chasser. Affamé à la veille de Noël, il ose s'approcher du village odorant. *Débutants.*

Aubry, Claude; Le violon magique et autres légendes du Canada français. Field, Saul (illus.). Les Editions de Deux Rives, 1968. 100 pages. $24.95

Dix contes canadiens-français racontés et illustrés avec art. *Moyens et plus.*

Barbeau, Marius; Il était une fois. Poirier, Claude (illus.). Héritage, 1976. 127 pages. $2.50 [0-7773-4403-3] (Pour lire avec toi)

Légendes canadiennes recueillies autrefois par Marius Barbeau. *Moyens.*

Beaugrand, Honoré; La chasse-galerie. Fides, 1979. 112 pages. $3.50 (Bibliothèque québécoise)

Paru d'abord en 1900. Recueil de légendes de traditions et de mythes de la fin du dix-neuvième siècle, par des écrivains qui ont tâché d'écouter les délicieuses histoires du peuple avant qu'il les ait oubliées. *Aînés.*

Chabot, Cécile; Contes du ciel et de la terre: v.1. - Imagerie: conte de Noël; v. 2 - Férie: conte du jour de l'An; v.3 - Paysannerie: conte des Rois. Beauchemin, 1962. $2.70 chacun.

Les aventures de Marie et de Joseph et de l'enfant Jésus au village de Sainte-Pétronille, situé sur la pointe de l'Ile d'Orléans, à l'occasion de Noël, du Jour de l'An et de l'Epiphanie. *Moyens.*

Choquette, Robert; Le sorcier d'Anticosti et autres légendes canadiennes. Théorêt, Michèle (illus.). Fides, 1975. 123 pages. $7.95 [0-7755-0560-9] (Goéland)

Seize récits qui appartiennent à la tradition orale du Québec. *Moyens et plus.*

Darios, Louise; Tous les oiseaux du monde: histoires et chansons. Beauchemin, 1975. 193 pages. $9.95 [0-7750-0315-8]

Contes écrits à partir de chants folkloriques canadiens. *Aînés.*

Dupont, Jean-Claude; Contes de bûcherons. Quinze, 1976, 1979. 215 pages. $12.95 [0-8856-5090-5]

Un conteur de "mentries" raconte à la façon des gens de la Beauce quelques bonnes histoires du répertoire québécois. *Aînés.*

Fielden, Hubert; Félix Leclerc raconte l'avare. Sander, Peter (illus.). Héritage, 1979. s.p. $2.50 [0-7773-2523-3] (Contes et légendes du Québec)

Album tiré d'une production Télé-Métropole, Radio-Canada, Sonolab et Peter Sander où cette légende québécoise est racontée par Félix Leclerc. *Débutants.*

Fielden, Hubert; Félix Leclerc raconte le violon magique. Sander, Peter (illus.). Héritage, 1979. s.p. $2.50 [0-7773-2524-1] (Contes et légendes du Québec)

Comme l'ouvrage précédant, tiré du film "Félix raconte." Bon texte, illustrations caricaturales. *Débutants.*

Fréchette, Louis; Les marionnettes. DesRoches, Roger (adapt.). Fortier, Michel (illus.). La Courte échelle, 1978. 32 pages. $4.95 broché. [0-88570-010-4] (Etoile filante)

Jos Violon raconte comment le violon ensorcelé de Tenfant Labranche fit danser les marionnettes (les aurores boréales). Folklore à l'intention des adolescents et des adultes. Vocabulaire difficile et présentation sévère. *Aînés.*

Fronval, George; Contes et récits du Canada français. Marin, Lise (illus.). Nathan, 1968. 250 pages. $6.65 (Collection des contes et légendes de tous les pays)

Ces contes sont de niveaux différents, d'intérêt de vocabulaire, mais d'excellents récits s'ils sont introduits à l'occasion de l'heure du conte. *Moyens, grands.*

Gallant, Melvin; Ti-Jean: contes acadiens. Leblanc, Bernard (illus.). Acadie, 1973. 165 pages. $4.50

Le héros, l'aventurier qui surmonte tout obstacle et qui survit tous les mauvais sorts. *Grands.*

Harvey, Azade; Contes et légendes des Iles-de-la-Madeleine. Editions Intrinsèque, 1979. 124 pages. $5.98 [0-919711-10-3]

Trente-cinq contes de lutins, de pirates ou de sorcières. Courtes histoires de coin de feu. *Aînés.*

Houston, James; L'archer blanc. Côté, Maryse (trad.). Héritage, 1978. 93 pages. $4.95 [0-7773-4103-4]

Cette légende, belle et dure, nous parle de vengeance, nous introduit aux traditions des esquimaux, et nous transmet subtilement bien des valeurs humaines. *Grands.*

Houston, James; Tikta'Liktak. Côté, Maryse (trad.). Héritage, 1978. 67 pages. [0-7773-3015-6]

Un jeune esquimau, parti à la chasse, se retrouve prisonnier d'un glacier à la dérive. Grâce à sa volonté et à sa bravoure, il survivra. Légende passionnante. Très beaux dessins en noir et blanc. *Moyens.*

Lemieux, Germain; Contes de mon pays. Héritage, 1980. 158 pages. $3.50 [0-7773-3010-5] (Katimavik)

Des contes amusants extraits de la collection "Les Vieux m'ont conté" présenté par le Centre Franco-Ontarien de Folklore. *Moyens, grands.*

Maillet, Antonine; Par derrière chez mon père. Recueil de contes. Scalabrini, Rita (illus.). Leméac, 1972. 91 pages. $5.95

Contes et légendes dans la langue savoureuse de l'Acadie. *Aînés.*

Melançon, Claude; Légendes indiennes du Canada. Jour, 1967. 156 pages. $5.95

Les fables les plus caractéristiques du folklore amérindien, racontées dans une langue claire et dans un style tout rempli de poésie. *Grands, aînés.*

Métayer, Maurice; Contes de mon iglou. Nanogak, Agnès (illus.). Jour, 1973. 128 pages. $6.95

Traduction de récits drôles ou tragiques qui donnent un intéressant aperçu de la culture des esquimaux du Canada. *Grands, aînés.*

St-Pierre, Georges; Légendes canadiennes illustrées. Garneau, 1975. $4.95 [0-7757-0575-6]

Quatre légendes illustrées par l'auteur. *Grands.*

Tonnerova, Maria; Les contes du Tsar. Decelles, Pierre (illus.). Héritage, 1979. 123 pages. $2.50 [0-7773-4416-5] (Pour lire avec toi)

Contes russes qui amènent le lecteur aux pays des princesses, des fées, des monstres, des diables. Déjà présentés à la télévision. *Moyens.*

Warnant-Côté, Marie-André; Les tours de Maître Lapin. Parsons, Michèle (illus.). Héritage, 1976. 126 pages. $2.50 [0-7773-4402-5] (Pour lire avec toi)

Légendes indiennes introduisant Maître Lapin, personnage inventé autrefois par les indiens, qui est un incorrigible joueur de tours. *Moyens.*

Wilson, Serge; Barbaro et la bête-à-sept-têtes. Poirier, Claude (illus.). Héritage, 1976. 14 pages. $0.39 (Contes de mon pays)

Conte adapté et illustré, d'après "*Barbaro-les-grandes-oreilles* parue dans le tome premier de *Les vieux m'ont conté. Débutants, moyens.*

Wilson, Serge; Ti-Jean et le gros roi. Poirier, Claude (illus.). Héritage, 1977. 126 pages. [0-7773-4409-2] (Pour lire avec toi)

Très bonne version de contes du centre franco-ontarien de folklore. Le lecteur ne peut que s'amuser de la malice de Ti-Jean profitant de la naïveté du roi. *Débutants, moyens.*

LITTERATURE

THÉÂTRE

Allard, Monic et **Major, Henriette;** Jeux dramatiques. Héritage, 1969. 124 pages. $2.50

Les auteurs donnent un aperçu d'une expérience théâtrale vécue avec un groupe de jeunes. Le volume suggère différents exercices corporels et vocaux, donne de nombreux conseils concernant les décors, les costumes et les accessoires ainsi que des idées pour la mise en scène de courtes pièces de théâtre. *Moyens, grands.*

Asllani, Luan; Les trois désirs de Coquelicot, suivi de Le retour de Coquelicot. Leméac, 1973. 152 pages. $5.95 (Théâtre pour enfants)

Des pièces de théâtre pour enfants où il arrive de nombreuses mésaventures à Coquelicot. *Moyens.*

Cailloux, André; François et l'oiseau du Brésil, suivi de Tombé des étoiles. Leméac, 1977. 151 pages. $5.95 [0-7761-9906]

Deux pièces de théâtre. Dans "François et l'oiseau du Brésil, un oiseau venu du Brésil apporte beaucoup d'imprévus à la forge du père Evariste. *Tombé des étoiles,* se déroule au laboratoire de monsieur Plume, astronome farfelu. *Moyens.*

Cailloux, André; Frizelis et Gros Guillaume. Leméac, 1973. 93 pages. $5.95 (Théâtre pour enfants)

Pièce de théâtre pour enfants où l'écureuil Tourbillon et le lutin Bigoudi bien connus des jeunes s'en donnent à coeur joie. *Débutants, moyens.*

Cailloux, André; Frizelis et la fée Doduche. Leméac, 1973. 91 pages. $5.95 (Théâtre pour enfants)

Pièce de théâtre pour enfants où on retrouve Frizelis, Tourbillon et Bigoudi mais cette fois avec l'intervention de la fée Doduche. *Tout-petits, débutants.*

Cailloux, André; L'île-au-sorcier. Leméac, 1974. 81 pages. $5.50 (Théâtre pour enfants)

Pièce de théâtre où le professeur, Béatrice et Jean-Sébastien passent par des aventures qui font jaillir les rires des enfants. *Tout-petits, débutants.*

Hébert, Marie-Francine; Une ligne blanche au jambon. Leméac, 1974. 90 pages. $5.95 (Théâtre pour enfants)

Petite pièce de théâtre où Bozébelle, Cruche, Escargot, Ciel de Lit et Petitbois amuseront l'enfant. *Tout-petits, débutants.*

Houle, Denise; Lune de neige. Castell, Frédéric (illus.). La Société de belles-lettres Guy Maheux, 1977. 64 pages. $4.95 broché [0-88585-024-X]

Prix Conseil des arts, 1978. Pièce pour être jouée à l'occasion de Noël, où, le Petit Prince, la Rose, le Renard et plusieurs autres personnages empruntés au conte de St-Exupéry, sont les héros. Manque d'originalité, sinon d'intérêt. *Débutants, moyens.*

Lepage, Roland; Icare. Léveillé, Jacques (illus.). Leméac, 1979. 125 pages. $5.95 [2-7609-9908-4] (Théâtre pour enfants)

Fantaisie mythologique pour enfants en quatre tableaux. *Grands.*

Morency, Pierre; Marlot dans les merveilles. Leméac, 1975. 114 pages. $5.95 (Théâtre pour enfants)

Une pièce de théâtre dont l'intrigue, captivante et fascinante, intéressera les élèves des écoles élémentaires. *Débutants, moyens.*

Péronnet, Jean; Pépère Goguen et les ratons voleurs. Acadie, 1975. 31 pages. $2.50

Pour le théâtre de marionnettes, la courte histoire d'un grand-père qui sème des graines de blé d'Inde, qui prend soin et protège les plantes jusqu'à ce qu'elles soient mûres. *Débutants.*

POESIE

Beaulac, Simone; Compti, Compta: comptines et rimettes. Jeunesse, 1962. 22 pages. $1.00 (Ménestrel)

Beaulac, Simone; Pompi pompette: exercices de prononciation, rimettes et chansons. Jeunesse, 1964. 22 pages. $1.00 (Ménestrel)

Beaulac, Simone; Gai patapon: comptines, rimettes et chansons. Jeunesse, 1964. 22 pages. $1.00 (Ménestrel)

Comptines, rimettes et chansonnettes remplies d'humour. *Tout-petits, débutants.*

Cailloux, André et **Fran Newman;** Fleurs et Frimas. Boulanger, Claudette (illus.). Héritage, 1979. s.p. $7.95 [0-7773-2519-5]

Un album captivant où 24 tableaux illustrent des poèmes sur les mois, les saisons et l'univers des enfants. *Moyens.*

Cailloux, Grand-père; Je te laisse une caresse. Tibo, Gilles (illus.). La Courte échelle, 1976. 24 pages. $2.95 [0-88570-006-6] (Etoile filante)

Poésies et comptines écrites et illustrées avec humour. Tirées du disque "Chansons et comptines de grand-père Cailloux," disponible chez l'éditeur. *Débutants.*

Cailloux, André; Lune en or. Béha, Philippe (illus.). La Courte échelle, 1979. $3.95 [2-89021-012-X]

Cailloux, André; Mon grand-père a un jardin. Béha, Philippe (illus.). La Courte échelle, 1979. $3.95 [2-89021-013-8]

Des comptines charmantes sur des thèmes que les enfants aimeront: animaux, fruits, amitié. Les illustrations chaleureuses donnent le goût de lire et relire le texte. Cassette et disques disponibles. *Tout-petits.*

Cailloux, Grand-père; Mon petit lutin s'endort. Tibo, Gilles (illus.). La Courte échelle, 1976. 24 pages. $2.95 [0-88570-007-4] (Etoile filante)

Poésies et comptines écrites et illustrées avec autant d'originalité que *Je te laisse une caresse* et tirées du même disque. *Débutants.*

Dor, Georges; Poèmes et chansons - 1; Poèmes et chansons - 2; Poèmes et chansons - 3. Leméac, 1970, 1971, 1972. $2.95, $3.75, $3.75 broché. (L'Hexagone)

"Ne cherchez pas de poésie
Dans mon poème
Cherchez l'enfant qu'on a trompé
En mil neuf cent quelque chose."
Moyens, grands.

Leclerc, Félix; Andante. Benoît, Nicole (illus.). Fides, 1975. 133 pages. $7.95 (Goéland)

Leclerc, Félix; Allegro. Fides, 1976. 156 pages. $7.95 [0-7755-0617-6] (Goéland)

Leclerc, Félix; Adagio. Dufour, Marcellin (illus.). Fides, 1976. 156 pages. $7.95 [0-7755-0618-4] (Goéland)

Trois recueils de contes, de fables et de poèmes qui célèbrent la nature et la vie canadienne. *Grands, aînés.*

Leclerc, Félix; Dialogues d'hommes et de bêtes. Fides, 1979. 235 pages. $4.50 [2-7621-0804-7] (Bibliothèque québécoise)

Aventures féeriques de visions d'étoiles filantes, de musiques d'oiseaux. Anthologie de fables. *Aînés.*

Leclerc, Michèle, Louise Méthé et **Yolande Chatillon;** Comptines traditionnelles du Canada français. Leméac, 1974. 32 pages. $5.95 (Littérature de jeunesse)

Des comptines populaires ou inconnues, illustrées avec goût et humour. Un album de qualité. *Tout-petits.*

Nelligan, Emile; Poèmes choisis. Fides, 1972. 166 pages. $3.95 [0-7755-0174-3] (Bibliothèque canadienne-française)

Un choix parmi l'oeuvre du poète du *Vaisseau d'or. Aînés.*

Poètes du Québec, 1860-1968; anthologie présentée par Jacques Cotnam. Fides, 1979. 222 pages. $4.50 [2-7621-0313-4] (Bibliothèque canadienne-française)

Une sélection assez variée et aussi représentative que possible, témoignant de la vitalité de la poésie Québécoise de Crémazie jusqu'à nos jours. *Aînés.*

Vigneault, Gilles; Les neufs couplets. Nouvelles éditions de l'Arc/Granger Frères, c1974. 76 pages. $4.00

"Petite chanson
Selon ma façon"
"Il nous reste un pays à comprendre
Il nous reste un pays à changer."
Aînés.

CHANSONS

Boucher, Pierrette; Je chante au jardin de Pierrot. Gagnon, Cécile (illus.). Société Radio-Canada et Héritage, 1974, 1975, 1976. $1.29 chacun. [0-7773-2041-X] [0-7773-2042-8] [0-7773-2043-6]

Trois albums contenant des chansons folkloriques accompagnées soit d'un jeu éducatif ou soit d'actions suggérées par les paroles. *Tout-petits, débutants.*

Butler, Edith; L'Acadie sans frontières. Leméac, 1977. 129 pages. $4.95 [0-7761-4660-2] (Mon pays mes chansons)

Répertoire de chansons traditionnelles et de chansons modernes de l'Acadie. *Aînés.*

Cailloux, André; Virginie chante . . . l'arc-en-ciel. Ladouceur, François (illus.). Héritage/Radio-Canada, 1980. s.p. $2.50 [0-7773-4321-5]

Cailloux, André; Virginie chante . . . Les instruments de musique. Ladouceur, François (illus.). Héritage/Radio-Canada, 1980. s.p. $2.50 [0-7773-4320-7]

Virginie, un gentil batracien ventriloque, propose aux petits une fort agréable leçon de solfège. D'après une émission télévisée. *Tout-petits.*

Le 100 plus belles chansons. La bonne chanson/Entreprises culturelles, 1956. 141 pages. $5.95

Folklore français et canadien. Illustré avec notation musicale. Reliure genre spirale. *Moyens.*

Lemieux, Germain; Chansonnier Franco-Ontarien. Centre franco-ontarien de folklore. Université de Sudbury, Sudbury, Ontario, 1974, 1975. 2 vols. $3.75 chacun.

Chansons folkloriques qui ont été transmises de génération en génération, avec accompagnements simples pour piano. *Moyens, grands.*

Méthé, Louise; La poulette grise. Leméac, 1973. 16 pages. $3.50 (Littérature de jeunesse)

Le texte d'une chanson et d'une comptine qui ravi les petits. *Tout-petits.*

Roy, Raoul; Le chant de l'alouette. Presses de l'université Laval/Radio-Canada, 1969. 104 pages. $2.00 [0-7746-6436-3]

Cinquante chansons folkloriques du Canada français. *Grands.*

SCIENCES NATURELLES

Cayouette, Raymond; Nichoirs d'oiseaux. Grondin, Jean-Luc (illus.). La Société zoologique de Québec, inc. 1978. 36 pages. $3.95

On y décrit 27 espèces qui occupent fréquemment ou occasionnellement les nichoirs artificiels et les oiseaux qui adoptent les bâtiments de l'homme pour nicher. Les oiseaux sont illustrés en couleurs, les nichoirs en noir et blanc. Illustrations claires et attrayantes. *Grands.*

Cayouette, Raymond et **Grondin, Jean-Luc;** Les oiseaux du Québec. La Société zoologique de Québec, inc., 1977. 117 pages. $5.95

On y traite de 243 espèces d'oiseaux du Québec avec illustrations en noir et blanc. Un *Guide sonore des oiseaux du Québec* de Jean Bédard en Album microsillon, London Zoo - 1 est aussi disponible chez cet éditeur. *Moyens et plus.*

Clarke, Arthur H.; Les mollusques d'eau douce du Canada. LaRocque, Aurèle (trad.). Musée National des sciences naturelles, 1980. 416 pages. [0-660-00023-7]

Manuel d'identification qui illustre 179 espèces. Illustrations en noir et blanc et planches en couleurs. *Grands, aînés.*

Douglas, Charles; Carnets d'histoires naturelle. Musée national des sciences naturelles. (Série no. 1), 1977. 108 pages. $2.00 [0-660-00093-8] (Série no. 2), 1978. 144 pages. $2.00 [0-660-00095-5] (Série no. 3), 1980. 114 pages. $2.00 [0-660-10341-9]

Des feuillets sur un choix d'animaux (oiseaux, poissons, mammifères) dont plusieurs sont menacés d'extinction. Textes courts et dessins intéressants. *Moyens, grands.*

Duchesney, Alice; Oiseaux de mon pays. Centre de Psychologie et de Pédagogie, 1970 (c1943). 117 pages. $3.95

Une étude zoographique sur les oiseaux du Canada. *Moyens et plus.*

Frison-Roche, Roger; Les seigneurs de la faune canadienne. Flammarion, 1976. 302 pages. $23.50 [0-88-554011-5]

Récit des observations et des recherches sur les bisons, les loups, les ours, les cervidés, les boeufs musqués et les grandes oies blanches. En appendice: les Parcs nationaux et un bestiaire des principaux mammifères. Illustrations magnifiques. *Grands, aînés.*

Gillett, John M.; Fleurs printanières de la région de la capitale nationale. Ottawa, Commission de la Capitale Nationale, 1973. 116 pages. $1.50

Livre bilingue qui présente cinquante fleurs printanières. Texte court et photographies en couleurs. *Grands, aînés.*

Grange, François de la; Le monde sauvage des Montagnes Rocheuses. Nathan, 1976. 48 pages. $14.25

Documentaire décrivant la formation des Montagnes Rocheuses et les principaux animaux qui les habitent. *Grands, aînés.*

Guide du botaniste amateur; édition revue et adaptée de *Le botaniste amateur en campagne* du R.P. Louis-Marie, o.c.s.o. Agriculture Québec, 1976. 110 pages. $2.50 [0-7754-2432-3]

Ouvrage illustré pour ceux qui veulent s'initier au monde végétal. Présenté sous forme de calendrier, facilitant la découverte des plantes propres aux mois mentionnés: avril à octobre. *Grands, aînés.*

Juchereau-Duchesnay, Elzéar; Mammifères du Québec. Juchereau-Duchesnay, St. Denys (illus.). Hurtubise, 1972. 123 pages. $6.25 [2-89045-190-9]

Guide illustré arrangé selon l'ordre systématique généralement accepté dans la description des mammifères. *Moyens, grands.*

Lamoureux, Gisèle; Plantes sauvages printanières. Editeur officiel du Québec, 1975. 247 pages. $3.90 [0-7754-2352-1]

Un manuel d'identification et d'utilisation. Photographies en couleurs. *Moyens et plus.*

McAllister, D.E. et **Crossman, E.J.;** Poissons de pêche sportive d'eau douce du Canada. Musée nationaux du Canada, 1973. 90 pages. $3.95

Sert à identifier les poissons, renseigne sur leurs habitudes et sur leur distribution. Surtout pour le pêcheur. *Grands, aînés.*

Mackenzie, Katherine; Fleurs sauvages du Québec. Toundra, 1976. 96 pages. $2.95

Un excellent guide accessible aux enfants sur la flore canadienne. *Moyens, grands.*

Marie, Jean-Pierre; Les mammifères canadiens. Jour, 1976. 77 pages. $4.95 broché. [0-7760-0714-9]

Vingt-cinq mammifères canadiens, du castor à l'ours polaire, sont regroupés en une présentation courte et simple. *Débutants, moyens.*

Melançon, Claude; Nos animaux chez eux. Jour, 1972. 174 pages. $3.00 [0-7760-0419-0]

Un guide qui vise à faire mieux connaître les mammifères de notre pays. *Moyens et plus.*

Melançon, Claude; Les poissons de nos eaux. Jour, 1973. 456 pages. $11.00 [0-7760-0583-0]

On retrouve dans cet ouvrage illustré presque toutes les espèces de poissons d'eau douce du Québec. *Grands, aînés.*

Mowat, Farley; Mes amis les loups. Arthaud, 1975. 256 pages. $21.00 [406-013-3B]

Traduction de *Never Cry Wolf.* L'auteur y étudie le comportement des loups. *Aînés.*

Plantes sauvages des villes et des champs, par le groupe Fleurbec. Fides/Editeur officiel du Québec, 1977. 273 pages. $6.95 [2-401-00079-8] [2-7621-0687-7] (La documentation québécoise)

Pour apprendre à reconnaître les plantes, le moment de leur floraison, leur habitat et leur folklore, leurs utilisations médicinales et culinaires, leur intérêt agricole. Y sont suggérées des méthodes d'éradication des "mauvaises herbes" sans l'emploi d'herbicides chimiques. *Aînés.*

Porsild, A.E.; Plantes sauvages des montagnes Rocheuses. Lid, Dagny Tande (illus.). Musée national des sciences naturelles, 1974. 454 pages. $6.95 [0-660-00069-5]

Permet d'identifier près de 400 espèces de plantes alpines et sub-alpines que l'on trouve partout dans les Rocheuses. Illustrations en couleurs. *Grands, aînés.*

Prévost, Bernard; Les papillons du Québec. Homme, 1976. $5.00 broché. [0-7759-0500-3]

Cent une photos, quelques clefs d'identification, un index et une claire description des moeurs et de l'aspect des papillons du Québec. *Grands, aînés.*

Les principaux insectes défoliateurs des arbres du Québec. Québec, Ministère de l'Energie et des Ressources, 1979. 188 pages. $7.95 [2-551-03428-0]

Un guide d'identification des insectes qui se nourrissent du feuillage des essences forestières. Limité aux espèces les plus importantes ou le plus communément rencontrées. Photographies en couleurs. Pas de texte. *Moyens.*

Provencher, Paul; Mes observations sur les insectes. Homme, 1977. $5.00 [0-7759-0537-2]

L'auteur y étudie l'anatomie et la physiologie générale et présente en détail quatorze espèces d'insectes et deux espèces d'arachnides que le lecteur pourra observer dans la nature québécoise. *Grands, aînés.*

Provencher, Paul; Mes observations sur les mammifères. Homme, 1976. 158 pages. $5.00 [0-7750-0503-8] (Sport)

Une étude illustrée des mammifères du Québec. *Grands, aînés.*

Provencher, Paul; Mes observations sur les oiseaux. Homme, 1977. $5.00 [0-7759-0534-8]

Une étude précise de l'anatomie et de la physiologie de douze espèces d'oiseaux du Québec, appuyée de schémas détaillés, précède les observations de l'auteur sur la vie des oiseaux. *Grands, aînés.*

Provencher, Paul; Mes observations sur les poissons. Homme, 1976. 124 pages. $5.00 (Sport)

Une étude illustrée des oiseaux du Québec par un spécialiste de la vie en plein air. *Grands, aînés.*

Québec. Ministère des Terres et Forêts; Petite flore forestière du Québec. Editeur officiel du Québec/Editions France-Amérique, 1974. 216 pages. $5.95 [2-89001-010-4]

Manuel pratique servant à l'identification des essences les plus courantes et de leurs principales caractéristiques. *Moyens et plus.*

Russell, Dale A.; Le monde disparu des dinosaures de l'Ouest canadien. Swibold, Suzanne M. (photos). Kish, Eleanor M. (illus.). Couchoud, Yves/Van Becelaere, Pascale (trad.). Musée national des sciences naturelles, 1977. 142 pages. $12.95 [0-660-00012-1]

Les reptiles géants, qui peuplaient autrefois la surface de ce qui est aujourd'hui le Canada, décrits par un chercheur et illustrés avec art. *Aînés.*

Sauvage, Louis; La faune qui nous entoure. Paulines, 1973. 69 pages. $9.75

Ce volume décrit les animaux les plus importants ou les plus curieux du Canada et inclut une bibliographie générale de la faune canadienne. *Moyens.*

Simard, Claire; Nature amie; sciences de la nature (tome 1). Fleury, Jean-Denis (illus.). Paulines (Documentation Video-Presse). 42 pages. $9.75 [0-88840-529-4]

En compagnie de Mimi et petit Jo, l'enfant de 4 à 7 ans apprend à explorer le monde qui l'entoure. *Tout-petits, débutants.*

Soper, James H. et Szczawinski, Adam F.; Plantes sauvages du Parc national du mont Revelstoke. Musée national des sciences naturelles, 1976. 112 pages. $2.95 [0-660-00002-4]

Cet ouvrage décrit 88 espèces de plantes sauvages que l'on trouve dans ce parc de la Colombie-Britannique. Elles sont groupées par couleur afin d'en faciliter l'identification. *Grands, aînés.*

Veilleux, Christian et **Prévost, Bernard;** Les papillons du Québec. Homme, 1976. $5.00 [0-7759-0500-3]

Une claire description des moeurs et de l'aspect des papillons du Québec. Un guide pratique. *Moyens et plus.*

BIOGRAPHIES

Barnett, Donald C.; Poundmaker. Bryns, George (trad.). Julienne, 1978. 61 pages. $2.95 (Célébrités canadiennes)

Description des conditions de vie des Cris et la biographie du fils adoptif de Crowfoot. Chef des Cris, Poundmaker lutta contre les autorités pour les droits de son peuple. *Grands, aînés.*

Bassett, John M.; Elizabeth Simcoe. Kelly, Patrick et Monique Auger (trad.). Julienne, 1976. 59 pages. $2.95 (Célébrités canadiennes)

Récit du séjour au Canada de John Graves Simcoe, premier Lieutenant-Gouverneur du Haut-Canada. *Grands, aînés.*

Bassett, John M.; Laura Secord. Ledoux, Albert (trad.). Julienne, 1976. 59 pages. $2.95 (Célébrités canadiennes)

La biographie d'une pionnière de l'Ontario, qui sauva son pays de l'attaque ennemie en 1813. Abondamment illustré. *Grands, aînés.*

Bassett, John M.; Samuel Cunard. Ledoux, Albert (trad.). Julienne, 1978. 60 pages. $2.95 (Célébrités canadiennes)

Histoire d'une compagnie de navires transatlantiques et biographie de son fondateur. Abondamment illustré. *Grands, aînés.*

Bassett, John M.; Timothy Eaton. Keely, Patrick et Monique Auger (trad.). Julienne, 1976. 59 pages. $2.95 (Célébrités canadiennes)

La vie de Timothy Eaton, fondateur des magasins Eaton. *Grands, aînés.*

Bassett, John M.; William Hamilton Merritt. Ledoux, Albert (trad.). Julienne, 1976. 61 pages. $2.95 (Célébrités canadiennes)

Biographie illustrée sur le "père du transport au Canada," à qui on doit la construction du premier Canal Welland. *Grands, aînés.*

Bassett, John M. et Petrie, A Roy; Allan Napier MacNab. Lamarche, Judith (trad.). Julienne, 1976. 61 pages. $2.95 (Célébrités canadiennes)

Avocat, militaire, politicien et homme d'affaires, constructeur du château Dundurn à Hamilton, défenseur de York durant la rébellion de 1837, instigateur du chemin de fer à Hamilton. *Grands, aînés.*

Clément, Béatrice; Jacques Cartier. Tousignant, Serge (illus.). Jeunesse, 1962. 24 pages. $1.00 (Panache)

Biographie illustrée, courte et facile à lire. ***Débutants, moyens.***

Damania, Laura; Egerton Ryerson. Bergeron, Richard (trad.). Julienne, 1976. 59 pages. $2.95 (Célébrités canadiennes)

Cette biographie d'un prédicateur méthodiste, journaliste, diplomate, éducateur et architecte raconte aussi une page de l'histoire de l'Ontario du 19e siècle. *Grands, aînés.*

DeRoquebrune, Robert; Testament de mon enfance. Fides, 1979. 204 pages. $3.95 (Bibliothèque québécoise)

Livre riche par les souvenirs qu'il rapporte sur une société raffinée. ***Aînés.***

Granatstein, J.L.; W.L. MacKenzie King. Byrns, Georges (trad.). Julienne, 1978. 62 pages. $2.95 (Célébrités canadiennes)

La vie du Premier ministre qui fut le plus longtemps au pouvoir. Photos intéressantes. *Grands, aînés.*

Hacker, Carlotta; Crowfoot. Fournier, Jean-Pierre (trad.). Julienne, 1978. 63 pages. $2.95 (Célébrités canadiennes)

Biographie imagée d'un grand pacificateur, le chef de la nation pied-noir qui sut demeurer neutre durant la révolte du Nord-Ouest et rester fidèle à son peuple et à ses principes. *Grands, aînés.*

Leclerc, Félix; Pieds nus dans l'aube. Fides, 1969. 216 pages. $4.50 [0-7755-0233-2] (Bibliothèque canadienne-française)

Raconte la jeunesse de l'auteur, son milieu natal, la vallée du Saint-Maurice, ses amis, et son goût de l'aventure. *Aînés.*

Mayles, Stephen; William Van Horne. Raymond, G. & F. (trad.). Julienne, 1978. 61 pages. $2.95 (Célébrités canadiennes)

Histoire de la construction du chemin de fer Canadian Pacific et la biographie de son premier directeur général. *Grands, aînés.*

Neering, Rosemary; Emily Carr. Ledoux, Albert (trad.). Julienne, 1976. 62 pages. $2.95 (Célébrités canadiennes)

Biographie d'une artiste peintre et d'un écrivain canadien. *Grands, aînés.*

Neering, Rosemary; Louis Riel. Fournier, Jean-Pierre (trad.). Julienne, 1977. 63 pages. $2.95 (Célébrités canadiennes)

Ouvrage abondamment illustré mettant cette tranche de l'histoire politique de l'ouest à la portée des jeunes. *Grands, aînés.*

Pedneault, Yvon; Guy Lafleur. Brodeur, Denis (photos). Homme, 1976. 94 pages. $4.00 [0-7759-0496] (Sport)

Document comprenant des témoignages, des statistiques et de nombreuses photographies traçant le portrait de Guy Lafleur, célèbre joueur de hockey. *Grands, aînés.*

Pellerin, Jean; D'Iberville. Leméac/Radio-Canada, 1967. $2.95

D'Iberville raconte à travers les faits et gestes de Pierre Le Moyne d'Iberville, grand navigateur et explorateur, l'histoire de l'amérique du Nord entre 1682 et 1697. *Grands.*

Petrie, A. Roy; Alexander Graham Bell. Ledoux, Albert (trad.). Julienne, 1976. 61 pages. $2.95 (Célébrités canadiennes)

La vie d'un grand inventeur canadien à la portée des jeunes. *Grands, aînés.*

Petrie, A. Roy; Sam McLaughlin. Kelly, Patrick et Monique Auger (trad.). Julienne, 1975. 61 pages. $2.95 (Célébrités canadiennes)

Cette brève biographie relate la vie de ce jeune homme qui commenca à travailler avec son père comme apprenti à l'atelier de rembourage et devint président de la General Motors du Canada. *Grands, aînés.*

Rudel-Tessier, J.; André Mathieu: un génie. Héritage, 1976. 364 pages. $3.95

Ouvrage largement documenté sur la vie d'un compositeur - interprète, enfant prodige, considéré comme le Mozart canadien. *Aînés.*

Smith, James K.; David Thompson. Ledoux, Albert (trad.). Julienne, 1976. 61 pages. $2.95 (Célébrités canadiennes)

La vie de ce cartographe qui fut nommé "le plus grand cartographe qui fut." *Grands, aînés.*

Spigelman, Martin; Wilfrid Laurier. Raymond, Gabrielle et François (trad.). Lidec (Célébrités canadiennes), 1978. 64 pages. $2.95 [2-7608-3019-5]

Texte et illustrations décrivent une époque de l'histoire tout en faisant connaître l'homme. Documentation et observations intéressantes. *Grands, aînés.*

Stewart, Roderick; Norman Bethune. Ledoux, Albert (trad.). Julienne, 1976. 60 pages. $2.95 (Célébrités canadiennes)

Courte biographie illustrée sur le chirurgien canadien qui donna sa vie au service de l'armée chinoise. *Grands, aînés.*

Tremblay, Gilberte; Bernier, capitaine à 17 ans. Leméac, 1972. 120 pages. $4.95

La vie aventureuse et héroique du capitaine Joseph Bernier (1852-1934), pionnier des explorations arctiques. *Grands, aînés.*

Weider, Ben; Louis Cyr, l'homme le plus fort du monde. VLB, 1976. 173 pages. $4.95

Une peinture exacte de ce Canadien qui fut considéré comme l'homme le plus fort de tous les temps. *Grands, aînés.*

Woodcock, George; Gabriel Dumont. Raymond, Gabrielle et François (trad.). Lidec, 1979. 63 pages. $2.95 [2-7608-3248-1]

Biographie d'un conducteur de ferry qui dirigeait les Métis lors de la Rébellion du Nord-Ouest de 1885. *Grands, aînés.*

AUTRES DOCUMENTAIRES

Allinson, Beverley et O'Kelly Barbara; "En voiture!" à la découverte du Canada. de Lorimier, Francine et Louis Rémillard (trad.). Héritage, 1979. 98 pages. $6.95 broché [0-7773-2529-2]

Toute seule, par bateau et par train, Evelyne fait le trajet de Port-au-Port, Terre-Neuve à Vancouver afin de visiter son père. Quelle aventure! *Moyens.*

Assiniwi, Bernard; Histoire des Indiens du Haut et du Bas Canada. Leméac, 1973-1974. v.1 - Moeurs et coutumes des Algonkins et des Iroquois. 151 pages. $8.50 v.2 - Deux siècles de civilisation blanche 1497-1685. 166 pages. $8.50 v.3 - De l'épopée à l'intégration, 1685 à nos jours. 189 pages. $8.50 (Ni-T'Chawama mon ami mon frère)

Ouvrage agrémenté de quelques illustrations. *Aînés.*

Assiniwi, Bernard et Fadden, John; Chasseurs de bisons. Leméac, 1973. 48 pages. $5.95 (Chicouté)

Vie d'un peuple de chasseurs. *Débutants, moyens.*

Assiniwi, Bernard et Fadden, John; Les Cris des marais. Leméac, 1979. 44 pages. $5.95 [2-7609-9881-9] (Chicouté)

Vie et coutumes d'un peuple. *Débutants, moyens.*

Assiniwi, Bernard et Fadden, John; Le guerrier aux pieds agiles. Leméac, 1979. 47 pages. $5.95 [2-7609-9880-0] (Chicouté)

"Chez les Agniers des monts Adirondacks, les hommes étaient évalués selon leur véritable mérite." *Débutants.*

Assiniwi, Bernard et Fadden, John; Les Iroquois. Leméac, 1973. 47 pages. $5.95 (Chicouté)

La vie dans la tribu et la vie d'aujourd'hui chez les Iroquois. *Débutants, moyens.*

Assiniwi, Bernard et Fadden, John; Makwa, le petit Algonquin, illustré. Leméac, 1973. 47 pages. $5.95 (Chicouté)

Une tentative de description didactique qui montre comment le garçon Algonquin Makwa devient le chasseur et chef Pontiac. *Débutants, moyens.*

Assiniwi, Bernard et Fadden, John; Les Montagnais et Naskapi. Leméac, 1979. 47 pages. $5.95 [2-7609-9882-7] (Chicouté)

Histoire sociale d'un peuple de chasseurs. *Débutants, moyens.*

Assiniwi, Bernard et Fadden, John; Sculpteurs de totems. Leméac, 1973. 47 pages. $5.95 (Chicouté)

Une histoire abrégée sur les totems de la côte de l'océan Pacifique. *Débutants, moyens.*

Bédard, Claude; Grunion et les basketteurs Algonquins. Robertson, John (illus.). Beauchemin, 1973. $2.95 (Sports Canada Série Sport-intro)

Un bref historique du jeu, une explication des règles ainsi qu'une définition précise des termes du jeu, entourés d'une aventure dans laquelle nous retrouvons cinq principaux personnages: Grunion le chat, Allumette, Granule, Super-Sport et Boum le pilote. *Moyens.*

Ber, André; Les fourmis en société. Fides, 1974. 44 pages. $2.50 (Satellite 2000,2)

Moeurs et caractéristiques des fourmis. Comment construire un formicarium. *Moyens.*

Bherer, Harold; Le Canada sans mythes. Paulines, 1973. 68 pages. $9.75.

"Ce volume essaie de situer la géographie de notre immense pays au niveau des problèmes des gens qui l'habitent." *Grands.*

Bordeleau, Charles; Les Alouettes de Sam Berger. Héritage, 1978. 80 pages. $5.00 broché. [0-7773-3821-1]

Les photos sont malheureusement en noir et blanc, mais ce livre écrit par un auteur bien informé plaira à tous les admirateurs des Alouettes de Montréal. *Grands, aînés.*

Bouchard, Michel; La pollution de l'air. Fides, 1974. 46 pages. $2.50 (Satellite, 2000,1)

Dans ce documentaire, on suit les démarches d'un étudiant qui part de connaissances rudimentaires sur la pollution de l'air mais cherche à aller au fond des choses en passant d'une question à l'autre. *Moyens.*

Bourret, Françoise; Le fléché; l'art du tissage au doigt. Homme, 1973. 222 pages. $4.00 [0-7749-0399-X]

Artisanat typiquement canadien, jadis pratiqué par les enfants. *Moyens et plus.*

Brisebois, Raymond; Le système métrique apprivoisé. Thomas, Eric & André (illus.). Lidec, 1974. 61 pages. $1.90 [0-7762-6181-9]

A l'aide de dessins amusants et de graphique comparatifs, l'auteur introduit le système métrique. *Moyens, grands.*

Canada. Ministère des Affaires indiennes et du Nord; Manuel de survie dans les régions nordiques. Opuscule, 1979. 208 pages. $4.95 broché. [2-89139-004-0]

Conseils et trucs utiles à tous les amateurs de plein air. Illustré. *Grands, aînés.*

Cibles; esprit et techniques des scouts et guides. Novalis, 1979. 382 pages. $8.00 [2-89088-001-X]

Une mise à jour de l'édition de 1954, qui met à la portée de tous des moyens techniques pour la vie de plein air. *Grands, aînés.*

Corkum, Nadja; Les aventuriers de l'Outaouais ou l'histoire de la capitale nationale. Chaput-Rolland, Solange (trad.). Hesse, Emma (illus.). Beauchemin, 1976. 59 pages. $4.95 [0-7750-0447-2]

L'histoire du développement de la région d'Ottawa dès l'arrivée des premiers défricheurs jusqu'à son ascension comme capitale nationale. *Moyens.*

Corriveau, Bernadette; Le chas de l'aiguille. Méthé, Louise (illus.). Fides, 1978. 119 pages. $7.95 [0-7755-9679-6] (Comment faire)

Introduit à la couture et stimule grâce à toutes sortes d'idées. Volume attrayant et très agréable à consulter. *Moyens, grands.*

Documents-recherches: encyclopédie audio-visuelle. Paulines (Video-Presse), 1976. 374 pages. $32.50 [0-88840-593-6]

Des articles tirés de la revue Encyclopédie audio-visuelle et reliés sous les grandes classes suivantes: Les communications. Hommes qui ont fait l'histoire. Merveilles de la nature. Peuples en voie d'extinction. Problèmes d'aujourd'hui. Sciences et techniques. Sports. Traditions musicales. Index à la fin du volume. *Moyens, grands.*

Dorge, Lionel; Le Manitoba, reflets d'un passé: les cartes et les recherches de l'illustration par Claude Dorge. Editions du Blé, 1976. 182 pages. $8.50

Un manuel d'histoire franco-manitobaine. *Grands, aînés.*

Doucet, Paul; Vie de nos ancêtres en Acadie: coutumes, croyances et religion populaire. Editions d'Acadie, 1979. 32 pages. $7.50 broché [2-7600-0036-2]

Doucet, Paul; Vie de nos ancêtres en Acadie: le vêtement. Editions d'Acadie, 1979. 40 pages. $8.50 broché. [2-7600-0037-0]

Ouvrage à l'intention des élèves, avec des questions dans les marges. Illustré. *Moyens, grands.*

Dumoulin, Gérald; Santé et joie de vivre par la bicyclette. Lidec, 1975. 72 pages. $2.25

Une initiation complète au cyclisme et à l'entretien de la bicyclette. *Moyens et plus.*

Fabi, Thérèse; Comment faire une recherche? Fides, 1975. 127 pages. $3.95 broché. [0-7755-0548-X] (Comment Faire)

Où trouver les renseignements; les choisir et les classer; rédiger la recherche; un certain art d'écrire et d'autres renseignements utiles - tous ces chapitres en font un très bon livre. *Grands, aînés.*

Fradet Harel, Louise et **Hélène Doucet Leduc;** Qu'est-ce qui mijote? La Presse, 1976. 139 pages. $6.95

Un livre de cuisine qui s'adresse aux jeunes et aux débutants de tous les âges. *Moyens et plus.*

Fronval, George; La véritable histoire des indiens peaux-rouges. Nathan, 1973. 125 pages. $22.00

Un beau livre sur les Indiens des Etats-Unis qui mentionne le Canada une dizaine de fois. *Grands, aînés.*

Gendron, Bertrand et **Poulin, Louis-Philippe;** L'imprimerie. Le Sablier, 1979. 24 pages. $1.00 [2-89093-000-9] (Reportage)

"Le miracle de la page imprimée est un des plus émouvants que le labeur des hommes puisse provoquer." Bien documenté. Illustrations claires. *Grands.*

Gendron, Lionel: La merveilleuse histoire de la naissance. Homme, 1969. 93 pages. $6.85

Le livre le plus complet sur ce sujet. *Moyens, grands.*

Gibbons, W.J.L.; Canada bibliothèque du Parlement. Tarte, Louis (trad.). KCB Publications. s.d. 64 pages. $12.95 relié.

Ouvrage admirablement illustré de photos en couleurs. *Aînés.*

Gigli, Amedeo; Anatomie humaine. Paulines, (Video-Presse), 1972. 44 pages. $5.95

Des articles tirés du magazine. *Grands.*

Hallamore, Elizabeth; Le système métrique en s'amusant. Bucholtz-Ross, Linda (illus.). Héritage, 1976. 95 pages. $3.95 [0-7773-4091-7]

La souris métrique présente des jeux, casse-têtes, problèmes, recettes pour aider l'enfant à se familiariser avec le système métrique. *Moyens.*

Hébert, Jacques; La terre est ronde. Fides, 1976. 185 pages. $6.95 [0-7755-0616-8]

L'histoire de l'entreprise "Jeunesse Canada Monde" commencée il y a six ans par l'auteur. Ce journal de voyage décrit l'enthousiasme et les difficultés des participants, la découverte des terres nouvelles et des cultures différentes, et surtout les amitiés avec les jeunes du monde périphérique du Tiers-Monde. *Aînés.*

Hill, Daniel G.; Les droits de la personne au Canada: regard sur le racisme. Congrès du Travail du Canada, Ottawa, 1977. 44 pages. $1.00

Analyse critique et informative de la discrimination au Canada. *Aînés.*

Lafortune, Ambroise; Le pays d'où je viens. Héritage, 1977. 122 pages. $2.95 [0-7773-3013-X]

Des anecdotes personnelles et des légendes recueillies par le père Ambroise font parcourir les différentes régions du Québec; l'île d'Orléans, Trois-Rivières, les Laurentides, la Côte Nord, les Iles-de-la-Madeleine, la Gaspésie, le Nouveau Québec et l'Abitibi. *Moyens, grands.*

Lafortune, Ambroise; Si le Québec m'était conté. Scriptomedia, 1977. 84 pages. $9.95 [0-88598-001-8]
Un maître conteur écrit une histoire du Québec à travers sa vision personnelle des beautés de la belle province. *Grands, aînés.*

Lafortune, Claude; Un beau coffre pour toi. Société Radio-Canada/ Héritage, 1974. 48 pages. $0.99 [0-7773-4001-1]
Un livret qui invite les enfants de six à dix ans à s'amuser avec des vieux journaux, du carton, de la colle et beaucoup d'imagination. *Débutants, moyens.*

Lavoie, Roger; Une technique artisanale dans la région de Sudbury-Nippissing: la raquette. La Société historique du Nouvel-Ontario. Université de Sudbury, 1975. 64 pages. $3.00 broché (Document historique no. 65)
Un document historique qui illustre la fabrication actuelle des raquettes de bois et qui analyse les autres types de raquettes. *Grands, aînés.*

Le Blanc, Monique; Parle-moi de la ceinture fléchée! Fides, 1977. 107 pages. $4.95 broché [0-7755-0661-3] (Comment Faire)
Seul ouvrage sur ce sujet à s'adresser directement aux jeunes, ce livre d'initiation au fléché traite de tous les aspects du sujet. *Moyens, grands.*

Lévesque, Gilbert; François de Laval, Seigneur de la Côte. Leméac, 1979. 93 pages. $4.95 [0-7761-9426-7] (Second regard)
Réflexions et reportage d'une marche organisée, par un scripteur-recherchiste, pour suivre les traces d'un fondateur. *Aînés.*

Louis-Hébert, Laviolette commandant de bord. Le Sablier, 1978. 27 pages. $1.00 broché [0-919428-49-5] (Reportage)
Description d'une profession. Didactique et agréable à consulter. *Grands.*

Magnin, Etienne; Ecologie: initiation à la biologie. McGraw-Hill, 1974. 215 pages. $13.00
Ce livre inculquera aux jeunes le goût de la recherche et leur montrera qu'on peut obtenir des résultats valables et utiles avec des moyens modestes. *Moyens.*

Major, Henriette; La Bible en papier. Lafortune, Claude (illus.). Fides, 1979. $10.95 [2-7621-0796-2]
Courtes histoires tirées de la Bible illustrées par le "magicien du papier." *Moyens.*

Major, Henriette; L'évangile en papier. Lafortune, Claude (illus.). Fides, 1977. 94 pages. $9.95 [0-7755-9641-9]
Ce livre nous présente les personnages de la Bible à l'aide des marionnettes présentées à l'émission télévisée du même titre. *Moyens.*

Maman c'est??? . . . Labelle-Jobin, Francine (trad.). Beauchemin, 1979. 62 pages. $6.95 [2-7616-0015-0]
Des réflexions d'enfants pour dire merci à toutes les mamans quelles qu'elles soient. Dessins en brun sur blanc, par des enfants. *Moyens et plus.*

Martel, Suzanne; A la découverte du Gotal. Fides, 1979. 424 pages. $13.95 [2-7621-0780-6]
L'auteur, dans le récit extraordinaire de son voyage en Inde, revit des situations et rencontre des personnages qu'elle a déjà décrits dans ses livres de la série des Montcorbier. Ce livre pour adultes sert de prélude aux romans de Paul et Arnaud de Montcorbier. *Aînés.*

Martel, Suzanne; Goûte à tout. Gagnon, Cécile (illus.). Fides, 1977. 80 pages. $7.95 [0-7755-0666-4]
Conçu pour les "cuisiniers paresseux, les gens pressés, les nouveaux mariés, les enfants cordons-bleus, les étudiants, les célibataires." Mise en page des recettes n'est pas toujours claire. *Grands, aînés.*

Martel, Suzanne; Tout sur Noël. Guberec, Josée (illus.). Fides, 1977. 179 pages. $7.95 [0-7755-0649-4] (Comment Faire)

Jeux, cantiques, décorations, recettes, bricolages, contes, historique . . . vraiment tout sur Noël! *Moyens, grands.*

Martel, Suzanne et **Alain;** Marmitons. Jeunesse, 1972. 160 pages. $3.95

Des recettes à la portée des jeunes cuisiniers. *Moyens.*

Meeker, Howie; L'ABC du hockey. Homme, 1973. 168 pages. $5.00 [0-7759-0401-5] (Sport)

Ce volume décrit les techniques de base du hockey afin d'aider les jeunes à jouer plus efficacement. *Moyens et plus.*

Mérinat, Eric; Les marionnettes de papier. Etincelle, 1975. 96 pages. $4.95

Ouvrage illustré qui amusera les enfants. *Moyens et plus.*

Méthé, Louise; Techniques d'impression. Fides, 1977. 120 pages. $5.95 [0-7755-0648-6]

Pour apprendre les techniques de base de l'impression: empreintes avec les doigts, les tissus, les pommes de terre et les fruits, etc. *Moyens, grands.*

Michaud, Josette; Montréal ma grand'ville. La Presse, 1979. 42 pages. $8.95 [0-89043-010-3]

Ecrit dans un français impeccable et surtout dans un niveau de langue abordable pour les enfants, cet ouvrage brosse un tableau intéressant et original de cette grande ville. *Moyens.*

Mignault, Marcel; Lise et Bruno dans l'univers des livres. St-Cyr, Normand (illus.). Société du stage en bibliothéconomie, La Pocatière/Centrale des bibliothèques, 1976. 94 pages. $6.75 [0-88546-077-4]

Initiation à la bibliothèque pour les jeunes de quatre à douze ans. Outil pédagogique. *Moyens, grands.*

Monet, Jacques; La Monarchie au Canada. Cercle du livre de France/Rideau Hall, Ministère des Approvisionnements et services Canada, 1979. 96 pages. $9.95 [2-89051-012-3]

Retrace l'évolution du rôle constitutionnel des représentants de l'autorité royale au Canada à partir des débuts où ces derniers gouvernaient véritablement le pays jusqu'à aujourd'hui où le pouvoir est confié à des premiers ministres choisis par le peuple. Illustrations bien choisies et de qualité. *Grands, aînés.*

Montpetit, Raymond; Le temps des fêtes au Québec. Homme, 1978. 285 pages. $8.00 [0-7759-0622-0]

A l'aide de textes et de documents iconographiques d'époque, du début de la colonie au 19ième siècle, cet ouvrage documentaire trace un portrait des Québécois en fête. *Aînés.*

Neering, Rosemary; La colonisation de l'Ouest. Bergeron, Richard (trad.). Gregory, Richard (illus.). Fitzhenry and Whiteside, 1978. 63 pages. $3.95 [0-88902-478-2] (Une nation en marche)

Neering, Rosemary; La construction du chemin de fer. Fournier, Jean-Pierre (trad.). Gregory, Richard (illus.). Fitzhenry & Whiteside, 1978. 64 pages. $3.95 [0-88902-477-4] (Une nation en marche)

Neering, Rosemary; La police montée du Nord-ouest. Bergeron, Richard (trad.). Gregory, Richard (illus.). Fitzhenry & Whiteside, 1978. 64 pages. $3.95 [0-88902-476-6] (Une nation en marche)

Neering, Rosemary; La ruée vers l'or. Bergeron, Richard (trad.). Gregory, Richard (illus.). Fitzhenry & Whiteside, 1978. 63 pages. $3.95 [0-88902-475-8] (Une nation en marche)

Neering, Rosemary; La traite des fourrures. Fournier, Jean-Pierre (trad.). Gregory, Richard (illus.). Fitzhenry & Whiteside, 1978. 64 pages. $3.95 [0-88902-479-0] (Une nation en marche)

Neering, Rosemary et **Stan Garrod;** Les Loyalistes. Fournier, Jean-Pierre (trad.). Smith, Merle (illus.). 64 pages. $3.95 [0-88902-482-0] (Une nation en marche)

Neering, Rosemary et **Stan Garrod;** La vie en Acadie. Bergeron, Richard (trad.). Smith, J. Merle (illus.). Fitzhenry & Whiteside, 1978. 64 pages. $3.95 [0-88902-480-4] (Une nation en marche)

Neering, Rosemary et **Stan Garrod;** La vie en Nouvelle-France. Ledoux, Albert (trad.). Smith, J. Merle (illus.). Fitzhenry & Whiteside, 1978. 64 pages. $3.95 [0-88902-481-2] (Une nation en marche)

Etude sociale et historique à travers une série de volumes sérieusement documentée. Illustrations authentiques. *Grands.*

Osgood, William; La raquette. Homme, 1974. 134 pages. $4.00 [0-7759-0434-1] (Sport)

Sport d'origine indienne de plus en plus en vogue. *Moyens et plus.*

Ouimet, Marie; Montréal et ses attraits. Tad, 1974. 96 pages. $5.95

Photographies en couleurs accompagnées de brèves descriptions, dépictant différents sites montréalais. *Moyens et plus.*

Ouimet, Marie; Québec et ses attraits. Tad, 1974. 96 pages. $5.95

Photographies en couleurs de sites Québécois très connus. *Moyens et plus.*

Papa c'est? Beauchemin, 1979. 63 pages. $6.95 [2-7616-0021-5]

Des réflexions d'enfants pour dire merci à tous les papas quels qu'ils soient. *Moyens et plus.*

Pednault, Yvon et **Brodeur, Denis;** Les Canadiens, nos glorieux champions. Homme, 1977. 95 pages. $5.00 broché [0-7759-0539-9]

Ce livre-reportage est très plaisant à lire. Les nombreuses photographies et les statistiques de toutes sortes ajoutent encore au tableau impressionant qui est peint des Canadiens. *Aînés.*

Perreault, Guy; Le manuel illustré du nouveau cavalier. L'Action Sociale, 1977. 189 pages. $12.95 broché.

Un ouvrage facile à lire et à utiliser par ceux qui possèdent ou sont sur le point d'acheter un cheval et qui trouveront quantité d'idées pratiques sur le cheval, son entretien, sa santé, son dressage, etc. *Grands, aînés.*

Rich-Plumet, Nicole; Poutoulik chez les Inouit de l'Ungava. Héritage, 1977. 64 pages. $5.95 [0-7773-4251-0]

Poutoulik et sa famille vont visiter les côtes du Nouveau-Québec et les îles de l'Ungava. D'excellentes et nombreuses photographies, un texte détaillé et familier. *Moyens.*

Rosenstiehl, Agnès; La naissance. La Presse, 1973. 46 pages. $6.50

Ce livre, traitant de la naissance, au premier abord très simple et sans grande prétention, est un des petits chefs-d'oeuvre du genre. *Moyens.*

Les Satellipopettes. Album d'activités. Héritage, 1979. 62 pages. Broché [0-7773-2526-8]

Jeux de mots, rebus, mots-mystères, acrostiche, questions, etc. Présentation matérielle très pauvre. *Moyens.*

Savoie, Robert; Les sports olympiques. Rinaldin, R. (illus.). Paulines (Video-Presse), 1973. 74 pages. $9.75

Des articles tirés du magazine Vidéo-Presse. *Grands.*

Scalabrini, Rita; L'Acadie et la mer. Leméac, 1973. 46 pages. $5.95

Un mélange savoureux de réflexions personnelles et de renseignements entremêlés et poursuivis au rythme de la mer. *Grands, aînés.*

Vaillancourt, Laurier; Je bricole. Héritage, 1979. 40 pages. $5.95 [0-7773-2522-5]

Guide pratique clairement illustré avec explications graduelles sur les outils et le travail du bois. *Moyens.*

REFERENCE

Almanach du peuple. Beauchemin, Annuel. $3.00

Les armoiries, drapeaux et emblèmes du Canada/The Arms, flags and emblems of Canada. Sécrétariat d'Etat et Centre d'édition, Approvisionnement et Services, 1978. s.p. $3.50 [0-88879-006-6]

Assiniwi, Bernard; Lexique des noms indiens en Amérique. Leméac, 1973. v.1 - Noms géographiques. 143 pages. $4.95 v.2 - Personnages historiques. 166 pages. $4.95 (Ni-T'Chawama Mon ami mon frère)

Banfield, Alexandre William; Les mammifères du Canada. Presses de l'université Laval, 1974. 432 pages. $25.00

Barbeau, Marius; Le rossignol y chante. Musée national de l'Homme, 1979. 486 pages. $10.95 [0-660-00140-3]

Bélisle, Louis-Alexandre; Dictionnaire nord-américain de la langue française. Beauchemin, 1979. 1196 pages. $32.50

Bélisle, Louis-Alexandre; Petit dictionnaire canadien de la langue-française. Aries, 1969. 648 pages. $7.95

Le Canada: revue annuelle préparée par Statistique Canada. Approvisionnement et Services Canada, Annuel. $6.00

Chiasson, Anselme; Les légendes des îles de la Madeleine. Landry, Denise (illus.). Acadie, 1976. 131 pages. $6.00 [2-7600-0019-2]

Dagenais, Gérard; Dictionnaire des difficultés de la langue française au Canada. Pedagogia, 1967. 679 pages. $5.40

Des Ruisseaux, Pierre. Le livre des proverbes. Hurtubise, 1978. 220 pages. $8.95 [0-7758-0132-1]

Dictionnaire biographique du Canada, 1 - De l'an 1000 à 1700. Université Laval, 1966. 800 pages. $35.00

Dictionnaire biographique du Canada, 2 - De l'an 1701 à 1740. Université Laval, 1969. 792 pages. $35.00

Dictionnaire biographique du Canada, 3 - De l'an 1741-1770. Université Laval, 1974. 856 pages. $35.00

Dictionnaire biographique du Canada, 4 - De l'an 1771 à 1800. Université Laval, 1980. 1034 pages. $35.00 [2-7636-6899-7]

Dictionnaire biographique du Canada, 9 - De l'an 1861 à 1870. Université Laval, 1977. 1060 pages. $35.00 [0-7746-6811-3]

Dictionnaire biographique du Canada, 10 - De l'an 1871 à 1880. Université Laval, 1972. 894 pages. $35.00

Dupont, Jean-Claude; Histoire populaire de l'Acadie. Leméac, 1978. 440 pages. $19.95 [2-7609-5278-9]

Dupuis, Hector et **Légaré, Romain;** Dictionnaire des synonymes et des antonymes. Fides, 1975. 607 pages. $14.95 [0-7755-0549-8]

Encyclopédie de la jeunesse. Grolier, 1979. 20 volumes. $349.50 et $284.50

Fortin-Jacques, Marcelle; Le savoir-vivre aujourd'hui. Homme, 1977. 192 pages. $5.00

Godfrey, W. Earl; Encyclopédie des oiseaux du Québec. Homme, 1972. 663 pages. $12.95 [0-7759-0317-5]

Le grand almanac. La Presse, Annuel. $3.25

Grand atlas du Canada et du monde. George Philip Raintree, 1979. 47 pages, 136 cartes, 96 pages. $30.00 [0-89810-003-8]

Hamel, Réginald; Hare, John et Wyczynski, Paul; Dictionnaire pratique des auteurs québécois. Fides, 1976. 724 pages. $19.95

Hosie, R.C. Arbres indigènes du Canada. Ministère de l'Environnement, 1975. 383 pages. $9.50

Légaré, Clément; La bête à sept têtes et autres contes de la Mauricie. Quinze, 1980. 276 pages. $4.95 (Mémoires d'homme)

Lemieux, Germain; Les vieux m'ont conté. Bellarmin, 1973-1980. 14 volumes.
v.1 - $12.00; v.2 - $13.00; v.3 - $13.50; v.4 - $15.00; v.5 - $14.00; v.6 - $14.50; v.7 - $14.00; v.8 - $14.50; v.9 - $15.00; v.10 - $15.50; v.11 - $16.00; v.12 - $16.50; v.13 - $16.50; v.14 - $16.50.

Le Mémorial du Québec. Les Editions du Mémorial (Québec) Inc., 1979. 8 volumes.
v.6 - 1939-1952 [2-89143-002-6]
v.7 - 1953-1965 [2-89143-001-8]
v.8 - 1966-1976 [2-89143-000-X]
v.1–2 - $50.00 chacun. v.3–8 - $55.00 chacun. $440.00 la série.

Michaud, Daniel; L'histoire du Canada et du Québec en quelques épisodes. Guérin, 1979. 86 pages. $4.95 [2-7601-0040-5] (Collection culture québécoise)

Montel, Suzanne; Mon pays le Canada. Ginn, 1978. 234 pages. $8.00 [0-7702-0590-9]

Mulligan, Gerald A.; Common weeds of Canada/Les mauvaises herbes communes du Canada. McClelland avec Information Canada, 1976. 140 pages. $7.95 paper [0-7710-6653-8]

Nungak, Zebedee et **Eugène Aruma;** Légendes inuit de Povungnituk, Québec. Musée national de l'Homme, 1975. 138 pages. $7.50 broché [0-660-00058-X]

Petit dictionnaire des écrivains. Union des écrivains québécois, 1979. 175 pages. $5.00

Le petit informateur Canadien. Grolier, 1978. 416 pages. $9.45

Préfontaine, Robert R.; "Demande à Isabelle," dictionnaire descriptif, phonologique, analogique et orthographique du vocabulaire actif. Le Sablier, 1974. 395 pages. $10.00 broché [0-919428]

Robinson, Sinclair et **Smith, Donald;** Practical handbook of Canadian French/Manuel pratique du français canadien. Macmillan, 1973. 172 pages. $6.95 broché [0-7705-1028-0]

Victorin, Louis-Marie; Flore Laurentienne. Université Montréal, 1964. 925 pages. $19.75 [0-8405-0018-1]

Vinay, Jean-Paul; Daviault, Pierre and **Alexander, Henry;** Dictionnaire canadien: The Canadian dictionary. Anglais-français/français-anglais. McClelland, 1962. 861 pages. $8.95

REVUES

Les Carnets de zoologie. Société zoologique de Québec, Inc. Rédacteur des Carnets de Zoologie, 8191, Avenue du Zoo, Orsainville, Québec, G1G 4G4. 4 nos. $2.00 par an. *Grands, aînés.*

Hibou; le nouveau magazine des jeunes. Héritage Inc., 300 rue Arran, St-Lambert, Québec. J4P 3N4. 10 nos. $10.00 par an. *Moyens, grands.*

Nos racines; histoire vivante des Québécois. Transmo Inc., 395, boul. Lebeau, St-Laurent, Québec. H4N 1S2. Hebdomadaire de 120 nos. $1.50 chacun. Abonnements: 30 nos. $42.00; 60 nos. $80.00; 120 nos. $45.00. *Grands, aînés.*

Passe-Partout. Presse-Import Léo Brunelle Inc., 307 Benjamin Hudon, St-Laurent, Montréal. H4N 1J1. 14 nos. $14.00. *Tout-petits, débutants.*

Québec Science. Université du Québec, C.P. 250, Sillery, Québec. G1T 2R1. 12 nos. $17.00 par an/$30.00 pour deux ans. *Grands aînés.*

Requiem; revue de la Science fiction et du fantastique. Norbert Spenner, 455, rue St-Jean, Longueuil, Québec. J4H 2Z3. $9.00 par an. *Aînés.*

Vidéo-Presse. Vidéo-Presse, 3965 est, boul. Henri-Bourassa, Montréal, Québec. H1H 1L1. 10 nos. Septembre à juin. $9.95 par an. *Moyens, grands.*

PRIX DE LITTERATURE DE JEUNESSE

LE PRIX LITTERAIRE DU CONSEIL DES ARTS POUR LA JEUNESSE/ THE CANADA COUNCIL AWARD FOR CHILDREN'S LITERATURE

Ce prix est décerné annuellement depuis 1975. Un prix de $5,000 était offert en reconnaissance d'une contribution marquante à la littérature enfantine de langue française. Deux prix de $5,000 sont maintenant attribués chaque année, une pour la texte et l'autre pour l'illustration. (Voir AWARD-WINNING BOOKS pour les prix de langue anglaise.)

1976 *Raminagradu:* histoires ordinaires pour enfants extraordinaires, par Louise Aylwin. Montréal, Jour, 1975.
1977 *Emilie, la baignoire à pattes,* par Bernadette Renaud. Montréal, Héritage, 1976.
1978 *Lune de neige*, par Denise Houle. Montréal, La Société de belles-lettres, Guy Maheux, 1977. (Texte); *L'évangile en papier*, par Henriette Major. Illustré par Claude Lafortune. Montréal, Fines, 1977. (Illustration).
1979 *La chicane,* par Ginette Anfousse. Montréal, La Courte échelle, 1978. *La varicelle,* by Ginette Anfousse. Montréal, La Courte échelle, 1978. (Texte et illustration).
1980 *Courte Queue,* par Gabrielle Roy. Montréal, Alain Stanké, 1979 (Texte); *Une fenêtre dans ma tête,* par Raymond Plante. Illustré par Roger Paré. Montréal, La Courte échelle, 1979 (Illustration).

CACL MEDAILLE DE BRONZE

Cette médaille de bronze était décernée par l'Association canadienne des bibliothécaires pour enfants (Canadian Association of Children's Librarians) aux livres pour enfants en français les plus marquants des années de 1954 à 1973.

1954 *Mgr. de Laval*, par Emile Gervais. S.J. Montréal, Comité des Fondateurs de l'Eglise canadienne, 1954.
1955 Pas de prix
1956 Pas de prix
1957 Pas de prix
1958 *Le Chevalier du roi*, par Béatrice Clément. Montréal, Les Editions de l'Atelier, 1955.
1959 *Une drôle de petit cheval*, par Hélène Flamme, Montréal, Editions Leméac, 1957.

1960 *L'été enchanté,* par Paule Daveluy. Montréal, Les Editions de l'Atelier, 1957.
1961 *Plantes vagabondes,* par Marcelle Gauvreau. Montréal, Centre de Psychologie et de Pédagogie, 1959.
1962 *Les îles du Roi Maha Maha II,* par Claude Aubry, Québec, Les Editions du Pélican, 1960.
1963 *Drôle d'automne,* par Paule Daveluy. Québec, Les Editions du Pélican, 1963.
1964 *Férie,* par Cécile Chabot. Montréal, Librarie Beauchemin, 1962.
1965 *Le loup de Noël,* par Claude Aubry. Montréal, Centre de Psychologie et de Pédagogie, 1963.
1966 *Le wapiti,* par Monique Corriveau. Montréal, Editions Jeunesse, 1964. *Le chêne des tempêtes,* par Andrée Maillet. Montréal, Les Editions Fides, 1965.
1967 Pas de prix
1968 *Légendes indiennes du Canada,* par Claude Mélançon. Montréal, Les Editions du Jour, 1967.
1969 Pas de prix
1970 *La merveilleuse histoire de la naissance,* par Lionel Gendron. Montréal, Les Editions de l'Homme, 1969.
1971 *La surprise de dame chenille,* par Henriette Major. Montréal, Centre de Psychologie et de Pédagogie, 1970.
1972 Pas de prix
1973 *Le petit sapin qui a poussé sur une étoile,* par Simone Bussières. Les Presses Laurentiennes, 1972.

PRIX ASTED-CLA

Prix offert en 1974 par l'Association pour l'avancement des sciences et des techniques de la documentation et la Canadian Library Association pour le meilleur livre de l'année pour enfants.

1974 *Ouram,* par Anne Vallières. Montréal, Leméac, 1973.

PRIX ALVINE BELISLE

Depuis 1974, l'ASTED distribue annuellement le Prix Alvine Bélisle pour le meilleur livre canadien pour jeunes paru en français durant l'année.

1975 *Jeanne, fille du roy,* par Suzanne Martel. Montréal, Fides, 1974.
1976 *Les saisons de la mer,* par Monique Corriveau. Montréal, Fides, 1975.
1977 *Emilie, la baignoire à pattes,* par Bernadette Renaud. Montréal, Héritage, 1976. (Pour lire avec toi.)
1978 *L'Evangile en papier,* par Henriette Major et Claude Lafortune, Montréal, Fides, 1977.
1979 *La petite fille aux yeux rouges,* par Gabrielle Grandbois-Paquin. Montréal, Fides, 1978.

PRIX MARIE-CLAIRE DAVELUY

Prix offert annuellement par l'ASTED pour le meilleur manuscrit écrit par un francophone de quinze à vingt ans.

1970 *Opium en fraude,* par Robert Chavarie. Sherbrooke, Paulines, 1971. *Miroir de l'âme,* par André Champagne. Non publié.
1971 *L'inconnue des Laurentides,* par Monique Sabella. Sherbrooke, Paulines, 1972.
Raie de lumière, par Aline Martinet. Sainte-Foy, La Liberté, 1972.

1972 *Lavabosse ou Légendes du pays perdu,* par Christian Desrosiers. Non publié.

1973 *Le naufrage,* par Jean-Pierre Charland. Montréal, Jour, 1975. *Les voyageurs du temps,* par Reynald Lefebvre. Montréal, Fides, 1978.

1974 *Raminagradu:* histoires ordinaires pour enfants extraordinaires, par Louise Aylwin. Montréal, Jour, 1975.

1975 *L'éveil d'un somnambule,* par Laurier Côté. Non publié.

1976 Pas de prix

1977 Pas de prix

1978 *Arabesque,* par Christina Sergi. Non publié. *Le lion des mers,* par Isabelle Berubé. Non publié.

1979 *Dont acte,* par Jean-François Chassay.

LITTERATURE PROFESSIONNELLE

OUTILS PROFESSIONNELS

Association Canadienne pour l'Avancement de la littérature de Jeunesse (A.C.A.L.J.). Dossier #1: Les besoins de lecture des enfants en difficulté. Octobre 1979. $1.00

Auteurs canadiens pour la jeunesse, v.1. Communication-Jeunesse, 1972. $1.95

Auteurs canadiens pour la jeunesse, v.2. Communication-Jeunesse, 1975. $1.95

Bélisle, Alvine; Guide de lecture pour les jeunes, 5 à 13 ans. ASTED, 1973. 164 pages. $5.75

Bourneuf, Denyse. Pédagogie et lecture; animation d'un coin de lecture. Québec-Amérique, 1975. 143 pages. $7.00

100 livres pour nous, 100 livres à nous. Communication-Jeunesse, 1978. Supplément *Lire du nouveau,* 1979. Gratuit.

Un choix de livres canadiens pour la jeunesse/Notable Canadian children's books; revu et mis à jour, y compris les meilleurs livres parus en 1973 et 1974. Bibliothèque Nationale du Canada, 1976. Suppléments: 1) 1975; 2) 1976-1977; 3) 1978. Gratuit.

Daveluy, Paule et Boulizon, Guy; Création culturelle pour la jeunesse et identité québécoise; textes de la rencontre de 1972. Communication-Jeunesse. Leméac, 1973. 188 pages. $5.95

Durand, Marielle; L'enfant-personnage et l'autorité dans la littérature enfantine. Leméac, 1976. 349 pages. $9.95 (Guides en littérature de jeunesse)

Enfin, je lis! Bibliographie sélective pour enfants 7-10 ans. ASTED, 1978. 72 pages $6.00

Illustrateurs canadiens pour la jeunesse. Communication-Jeunesse, 1977. $1.50

Images pour tous; illustration de livres canadiens pour enfants/Pictures to share; illustration in Canadian children's books. Catalogue annoté préparé par Irene E. Aubrey pour célébrer l'Année internationale de l'enfant, 1979. Bibliothèque nationale du Canada, 1979. Gratuit.

Les Indiens; une liste de livres à leur sujet. Ottawa, Ministère des Affaires indiennes et du Nord/ Approvisionnement et Services Canada, 1977. Gratuit.

Lalonde, Agathe; Guide annoté: instruments de choix et de commande de documentation en langue française pour les centres multi-media scolaires. Association des enseignants franco-ontariens, 1979. 23 pages. $1.25

Lemieux, Louise; Pleins feux sur la littérature de jeunesse au Canada français. Leméac, 1972. $14.95 (Guides en littérature de jeunesse)

Potvin, Claude; La littérature de jeunesse du Canada français. Association des bibliothécaires de langue française (ASTED), 1972. $3.50

Sources d'information sur les livres canadiens-français pour enfants/ Sources of French Canadian materials for children. Compilée par Irène E. Aubrey. Bibliothèque Nationale du Canada, 1979. Gratuit.

Tétreault, Raymond; Le livre dans la vie de l'enfant; actes du colloque 2 au 4 juin, 1977. A.C.A.L.J., 1980. 200 pages. $6.00

PERIODIQUES

Bibliographie du Québec. Bibliothèque Nationale. 1700, rue Saint-Denis, Montréal. H2X 3K6. Mensuel. Gratuit.

The Book trade in Canada/ L'industrie du livre au Canada. Ampersand Publishing Services Inc. Annuel. $25.00 [0-920262-06-6]

Canadian children's literature: a journal of criticism and review. Canadian Children's Literature Association. C.P. 335, Guelph, Ontario. N1H 6K5. 4 nos. $11.00 par an.

Canadiana: publications se rapportant au Canada notées par la Bibliothèque Nationale, Ottawa. Tel: 1-613-996-7275. Mensuel. $7.50. Refonte annuelle avec index. $50.00

Des livres et des jeunes. A.C.A.L.J., C.P. 2152, Succursale Jacques-Cartier, Sherbrooke, Québec. J1J 3Y2. 3 nos. par année. $5.00 [0706-795X]

Documentation et bibliothèques. ASTED, 360 rue Le Moyne, Montréal. H2Y 1Y3. 4 nos. Gratuit pour les membres de l'ASTED. Non-membres, $6.00

In review: Canadian books for young people. Libraries and Community Information branch, 7th floor, 77 Bloor St. W., Toronto. M7A 2R9. Gratuit en Ontario. Ailleurs: $14.00 pour trois ans.

Le livre d'ici. S.P.L. 445, rue Saint-François-Xavier, Montréal. H2Y 2T1. Hebdomadaire. Gratuit. [0226-1103]

Livres et auteurs québécois, revue critique de l'année littéraire. Université Laval. Annuel. $10.00

Lurelu; bulletin d'information sur la littérature de jeunesse. Communication-Jeunesse, 445 rue Saint-François-Xavier, Bureau 28, Montréal. H2Y 2T1. 4 nos. par année. $3.00 par an.

Nos livres: Evaluation systématique des livres canadiens d'expression française. 4635, rue Delorimier, Montréal. H2H 2B4. 10 nos. $8.00

Périodex: Index analytique de périodiques de langue française. Montréal. Centrale des bibliothèques. 10 nos. et refonte annuelle. $160.00

Canadian publishers directory: including the names of foreign publishers and their representatives in Canada. Publié par Key Publishers Company Ltd. comme supplément à Quill and Quire, Avril et Octobre. Gratuit avec abonnement ou $6.00 chacun.

Radar: Répertoire analytique d'articles de revue du Québec. Québec, Ministère des Affaires Culturelles/Bibliothèque Nationale du Québec. 6 nos. et refonte annuelle. $75.00

Répertoire de l'édition au Québec. Edi-Québec, 1976. $50.00

Index

www.ingramcontent.com/pod-product-compliance
Lightning Source LLC
Chambersburg PA
CBHW082101090726
47910CB00008B/2554

* 9 7 8 1 4 8 7 5 8 6 9 8 0 *